EXPLORING THEOLOGY

Making Sense of the Catholic Tradition

Edited by
Anne Hession & Patricia Kieran

VERITAS

First published 2007 by
Veritas Publications
7/8 Lower Abbey Street
Dublin 1
Ireland
Email publications@veritas.ie
Website www.veritas.ie

ISBN 978 1 84730 025 6

10 9 8 7 6 5 4 3 2 1

All Scripture quotations taken from the *New Revised Standard Version Bible* © 1993 and
1998 by the Division of Christian Education of the National Council of the Churches of
Christ in the United States of America, except where otherwise stated.

'A Giving' by Brendan Kennelly from *A Time for Voices*, Bloodaxe Books, 1990.
'Natural Resources' by Adrienne Rich from *The Dream of a Common Language: Poems*,
W&W Norton, 1978.

A catalogue record for this book
is available from the British Library.

Printed in the Republic of Ireland
by Betaprint Dublin

Veritas books are printed on paper made from the wood pulp of managed forests. For every
tree felled, at least one tree is planted, thereby renewing natural resources.

Sept 09

Dearest Mam,

As you explore theology may this book enrich your thirst for knowledge and zest for life. May this year be filled with all that is good and may the future burn brightly and that which is past evaporate! Happy Birthday!! Lots of love,

Bernadette

xxxx

With gratitude for the three Johns who have shaped my life:
My father, John Francis Kieran (1910–1978)
My husband, John Mc Donagh
My firstborn, John Kieran Mc Donagh, big brother to Brigid,
Patrick, Michael and Meabh

For Donal,
Sacrament of God for me
With gratitude, admiration and love

TABLE OF CONTENTS

ABBREVIATIONS

AG: *Ad gentes divinitus*: The Decree on the Church's Missionary Activity (Vatican 11, 1965)

ARCIC: Anglican-Roman Catholic International Commission

CCC: *Catechism of the Catholic Church* (John Paul II, 1992)

CDF: *Congregation for the Doctrine of the Faith*

DM: *Dialogue and Mission* (The Pontifical Council for Interreligious Dialogue, 1984)

DP: *Dialogue and Proclamation* (The Pontifical Council for Interreligious Dialogue, 1991)

DV: *Dei Verbum*: The Dogmatic Constitution on Divine Revelation (Vatican II, 1965)

Ger.: German

Gk: Greek

GS: *Gaudium et spes*: The Pastoral Constitution on the Church in the Modern World (Vatican II, 1965)

L.: Latin

LG: *Lumen gentium*: The Dogmatic Constitution on the Church (Vatican II, 1965)

MM: *Mater et Magistra* Encyclical on Christianity and Social Progress (John XXIII, 1961)

NRSV: New Revised Standard Version

NT: New Testament

PCPCU: Pontifical Council for Promoting Christian Unity

RSV: Revised Standard Version

SRS: *Sollicitudo rei socialis* (John Paul 11, 1987)

SPCU: Secretariat for Promoting Christian Unity

UR: *Unitatis redintegratio*: The Decree on Ecumenism (Vatican II, 1964)

VS: *Veritatis splendor*: The Splendour of Truth: Encyclical on Social Teaching (John Paul II, 1993)

ACKNOWLEDGEMENTS

Both Anne and Patricia would like to acknowledge the support, encouragement and expertise of their colleagues in St Patrick's College, Drumcondra and Mary Immaculate College, Limerick.

In particular they would like to acknowledge and thank their respective Heads of Department for the professional leave of absence, which enabled them to complete this research project. Dr Raymond Topley, Head of the Department of Religious Studies and Religious Education at St Patrick's College and Dr Teresa O'Doherty, Dean of the Faculty of Education at Mary Immaculate, provided support, advice and encouragement throughout the project. Particular gratitude is also due to wonderful colleagues in both colleges, especially Rev. Fachtna McCarthy, Carol Barry, Niamh Middleton, Rev. Joe McCann, Sr Eileen Lenihan, Fiona McSorley, Sr Delia O'Connor and Rev. Michael Wall.

Finally, Anne and Patricia wish to acknowledge the continuing love and support of their families: Martin and Ena Hession; Mary, James and Sarah-Kate O'Donovan; Catriona, Ger and Grace McNally; Helena Hession and Columba McGarvey; and Donal Casey.

Mary (Cregan) Kieran, Anne Mc Carthy, Florrie, Jack, Kieran and Denis Mc Carthy; Michael Kieran, Christian Burke, John, Siobhan and Mairead Kieran; Jim, Tadhg and Conor Kieran; Margaret and Turlough Mc Keown, Turlach Jnr., Tomás, Sean and Caoimhín Mc Keown, Mary Kieran and Michael, Kieran and Suzanne Lillis; Brigid Kieran and Norbert Coyle and Oisin and Muireann Kieran-Coyle; John Mc Donagh and John, Brigid, Patrick, Michael and Meabh Kieran-Mc Donagh.

We are deeply grateful to all our contributors whose multiple voices provide a fascinating introduction to the Catholic theological conversation at this time. We wish to extend our gratitude to Caitriona Clarke and Ruth Kennedy who provided valuable editing and proofreading of all the chapters in this book. It would not be of such quality without their careful attention to detail and constant support to us throughout the editing process. Go raibh míle maith agaibh! Thanks also to Niamh McGarry for the cover design and layout, to the marketing department and sales representatives, and finally to the director of Veritas, Maura Hyland, for her continuing belief in us and in the projects we undertake. We are honoured to bring the essays together for you and we hope you enjoy this book.

BIOGRAPHICAL NOTES

Una Agnew SSL is Associate Professor of Spirituality at Milltown Institute, Dublin and Head of the Spirituality Department. She is a founding member of the All-Ireland Spiritual Guidance Association (AISGA) and its Company Secretary. She is author of *The Mystical Imagination of Patrick: A Buttonhole in Heaven* (Columba, 1998). She has contributed to D. Marmion and G. Theissen (eds) *Theology in the* Making (Veritas, 2005) and J. Putti (ed.) *Time to Change* (Veritas, 2006).

Michael Barnes SJ is a lecturer at Heythrop College in the University of London. A specialist in the Buddhist-Christian dialogue, he has written several books on the theology of religions, notably *Theology and the Dialogue of Religions* (Cambridge University Press, 2002). He lives and works in Southall, West London, where he runs a small centre for dialogue which involves local Sikhs, Muslims, Christians and Hindus – and the occasional Buddhist.

Carol Barry lectures in the areas of theology, scripture and spirituality at St Patrick's College, Drumcondra, a linked college of Dublin City University. She has extensive experience at home and abroad in directing retreats for youths, adults, religious and educators. Her research interests include the significance of spirituality for educators and the in-career personal development of teachers.

Patrick Connolly is a priest of the diocese of Clogher. He is a Lecturer in the Department of Theology and Religious Studies at Mary Immaculate College, University of Limerick, where he teaches in the areas of moral theology and canon law, as well as being the co-ordinator of the Department's taught post-graduate programmes. He was previously Assistant Professor at St Paul University in Ottawa and he has also served in parish and Church tribunal work. He has published articles on the relationship between the theology and law of marriage in the Eastern and Western Churches, on the canonical dimensions of the abuse crisis as well as on pastoral theology.

Eamonn Conway is a priest of the Tuam archdiocese. He is Head of Theology and Religious Studies at Mary Immaculate College, University of Limerick, where he also co-directs the Centre for Culture, Technology and Values. He is author of *The Anonymous Christian – A Relativised Christianity? An Evaluation of Hans Urs von Balthasar's Criticisms of Karl Rahner's Theory of the Anonymous Christian* (Peter Lang, 1993), and has edited a number of volumes including *Twin Pulpits: Essays in Media and Church* (Veritas, 1997), *The Splintered Heart* (Veritas, 1998), *Child Sexual Abuse & the Catholic Church – A Pastoral Response* (Columba, 1999), *Technology and Transcendence* (Columba, 2003) and *The Courage to Risk Everything, Essays Marking the Centenary of Karl Rahner's Birth* (Louvain Studies, 2004). Dr Conway is a member of the American Academy of Religion, the European Society for the Study of Science and Theology, the Irish Theological Association, the European Society for Catholic Theology and the American Catholic Theology Association, and is a member of the Board of Directors of Concilium.

Owen F. Cummings is Regents' Professor of Theology at Mount Angel Seminary, Oregon, the principal seminary for the Pacific North-West. Most of his writing is in the area of liturgical/sacramental theology. He is author of numerous works and his most recent book is *Eucharistic Doctors* (Paulist Press, 2006).

Lawrence S. Cunningham is John A. O'Brien Professor of Theology at the University of Notre Dame. He is the author or editor of twenty books, the most recent being *A Brief History of Saints* (Blackwell, 2005). The recipient of two honorary doctorates from American Universities and several teaching awards, he was honored by his own university with a Presidential Award in 2002 for services to the academy and the Church. His most recent project is a book on Roman Catholicism commissioned by Cambridge University Press.

Donal Dorr is a missionary priest who has lectured in various colleges in Ireland and abroad. He is the former holder of a research fellowship in the theology of development and a former consultor to the Pontifical Commission on Justice and Peace. Donal has been involved over many years in founding and staffing training programmes and support networks for community activists in several African countries and in Ireland. He is the author of nine books, dealing with various aspects of justice and spirituality, including *Spirituality and Justice*, *Option for the Poor*, *The Social Justice Agenda* and *Time for a Change*. His most recent book is *Spirituality of Leadership* (Columba, 2006).

Mary Grey is Professorial Research Fellow at St Mary's University College, Twickenham UK, and D.J. James Professor Emerita of the University of Wales, Lampeter. She is also Founder trustee of the NGO *Wells for India* and Patron of *Friends of Sabeel*, UK. Recent works include: *Sacred Longings: Ecofeminist Theology and Globalisation* (SCM, 2003; New Delhi, 2004), *The Unheard Scream: The Struggles of Dalit Women in India*, with Rabbi Dan Cohn Sherbok (New Delhi, 2004), *Pursuing the Dream: A Jewish Christian Conversation* (Darton, Longman and Todd, 2005) and *Struggling with a Reconciling Heart: A Christian Feminist Spirituality of Reconciliation* (Darton, Longman and Todd, 2007).

Anne Hession is a lecturer in Religious Education at St Patrick's College, Dublin, a linked college of Dublin City University. She is a member of the Irish Episcopal Commission for Catechetics. Her fields of academic research are in the religious education of children and the spirituality of children. She is co-author with Patricia Kieran of *Children, Catholicism and Religious Education* (Veritas, 2005). She is co-editor with Patricia Kieran of a forthcoming book on Religious Education (2008).

Patricia Kieran is a Chevening Scholar who has taught Theology and Religious Education in the UK and Ireland. She currently teaches Religious Education at Mary Immaculate College, University of Limerick. She is co-author of *Children, Catholicism and Religious Education* (Veritas, 2005) and has published a number of chapters and articles on the subject of Roman Catholic Modernism, gender and inter-religious education. She is currently working on the next book in this series.

Dermot A. Lane is President of Mater Dei Institute of Education, Dublin City University and a priest of the Dublin diocese, serving in Balally Parish. He is author of numerous works including *The Experience of God: An Invitation to do Theology*, revised and expanded (Veritas/Paulist Press, 2003) and editor with Brendán Leahy of *Vatican II: Historical and Theological Perspectives* (Veritas, 2006).

Brendán Leahy is Professor of Systematic Theology at St Patrick's College, Maynooth and secretary of the Irish Episcopal Conference's Advisory Committee on Ecumenism. He is author of *The Marian Profile of the Church* (New City, 2000) and co-author with Thomas Norris of *Christianity: Origins and Contemporary Expressions* (Veritas, 2004).

Gerard Mannion is Associate Professor of Ecclesiology and Ethics at Liverpool Hope University where he is Director of the Centre for the Study of Contemporary Ecclesiology and co-director of the Applied Ethics Initiative. The Archbishop Derek Worlock Research Fellow for 2006–07, he previously taught at Church Colleges of the Universities of Oxford and Leeds and was a 2004 Coolidge Fellow at Union Theological Seminary, New York. His publications include *Schopenhauer, Religion and Morality* (Ashgate, 2003), *Readings in Church Authority – Gifts and Challenges for Contemporary Catholicism* (co-editor) (Ashgate, 2003) and *Ecclesiology and Postmodernity – Questions for the Church in our Times* (Liturgical Press, 2007). He is the co-editor of two forthcoming volumes, *The Routledge Companion to the Christian Church* (2007) and *Catholic Social Justice: Theological and Practical Explorations* (Continuum, 2007). Mannion is also presently chair of the Ecclesiological Investigations International Research Network, and founding co-chair of the Ecclesiological Investigations Program Unit of the American Academy of Religion.

Fachtna McCarthy is a Lecturer at St Patrick's College of Education, Drumcondra, a linked College of Dublin City University. His writings include contributions to *Faith and Culture in the Irish Context* (Veritas, 1996) and *Religion and Science: Education, Ethics and Public Policy* (St Patrick's Publication, 2003). With Joseph McCann he is the author of *Religion and Science: Into the Classroom* (Veritas, 2003) and the textbook for the Leaving

Certificate Religious Education Syllabus, *Religion and Science* (Veritas, 2006).

Sean McDonagh is a Columban missionary priest. He spent over two decades in the Philippines. He has written widely on ecology, theology and justice issues. He is author of *To Care for the Earth* (Continuum, 1986), *Dying for Water* (Veritas, 2003), *The Death of Life* (Columba, 2004) and *Climate Change* (Columba, 2006).

David McLoughlin is Senior Lecturer in Theology at Newman College in Birmingham. He is the former President of the Catholic Theological Association of Great Britain and Vice President of the European Association of Catholic Theology. He serves as a theological consultant to CAFOD, Caritas and the national and international Christian Worker Movements. His present research, with the Urban Theology Unit in Sheffield, is on the changing use of the Scriptures in radical Christian movements. His most recent publications are: 'Remembering who and what we are – Ecclesial self-identity in the face of globalisation: A Roman Catholic Perspective', *New Blackfriars*, March 2005 and 'Women and Children First? Jesus Teaching on Family', *The Pastoral Review*, July/August 2006.

Niamh Middleton lectures in Religious Education and Moral Theology at St Patrick's College of Education, Drumcondra, a linked college of Dublin City University. Her research interests include the implications of Darwinian evolutionary theory for the natural law and the role of psychology in moral formation.

Bruce T. Morrill is Associate Professor and Director of Graduate Studies in the Theology Department at Boston College. He is the author of *Anamnesis as Dangerous Memory: Political and Liturgical Theology in Dialogue* (Liturgical Press, 2000) and contributing editor to three other books: *Practicing Catholic* (Palgrave Macmillan, 2006), *Bodies of Worship* (Liturgical Press, 1999) and *Liturgy and the Moral Self* (Liturgical Press, 1998). A Jesuit priest, he has lectured widely in the United States and Europe.

Pat Mullins OCarm STD is Associate Professor of Systematic Theology and Director of Online Modules at Milltown Institute, Dublin, where he has recently completed a six-year term as Dean of Theology. He is Director of Studies of the recently established Carmelite Institute of Britain and Ireland. He is author of numerous articles in the field of Pneumatology and Ecclesiology, including 'Pentecost as the Hermeneutical Key to Vatican II's Presentation of Mary as the Type of the Church' (2003), 'The Spirit Speaks to the Churches: Continuity and Development in Congar's Pneumatology' (2004), 'Pope John Paul II: Doctrine and Dissent' (2005) and 'The Ecumenical Movement and the Transmission of the Word of God in Vatican II's *Dei Verbum*' (2006).

Paul D. Murray is a married lay Roman Catholic theologian who teaches Systematic Theology at Durham University. He has previously taught at St Cuthbert's Seminary, Ushaw College, Durham and Newman College of Higher Education, Birmingham and has worked as an Adult Christian Educator within the Department of Pastoral Formation of the Archdiocese of Liverpool. He serves on the British Methodist-Roman Catholic Committee and is the Director of the emergent Durham Research Centre for Contemporary Catholic Studies. His first monograph was 'Reason, Truth and Theology in Pragmatist Perspective' (Peeters, 2004). In addition to a number of essays in leading journals and scholarly collections, he is editor of *Receptive Ecumenism and the Call to Catholic Learning* (Oxford University Press, 2007).

Martin O'Kane is Senior Lecturer in Biblical Studies at the University of Wales, Lampeter, director of the research centre, *The Bible and the Visual Imagination* and Chair of The Bible and Visual Culture Seminar of the International Society of Biblical Studies. His most recent publication is *Painting the Text: The Artist as Biblical Interpreter* (Sheffield Phoenix Press, 2006). His current research interests centre on interdisciplinary approaches to the Hebrew Bible.

Anne O'Leary PBVM is Assistant Professor of New Testament at St Mary's University, San Antonio, Texas. She is author of *Matthew's Judaization of Mark* (Continuum/T & T Clark, 2006) as well as of several articles. She has lectured in the areas of Sacred Scripture and Spirituality, directed retreats and facilitated Ignatian Communal Discernment with groups in several countries – Canada, England, Ghana, Israel, Italy, Pakistan, the Philippines, Turkey, New Zealand and Wales – as well as in her home country, Ireland.

Ethna Regan is a lecturer in theology at the Mater Dei Institute, Dublin City University. She was previously Lecturer in Theology and Ethics at the University of the West Indies in Trinidad. She studied at the Mater Dei Institute, Fordham University and holds a Ph.D. from the University of Cambridge. She recently contributed to *The Modern Theologians* (Blackwell 2005, ed. David Ford with Rachel Muers) and has written on social justice, human rights and the death penalty. A Holy Faith Sister, she has worked in Samoa and the Caribbean.

Caroline Renehan is a lecturer in education and Teaching Practice Coordinator at Mater Dei Institute of Education, Dublin. A founding member of the Religion Teachers' Association, she holds a doctorate in Theology as well as a doctorate in Education. Her fields of academic research are in Feminist and Marian Theology and Gender Differences in Initial Teacher Education. She is author of *Different Planets? Gender Attitudes and Classroom Practice in Post-Primary Teaching* (The Liffey Press, 2006). She is co-author with Luke Monaghan of *The Chaplain: A Faith Presence in the School Community* (Columba, 1998).

Raymond Topley is Head of Religious Studies and Religious Education at St Patrick's College of Education, Drumcondra, a linked college of Dublin City University. He lectures in the areas of liturgical catechesis and religious education methodology. His publications include a pastoral video trilogy on the sacraments of initiation, a book on prayer assemblies, as well as an edited work with Gareth Byrne, *Nurturing Children's Religious Imagination: The Challenge of Primary Religious Education Today* (2004), all published by Veritas.

INTRODUCTION

Nothing is more practical than finding God, that is, than falling in love in a quite absolute, final way. What you are in love with, what seizes your imagination, will affect everything. It will decide what will get you out of bed in the morning, what you will do with your evenings, how you will spend your weekends, what you read, who you know, what breaks your heart, and what amazes you with joy and gratitude.

Attributed to Pedro Arrupe SJ (1907–1991)

This book explores and attempts to make sense of Catholic theology. Its twenty-six short chapters invite the reader to listen and respond to the creative voices of contemporary Catholic theologians as they investigate the major areas of study, themes and challenges in the Catholic theological tradition. These rich and distinctive voices attempt to speak of the Catholic tradition in a reader-friendly, accessible manner while simultaneously providing a comprehensive introduction, overview and analysis of key areas in contemporary Catholic theology.

While the text sets out to explain the Catholic theological tradition and make it accessible to the theological initiate, the volume also explores issues that are of relevance to those who have a deep and long-held interest in and passion for theology. Each chapter is crafted by an expert who provides a substantive and challenging overview of their subject area in a clear, simple manner which excites interest and evokes the desire for further analysis and exploration.

A reading of this text should banish the assumption that Catholic theology is about abstract concepts and arid definitions that are of little relevance to contemporary life. Catholic theology is about people and their experience and understanding of a loving God. It is deeply personal as it explores, challenges and transforms how we understand ourselves as people and how we relate to others, to the environment and to God. Catholic theology is the end product of a divine-human love story. It represents a human desire to respond to and reflect upon the God whom we know as love. The fact that theologians are called to think and talk about this experience of unconditional divine love in an intellectually rigorous manner does not annul the fact that 'theology is about people, loved by a passionate God'.[1]

In Catholic theology we seek to understand God who loves us, seeks us out and invites us to fullness of life, through participation in, and celebration of, the universal redemptive activity and power of Christ in the Holy Spirit. To explore and understand the wisdom of the Catholic theological tradition is to join a conversation that has been going on for centuries in the Church. This 'handing-on' and re-interpretation of the tradition is grounded in revelation, in Church teaching and in the scholarship of theologians down through the ages. Nevertheless, immense creativity, imagination and critical openness is required on the part of each new generation of learners, so that their engagement with the tradition becomes at the same time a contribution to its ongoing development.

The subject matter of the theological conversation is limitless; however, some classic themes recur: Revelation, Trinity, Jesus, Holy Spirit, Scripture, Mary, Sacraments, Morality, Saints, Church, Spirituality, Eschatology and so on. Other themes and questions rise to prominence because of the particular age in which we live. From the raw ingredients of God's self-disclosure in Jesus Christ, Scriptures, Tradition and the Church, Catholic theology is shaped in a manner that reflects human experience and understanding of God as it is manifestly expressed in different contexts and at different times.

Contemporary Catholic theology engages with the dominant ideas and concerns of our time. For example, since it is now recognised that God's grace is found in other Christian churches as well as in other religions, the concepts and skills of ecumenical and inter-religious dialogue are constituent parts of Catholic theological literacy. In the context of impending ecological crisis and the predicted extinction of up to eleven thousand species in the next fifty to one hundred years, the Catholic theological tradition faces the challenge of developing a new Catholic theology of creation that will enable a creative response to this environmental disaster.[2] In a post-modern world of diversity and choice, the question of what it means to uphold a distinct religious identity has also come to the fore. In an age where all foundations are subject to question, where all 'is now plural and seemingly relative and one thing as good as another' questions about the truth status of Catholic beliefs and the sustainability of the Catholic way of life need to be explored anew.[3]

The problem of marginalisation or domination on the basis of gender is another concern of contemporary Catholic theology. Aided by gender studies, feminist theory and men's studies, Catholic feminist theology addresses the traditional theological tendency to speak of God in predominantly male terms (God-he language) while simultaneously taking cognisance of women and men's experience and reflection upon their faith in God. Theologians also attempt to reclaim and celebrate the voices of women mystics and theologians who, in previous ages, were deemed marginal to the theological enterprise. Much contemporary Catholic theology arises out of people's experiences of God in situations of injustice, inequality and oppression. It aims to respond to the challenge of Vatican II to read these and other 'signs of the times' in the light of the Gospel and the tradition of the Church.

Fayette Veverka has argued that Catholic religious identity is 'constantly renewed in learning communities that honour and engage its diverse voices in vigorous and passionate conversation about the meaning and purposes of its common life'.[4] The responsibility of theologians is to ensure that communities are equipped with the necessary critical tools (e.g. basic theological language, concepts, attitudes and methods) to engage fruitfully in that ongoing conversation. This approach finds an echo in Alasdair MacIntyre's concept of tradition. For him, a tradition is 'partially constituted by an argument.'[5] Every tradition pursues certain 'goods', which give to that tradition 'its particular point and purpose'. When a tradition is 'living' its members are engaged in a vibrant, embodied 'argument' about what the fullest participation in its particular goods would entail.

MacIntyre advocates 'the virtue of having an adequate sense of the traditions to which one belongs or which confront one.'[6] This does not mean an attempt to reify the past and impose an antiquated vision on future generations. Instead it means grasping the future possibilities which the past makes available to the present. It means judging how the wisdom bequeathed by the Catholic tradition enables the contemporary Catholic community to pursue our own good as well as the good of the tradition of which we are the contemporary bearers. To this end, each new generation of Catholics needs to be able to engage the tradition in an intellectually serious way, so that they will be enabled to extend the tradition and disclose new aspects of the goods that the tradition has been pursuing for centuries.

Lucien Richard argues that before students of theology can engage in a critical dialogical conversation with tradition, they must belong to a 'community of memory'. Theological knowing arises from reflection on one's own experiences, knowledge and values in relationship with the experience, knowledge and values of the community.[7] This entails a certain fidelity to the tradition, to the work of memory, as well as a commitment to hearing a truth not of one's own making, so that one is open to being informed, formed and transformed by it. Cardinal Avery Dulles echoes this insight arguing, that the first attitude of the believer toward tradition ought to be one of trusting receptivity. He describes the Catholic principle as an acceptance of visible mediation. 'It asserts that God ordinarily comes to us through the structures that are given, especially those to which his gracious promises are attached, such as Incarnation, Scripture, sacrament and apostolic ministry.'[8] Premature criticism weakens faith. Therefore, it is important for Catholics to be able to appreciate, articulate and explain Catholic beliefs and practices. If it later appears that there are reasons for suspecting a mediation the time will come for prophetic criticism and even protest.

This book brings together the work of a wide variety of theologians from Britain, the United States and Ireland. Despite the great variety of writing styles and approaches found herein, the book exemplifies the extent to which both fidelity and resistance are essential ingredients in the task of Catholic theology. The writers introduce the reader to a variety of voices and perspectives within the contemporary Catholic theological conversation. Readers should expect some aspects of Catholic theology to challenge and confront them, calling at least some aspects of their lives into question. At other times they may find that their own spirituality and ethic of life is affirmed, strengthened and enriched. Ultimately, readers will internalise, process and translate what they have learned. In this way the study of Catholic theology contributes to the search for truth and goodness which is the ultimate goal.

Overview of the book

After an initial introduction to the general nature of Catholic theology and an exploration of the contribution of Catholicism to western culture, Section 1, 'Christian Foundations', outlines the basis upon which all Catholic theology is built; that is, Revelation, Scripture and Tradition. Section 2, 'Christian Creed', consists of six chapters which focus on the central beliefs of Catholic Christians. These are: Jesus Christ, Trinity, the Holy Spirit, Church, Mary and Eschatology. We recommend that the chapters on Jesus Christ and the Holy Spirit are read in conjunction with the chapter on Trinity for a deeper and enriched understanding.

In Section 3, 'Christian Morality', the focus moves more explicitly to the Christian life. The section opens with an exploration of how Catholic theology speaks of human nature (Catholic anthropology) and follows with an introduction to the Catholic moral life and to the place of conscience and Church authority in the life of a Catholic. An introduction to Catholic social teaching and a Catholic theology of creation complete this section.

Section 4, 'Christian Prayer', explores the Catholic spiritual and prayer tradition. It outlines the liturgical year and its role in enabling Catholics to become holy. An introduction to the place of sacraments in the Christian way of life and a study of the sacraments of initiation (Baptism, Confirmation and Eucharist) and reconciliation follows. Finally, the reader is introduced to Christian spirituality and our inborn capacity and hunger for the Divine: a desire that is nourished, deepened and given meaning through a life of personal discipleship and loving service in imitation of Christ.

The final section, 'Contemporary Catholic Identity', explores a number of themes central to the search for Catholic identity today. The first chapter in this section offers a broad vision of the kind of personal identity proposed by Catholicism. Catholicism upholds an understanding of the human person-in-relationship to God and Catholics are committed to the vision that it is God rather than ourselves who ultimately gives human life meaning and purpose. Chapter 23 examines the difference gendered thinking makes to our understanding of the human person, community, relationships and

God. The origins of feminist theology are examined and some of the questions it presents for anyone doing theology are raised. Chapter 24 (on interreligous dialogue) and Chapter 25 (on ecumenism) enable us to see that it is possible to develop a distinct Catholic identity and a pluralistic and ecumenical openness to other religious faiths at the same time.

The collection ends with a reflection on the task of theology and on those responsible for its development. It is proposed that theological reflection is an activity engaged in by people of varying commitments to faith, professional and non-professional alike. Catholic theology is a conversation that is open to all. Thus we come back to our starting point and to the reason for this compilation. Perhaps we are facing a new educational moment where the central issue is not simply the ability to critically analyse or 'deconstruct' religious traditions but the ability to appreciate and engage their wisdom. This book aims to assist students of Catholic theology everywhere with this noble task.

Anne Hession and Patricia Kieran
Feast of the Epiphany
6 January 2007

Notes

1   J.J. Mueller, *What is Theology?*, Collegeville, Minn: The Liturgical Press, 1988, p. 10.

2   Sean McDonagh, *The Death of Life: The Horror of Extinction*, Dublin: Columba, 2004.

3   Gerald Loughlin, 'Christianity at the End of the Story or the Return of the Master-Narrative' in *Modern Theology*, Vol. 8, No. 4 October, 1992, p. 365.

4   Notes from a course given by Fayette Veverka at Boston College, October 1999.

5   Alasdair MacIntyre, *After Virtue: A Study in Moral Theory* (2nd ed.) London: Duckworth, 2000, p. 222.

6   Ibid., p. 223.

7   Lucien Richard, 'Theology and Belonging: Christian Identity and the Doing of Theology,' *Religious Education*, Vol. 79, 1984, p. 403.

8   Avery Dulles, *The Catholicity of the Church*, Oxford: Clarendon Press, 1985, p. 7.

CHAPTER 1

AN INTRODUCTION TO CATHOLIC THEOLOGY

Gerard Mannion

INTRODUCTION

Catholic theology is a discipline that seeks to make sense of and to understand the God whom Christians profess belief in. It literally means 'God-talk' or discourse about God, coming from two Greek words – *theos* (God) and *logos* (words or discourse). Just as sociology is discourse about society and anthropology is discourse about human beings (Gk *anthropos*), so too, then, is theology discourse about God. The term 'Catholic' means 'universal' or 'relating to the whole' (Gk *katholikos*). Christianity is a religion that believes in universal salvation, that is to say that God calls *all* human beings to ultimate fulfilment and community with God's own self. The Catholic Church is the community that seeks to bear witness to this promise that God has made to the human family and which seeks to help people along the way towards closer unity with one another and with God.

However, Catholic theology is about a great deal more, not 'in addition to' the above, but *because of* the above. In other words, because Catholic theology is discourse about the God whom Christians believe in, whose most defining characteristic Christians believe is *love* (in Latin, *caritas*, from where we get the word 'charity'), whom Christians believe calls all the human family to community with one another and with God's own very self: *because* of all this, theology has so much more to say, so many more 'words' to speak. This volume in its entirety will seek to illustrate this in a variety of ways. This introductory essay will seek to touch upon and explain some of the fundamental aspects of what Catholic theology is about and what it seeks to achieve.

Understanding the Christian God

Catholic theology attempts to understand the God that Christians believe in. I wish to start with a quotation from a well-known Catholic theologian and, in the remainder of the essay, to try and make sense of what this statement means. In the following quotation, Richard P. McBrien, an American scholar, attempts to summarise the nature and significance of Christian doctrine (doctrine means 'teaching', so he is referring to the important teachings and beliefs that Christians hold):

> The interlocking character of Christian doctrine is ... unmistakably clear. Our understanding of Jesus Christ is a function of our understanding of God, and our understanding of God is, in turn, a function, at least correlatively, of our understanding of human existence.[1]

Theology seeks to explain, to make sense of and, when necessary, to put into terms that will make sense for particular times and particular places, these most fundamental doctrines that concern the God whom Christians believe in and seek to relate to in their daily lives. McBrien indicates that doctrine seeks to be coherent, complementary and consistent in its character. We can add, so also does theology in general. It is not a question of being satisfied with a disparate range of beliefs that come from differing times and places and do not relate to one another. Theology tries to show that making sense of what Christians believe about Jesus of Nazareth, a wandering charismatic preacher who lived in first-century Palestine, depends upon and relates to our understanding of God. In turn, our understanding of God is also bound up with our understanding of what it is to be a human person and to live out a human life in community with others. All three areas are interdependent and inform one another. One might say that our *Christology* (understanding of Jesus Christ) interacts in a fundamental way with our *theology* (understanding of God), and both interact in a fundamental way with our *anthropology* (understanding of being human).

I   THE QUEST FOR MEANING: KEY QUESTIONS

Our hearts are restless until they find rest in you, O Lord.
(St Augustine of Hippo, *Confessions*, Bk I, 1)

Human beings are naturally curious creatures. We ask questions of the world and of ourselves and probe on and on until we find some answers. Human life is a life that inherently seeks to make sense of, understand and explain itself. In other words, much of human existence can be said to be a quest for *meaning* – the meaning of that existence itself. Humans often want to know where they came from, where they are going (or should go) in life, and how to get there.

1.   Being Human – Direction and Fulfilment

Yet we are not curious just for the sake of it (or at least not always!). We seek to give our lives not just meaning but also some purpose and direction. For that, purpose and direction is aimed towards some end – and when that end is deemed a good one, indeed when our overall purpose and direction in life is 'in the right direction', then we are moving along the path towards fulfilment – what some might call well-being or, put into theological language, 'salvation' (which literally means 'well-being', 'health'). Throughout history, the human quest for meaning, purpose and fulfilment has been linked to faith and religion, but not every human being or community has sought to give order to their existence by turning to religion to help with the answers.

2.   Atheism

For some people, religion does not seem to provide satisfactory answers. Indeed, some quite openly reject or refuse to entertain the value of religious answers to life's most important questions. They do not feel that the meaning, purpose and fulfilment provided by a life lived in accordance with religious beliefs and practices is the best way to make sense of and guide one's life in the world. Sometimes such critics of religion make the common mistake of blaming the bad and evil things, as well as the human mistakes that some religious people often do or make, on the religion they claim to profess. But this is a confusion that really is ultimately illogical, for humans will always be prone to making mistakes and doing bad and even evil things, even those who attach themselves to a particular religion and even some who earnestly try to follow that faith. However, this does not necessarily mean the religion itself is harmful or that what it teaches is wrong.

To take an extreme example: a bomb dropped upon civilians in Iraq by armed forces of the US or Britain, even if the military personnel involved are Christians, is no more representative of something which is the fault of genuine Christianity than the horrific Twin Towers attack of 11 September 2001 was representative of true Islam. Just because some people might wander off the path and get lost does not mean that the path was the wrong one or that the path caused them to be lost. Nonetheless, some choose a life without religion – and often this is called 'atheism' (meaning 'without belief in God').[2] Thus, one answer to the human 'quest for meaning' is to refuse to try and explain this world and our place within it with reference to any 'being', God or the like, deemed to 'be' beyond the normal confines and modes of human existence.

3.   Agnosticism

Another route does not claim to possess the certitude that much atheism claims to have about life and its meaning. Nor indeed does this route claim to have the certitude that more fundamentalistic religious believers claim to have (those who insist on rigid and absolute fundamentals and who refuse to allow anything to shake their particular interpretation of the world and their faith). This is the path of 'agnosticism' (literally meaning 'without knowledge') and it also has many forms. Fundamentally, it involves admitting that there is a limit to what we can know about the origins, meaning, purpose and best direction for fulfilment of human life. This does not mean that all such people would reject religion – indeed many religions have a very healthy strain of agnosticism running throughout the very heart of their beliefs (Christianity being no exception). It simply means that some humility and realism is present and that there are questions that we cannot as yet answer in a definitive fashion.

4.   Conditions of the Possibility of Knowing

Of course, this all relates to further considerations of what we *can* know. Both the agnostic path and many religious quests for meaning alike would readily admit that the 'ultimate' questions about where we and the universe came from, where we are going and how best to get there will *necessarily* evade any attempt to gain a definitive answer because such answers involve an attempt to try and think 'outside the box' that is human existence and our mental capacities to make sense of it. For example, if we try and imagine how the universe came into being, then we are trying to imagine what may have 'existed' (and how it existed) before any of our means of imagining and of understanding existence actually existed themselves. That is a task that will frustrate even the greatest minds for we are thinking up to the very limits of human knowledge itself – we are trying to think 'beyond' the limits of our 'tools' (our mental 'software') for knowledge itself. For our mental 'software' and sensory means of experiencing are designed, in the main, to make sense of *this* world, this mode of existence and our place within it. In other words, we are trying to understand, to 'know', what is literally beyond what we are equipped to know beyond, as one famous philosopher might have put it, 'the conditions for the possibility of knowledge' itself. Still none of this means that the attempt to answer such 'ultimate questions' is futile and doomed to failure.

II.   GOD THE ANSWER

A third way *does* embrace the religious quest and does not rule out trying to understand what might be beyond this mode of existence, even what might be beyond the (normal) conditions for the possibility of knowledge itself. For religions that believe in a deity, a supreme being, a god, this pathway is a *theistic* pathway and Christianity is such a pathway. For Christians, 'God' is the unifying being (and for theology, the unifying 'concept') that enables us to make sense of life, to gain meaning, to find direction, purpose and to move along the pathway towards true fulfilment (salvation).

1.   Faith and Existence – The Classical Theological Tradition

How does this link to the notion we just mentioned that some things are beyond our capacity for knowing? How can we know what we do not ordinarily have the means to know? In one sense, we must come to appreciate that there are differing ways of 'knowing' and, indeed, different forms of 'knowledge'. However, another fundamental factor is that many faiths and especially Christianity can happily live without black and white definitive 'answers' to each and every ultimate question. Some questions, some aspects of the origin, meaning and purpose of the universe and life within it can never be answered in the definite way in which we might answer other questions. We cannot 'know' and understand who or what brought the universe into being in the same way that we can know what the capital of Sri Lanka is or can even give the answer to the question, 'what is the sum of two plus two?'

Some aspects of the quest for meaning, purpose and fulfilment involve *believing* in certain things, committing oneself to their truth *without* having definite proof, in the way that we can prove such other things. In other words, they involve taking such things on *trust* – they are a matter of *faith*. Christian theology seeks to illustrate that a disposition of faith is absolutely vital to the quest for meaning, purpose and fulfilment in life: there are very important truths about the world, its origins, reason and purpose, why it and we within it exist and the ultimate destiny of all, which cannot be proven in the way in which one might prove that 'two plus two equals four'. We take them on *faith*.

And yet the classical Christian theological tradition (despite what many of its atheistic critics might think) does *not* then say, 'So that's all you do, you take these things on trust, you just believe them without factual proof'. No. Instead, equally important to the science of Catholic theology is *reason*. For theology *is* a science. The word 'science' means knowledge and a science is simply a 'pathway to greater knowledge and understanding', so physics, biology and chemistry are pathways to greater knowledge of the physical and natural world. When it comes to the science of theology, the capacity we humans have for weighing things up, for applying our inbuilt skills (our 'software' again) for rational thought, is crucially important to the Catholic Christian way of life. For faith and reason go hand in hand.

So, just as you would be ill-advised simply to believe a man who told you his jumper was white when your eyes and means of perception told you it was black, so too does Catholic theology allow *reason* to inform, explain and articulate what it is that Catholics believe – in other words, the classical tradition in Christian theology, for the most part (though there are always exceptions) believes that faith and reason go hand in hand: one complements the other. So our rationality, our capacity to reason, to apply the laws of logic, to weigh up probabilities, to discern the likelihood and trustworthiness of various propositions, informs our understanding of the faith.

This is not simply about crudely putting faith to the test. For example, if someone proclaimed that God existed and yet also proclaimed God did *not* exist, our capacity for rational thought would quickly lead us to conclude that, because of the law of contradiction, both could not be true and therefore one statement must be false. Thus, St Anselm of Canterbury

(c. 1033–1109) described the task of theology as 'faith seeking understanding'. In a famous work (the *Proslogion*), he prayed to God, saying, 'Lord, I do not seek to understand in order that I may believe, but I believe in order that I may understand'. This means that theology does not go about trying to find proofs and rational demonstrations of 'facts' and 'truths' about God, Christ and human existence, *in order that* they be more attractive for people to believe in them, in the manner that a scientist would seek to conduct experiments to prove to people the truth of his hypothesis. On the contrary, theology starts from those positions of what may be factual uncertainties in the normal sense, that nonetheless Christians are firmly committed to believing, in other words, what they take on trust as a matter of faith. Theology seeks to come to a greater understanding of God, Christ and human existence *by building upon* this starting point of faith. We believe in order to understand – we are not like Thomas in the Gospel who (at first) would not believe Jesus had risen from the dead until he had definite proof and had seen him with his own eyes. Faith, then, comes first, but it works in tandem with reason in order to increase our understanding.

And lest anyone think that such a method of procedure is open to question, we proceed in this manner in all sorts of ways in life and on a daily basis – and not simply in religious matters. We take things on trust; we have 'faith' in them all the time. For example, when we walk down the street, placing one foot before the other, we have no way of knowing *for certain* that the pavement will not disappear before our foot touches the ground again. But we proceed 'as if' we did know. We take it on trust that it is reasonable to assume the pavement will be there. Indeed, how could we ever live without taking many, many things on faith first? Who knows when preparing their clothes and papers for work or school the next day that they will wake up the next morning *for certain*? Yet the act of preparing for the next day is an act of faith informed by reason. Or who is it that only ever falls in love with the absolute certain proof that the other person loves them in return? Such proof is impossible. But an act of faith, taken on trust, albeit (although not always!) informed by reason, is the basis for most successful relationships.

Finally, is not every great scientific discovery the result of a significant act of faith? By its very definition, faith is not necessary when definite proof has been supplied. Who needs trust, faith, when they have evidence? But what would be the point of conducting many experiments to prove something you already knew to be true, because you had definite proof that it was true? Instead, every great scientific discovery starts out as a *hypothesis*, a 'hunch', on the part of the scientist. Not a wild hunch, in most cases, but a *reasonable* one – a hunch the scientist thinks is possible/likely/probable to be proved right. The scientist then sets about conducting experiments to test the hunch and, if all goes well, verification is later supplied. So life itself is filled with instances when faith informed by reason is our guiding principle. We would find it difficult to achieve anything without faith.

2.   The Social Sciences

The development of other sciences which seek to understand and explain human beings, human nature and human social existence in communities and societies all point towards the prevailing significance, importance and value of human beings turning to religion to give their lives hope through giving them meaning, purpose and fulfilment, through helping them to make sense of the world and their part in it and of the challenging events which take place throughout all human lives. Across millennia, continents and cultural contexts, religion has served this purpose and, indeed, has often served it very well.

3.   God as an Explanatory Hypothesis

Thus, in one sense, what Christians refer to as 'God' – that which brings the world and all within it (including us humans) into existence and, crucially, *sustains* them in that existence – *is* the answer to our quest for meaning, purpose and fulfilment. Theology and indeed another discipline, philosophy (the 'study or love of wisdom'), which also plays a major part in the Catholic Christian story, do not seek to explain and give meaning to things in exactly the same way that natural science might, but they do seek to try and make sense of things, to explain them, to bring people to a greater understanding of them. In this sense, our understanding of 'God' really acts as the pinnacle of all our quests for meaning, purpose and fulfilment – in God we discern, however imperfectly and provisionally, the meaning, purpose and fulfilment of all that is, including our own lives. Lest this be misunderstood, this is not simply to relegate 'God' to being *merely* a means of explaining things – God is so much more than that. Much more, indeed, than we can ever, in this mode of earthly existence, hope to comprehend fully.

III. ARGUMENTS AGAINST GOD AS AN ANSWER

As indicated earlier, not everyone would accept the idea of God as the key to the answers in the human quest for meaning, purpose and fulfilment. Indeed, there are a number of crucial arguments which might cast doubt upon the notion of God as an answer to such yearnings. The presence and sheer prevalence of suffering and evil, the sense of meaninglessness, literally that life has *no* meaning, that prevails in the lives of some individuals, particularly at certain points of history and cultural development (e.g. in the nineteenth and twentieth centuries), the aforementioned challenges of philosophical and scientific reason, the prevalence of several different major world religions, all with claims to represent the 'true' or 'right' path in life, the rise of 'subjectivity', where objective 'truths' and certainties are increasingly rejected in favour of self-chosen ways of living, along with the increasing 'post-modern' emphasis upon consumerist choice in all areas of life, even a 'pick and mix' approach to religion itself, all pose particular problems for religious belief, which theology has the ongoing task of seeking to address.

One Possible Solution: The Christian God

There are many challenges to finding satisfaction in our ongoing quest for meaning, purpose and fulfilment as human beings. Just as it had to face challenges in the past, Christian theology provides many responses, which suggest that perhaps these challenges are premature in dismissing the ongoing validity of the Christian path towards meaning and salvation. For Christian theology has encountered many of the doubts and fears of human communities along the way before and it has sought to articulate a coherent and hope-filled way of explaining exactly why the Christian path towards meaning and salvation can meet with such challenges and can continue to prove a valid path even in the postmodern world. It does not claim to have definite and absolute answers – to do so would be misleading (for, as we said, some questions cannot be answered in such a way). Instead, Christian theology proceeds by means of pointing towards those greater and ultimate truths, towards meaning, purpose, direction and fulfilment. Our language, for example, about God's very self is always provisional and, from our standpoint, never the 'full picture'.

So, theological language is always *analogical*, that is, it tries to say something about God by drawing upon the words and concepts we have to work with, whilst realising that we are not quite comparing like with like. Hence, for example, when Robbie Burns, the Scottish poet, said, 'My love is like a red, red rose', he was not saying that the woman he loved was all prickly from the neck down and would wilt after a few days. He was not speaking *literally*. Rather, he was speaking *analogically* – he was trying to communicate to his readers that his love was beautiful, fragrant, etc.

Christian theology is rich with symbolism, for it seeks to bring people closer to an understanding of human truths by painting a rich tapestry of meaning and understanding. Therefore, theological language is often misunderstood or indeed misrepresented if it is only taken in a literal sense. As the British Catholic theologian, Nicholas Lash, has said, 'The crucial question is not whether we can speak of God "literally", but whether we can speak of God truthfully'.[3]

Let us thus explore some of the fundamental (here understood as 'foundational' or most important) ways in which Christian theology offers meaning, purpose and fulfilment in our world.

1.   Creation–Providence

Christian theology does not simply speak of God bringing the world into being. Indeed, to understand the doctrine of creation in terms of a one-off event in the distant historical past is to completely misunderstand the doctrine altogether. For (going back to the 'conditions for the possibility of knowing') if God created, i.e. brought into existence (into being), the universe and everything in it, then God also brought time itself into existence: there was no 'time' when the universe was not, so to speak. Time began with the universe. And God did not (despite what some believe) bring the world into being and then leave it at that. The classical Christian understanding of creation is that God 'creates' the universe in every moment of its existence. What does this mean? That God not only 'creates' but 'sustains', 'take cares of', 'provides for' the universe in each and every moment and for everything within it. Creation–sustenance then is a continuum, not two separate ways in which God has 'acted' for the world.

The theological term for all of this is the doctrine of 'providence'. It does *not* mean that God controls, like a puppeteer, every event that takes place in the world. For, made in the image and likeness of God, humans have been given the dignity of *freedom*. And this freedom even allows us to go astray from God's own love. Nonetheless, it does point towards the fact that God relates to the world and all within it in every moment of their existence and wills for them to say 'yes' to that love and to come closer to God's own being.

2.   Fall and Grace

Christianity does not try to paint an overtly and misleadingly optimistic picture of human existence. It realises that, whatever the best pathway for humans to travel along in their lives, we frequently choose the wrong path or stray from the right one. In trying to follow the path that leads us towards fulfilment (for Christians, that is communion with God and salvation), we often fall short, like an archer missing the target. We go the wrong way and do the wrong things. Hence the concept of 'sin' – which (in the Greek *hamartia*) literally means 'missing the mark' (hence an *analogy* taken from archery). Christian theology, then, explains that humans have a propensity towards going the wrong way, missing the mark, towards 'sin' (and it explains this in a variety of ways).

Yet that is not the end of the story, for theology also tries to explain that Christians believe God does not leave us alone to go further astray. God wants us to follow the right path which leads towards unity with God's own self. Thus, God continuously points the way for humans to return to the right path that leads towards meaning, purpose, fulfilment and salvation. God tries to bring 'lost sheep' back into the fold and God does this whether we deserve it or not. It is not a question of God choosing only to rescue (to 'save') those who previously did the best in following the right path – God freely (for God is under no obligation to do anything) offers us the means to return to the path to salvation. It is, if you like, a pure 'gift' of God. The theological term for this is *grace* (which comes the term for 'gift', or 'freely given').

What does this gift consist of? It is nothing other than the gift of God's own self, which God 'discloses' or communicates to us in the midst of our everyday lives. Christianity believes (on rational grounds as well as those of faith) that the most defining characteristic of God's very self is limitless love (a very hard concept to imagine, admittedly, but theology has plenty of symbols that try to explain this further). God's self-communication then is that wondrous gift of the love that God *is*. Pope Benedict XVI chose this theme for the subject of his very first letter to all Catholics; in other words, he chose to write about the fact that God *is* love (*Deus caritas est*).

3. Experience

A further fundamental source for Christian theology is found in the very lives of Christians themselves. Our lived existence, our 'experience', along with those experiences of other Christians before us and, indeed, of those of other faiths and of none, is believed to also disclose to us something of the nature and truth of this God who is love. From the depths of God's very self, God graciously (hence the term *ex gratis*) gives of that love in order to bring us closer to that same self, towards unity with God (being at one with God, i.e. 'at-one-ment'). Certain Christians in history have lived such extraordinary lives, whether in terms of faith or their steadfast and exemplary practicing of the love that God reveals (their 'heroic virtue'), that they are said to embody and point the way towards the true path of salvation for us all. These people are special, seen to be particularly 'close' to God, to be 'holy', the Latin for which is *sanctus*: they are 'saints'.

4. Emmanuel

God's providence is not limited to all that we have outlined above, nor, even, through the ongoing self-communication of God's love to the world. Christian theology teaches that God was so moved to orient human existence back towards the rightful path of love, meaning and fulfilment (to bring about salvation), that God – with the most astonishing display of humility conceivable – actually came amongst humanity in first-century Palestine in the person of Jesus of Nazareth. The early Christians further built upon the Jewish understanding of God's promises ('covenant') to the human family here and adopted the name of 'Emmanuel' as one of many names for Jesus of Nazareth – a name which means 'God is with us'.

5. God-Talk

Such beliefs and teachings (doctrines) of the Christian Church obviously need further explanation. Some explanations, which were formulated in a particular century and region and therefore in a particular cultural and intellectual context, sometimes subsequently seem less clear in later and different contexts. So the Church believes there is an ongoing challenge to articulate the essentials and life-transforming beliefs that Christians hold most dear for each and every generation and location. Indeed, as Christians believe God continues to offer the self-communicating love in each and every part of the world at each and every moment, obviously we can learn new ways in which to bear witness to and make sense of that love of God. Therefore, Catholics believe that doctrine *develops* – it does not remain static and 'set in stone', only to be explained in a rigid and particular way once and for all.

Theology is charged with making sense of all this, with trying to explain these beliefs for each and every generation. Thus, 'God-talk' is an ongoing task and challenge.

IV. THE TRIUNE GOD

One of the most distinctive features of the Christian faith that sets it apart from most other religions is the fact that, although Christians believe in just *one* God (monotheism), they nonetheless bear witness to and understand their relationship to God, indeed, they explain the very being of God itself in a *threefold* way. The Christian God is *triune*. God is one (unity) in three distinct ways (trinity). This is further explained by theology in a variety of ways.

1. Mystery

As we have previously stated, Christian theology acknowledges the limitations of human knowledge (conditions for the possibility of knowledge). So, in the very 'depths' of God's innermost being, we cannot hope to know in a certain and definitive fashion what God is actually like. Much Christian theology (in common with some other faiths) has a concept of divine 'mystery'; that is, that there are truths about the being of God that remain hidden from human understanding (hence 'mystics' and 'mystical theology'). But this is not a 'cop-out', resorting to the claim that some things are a 'mystery' because we cannot answer the challenges posed to religion by its critics. Indeed, mystical theology involves some of the most complex epistemological (the study of knowledge) challenges one can possibly attempt to discuss. In any case, whilst some aspects of God's being remain hidden from us thus far in this mode of existence, the story, happily, does not end there.

2. Self-Giving

We have already spoken about the most defining characteristic of God being love. Christians believe that, by God's very nature, God is 'self-giving' in each and every act that God engages in. If love is the most fundamental aspect of the very self of God, how could this be otherwise? And so God does not 'leave us alone' to dwell upon the 'mysteries', for, as we said earlier, the self of God is love and God seeks to transform, to save human lives by communicating that fact, by God's offer of 'grace', through the self-communication of the divine being itself (love).

3. Revelation

God, Christian theology tells us, *makes known*, 'reveals' aspects of that divine being. God discloses to us aspects of what God is truly like and adds to our understanding of God's love and plan for our salvation. The theological term for this is 'revelation'. Revelation is not to be understood as being like a savings account, where each 'bit' of revelation, like euros or pounds or dollars paid into the bank account, 'adds' to the total, making the 'amount' of revelation rise over the years. Rather, revelation has only one object (and indeed subject) – the being of God. Revelation is simply the self-revealing of the threefold God. Of course, Christianity believes that the Bible, Holy Scripture (sacred writings), captures in a special way much of the truth of God's self-disclosure. Further, in the person of Jesus of Nazareth, the most definitive, and in numerous ways, once-and-for-all disclosure of God's very self has been made in the midst of human history. Yet, *Catholic* theology also believes that there is an ongoing task to make sense of, shed light upon and understand anew or better God's self-disclosure and loving purpose for the world. Hence the Church, theologians, Christians, communities, saints and anywhere human experience discloses the God of love all add to the store of *interpreting* the self-revealing of God. Much of it is 'handed on' (tradition, which comes from the Latin to 'hand over') and, in turn, reinterpreted for differing times, locations and contexts.

4. Trinity and Creation

The doctrine of the Trinity answers the questions 'Who is God?' and 'What is God like?' For it bears testimony to the three-fold *experience* of God to which Christians, from the very beginning of the faith, have borne witness to. It also makes sense of the self-giving, loving nature of God, who would otherwise remain mostly mystery to our limited intellectual and spiritual capabilities. Additionally, it points towards further explaining why and how the world came to be and remains in existence. The self-giving nature of God led to God uttering forth God's 'Word', and the world, creation, is the result of such utterance. God could have remained silent. God, being self-giving love, did not. If I speak, some meaning comes forth. If God speaks (we are employing analogy again here), the world is what results. Indeed, God chose to 'speak' again in a most definitive fashion: for, as the beginning of John's Gospel tells us, God's 'Word' was there from the start; it represents God's creative and self-giving nature. However, the 'Word' became flesh (incarnation) and 'dwelt amongst us' (Emmanuel). Hence, Jesus of Nazareth, the Christ, is also understood to be God's Word.

The ongoing gift of God's self, the presence of God's love, the transformative energy by which God relates to the world is the third and final aspect of this threefold understanding of God's being. God, the mystery, speaks and what comes forth is the magnificent 'Word' that brings the very world into existence and attempts to sustain it in that existence on the right path. The result of all this is the 'Spirit of God' dwelling throughout the world, transforming lives and creation itself – seeking to bring the love of God, the 'Spirit of God' into the hearts and minds of human beings anew.

5. Relational

Christianity believes in a God who, in the very depths of divine being, is understood to be the most perfect and loving *community* of persons. However, 'person' is not understood here as isolated individual in the modern sense. Rather, it points to the ancient world's understanding that one's 'persona' referred to one's role within a community (it originally meant the mask an actor wore and so 'role' they were playing). Thus, God is God in three very different ways and yet God is always one. God is not God in any fuller sense as 'Father' than God is as 'Son', nor is God any fuller or more divine when God is experienced as 'Spirit'. God is a trinity of 'co-equal, co-divine and co-eternal persons'. God relates to the world in three distinct 'ways (or modes) of being' God. God is threefold even in the hidden depths of God's very being. For the same God who is mystery *is* the God who relates to the world in a threefold way and brings us towards salvation (communion with God). God is the perfect, all-loving, all-equal community.

6.   Athens and Jerusalem

Much of Christian doctrine then, and the theology which seeks to make sense of it, has been necessarily complex in form. It is important to remember that we are dealing with things that stretch up to the very limits of what is currently knowable to humans. Just as we said earlier that Christian theology has always championed the value of faith and reason working in tandem, so here it is worth pointing out that this was the case from very early on in the Church's history (though not to everyone's liking!). For the fundamental doctrines in the Christian faith, in their classical formulations, owe just as much to the philosophical traditions of the Ancient Hellenistic world (i.e. those regions of the world influenced by Greek learning and culture), as they do to Jewish religious and theological traditions. So, despite the objections of the second- and third-century Church father, Tertullian, and numerous Christians since, in Christian theology 'Athens' (philosophy) has always had a great deal to do with 'Jerusalem' (faith).

V.   GOD INCARNATE

Now we turn to that most distinctive aspect of the Christian faith: that God came amongst the human family and we are brought back to 'Emmanuel'. The fact that God came amongst humanity in the person of Jesus is so distinctive a feature of the Christian faith that Christianity takes it name from this occasion when God became 'flesh' (incarnation means 'enfleshment').

1.   Jesus the Christ

The notion of 'Emmanuel' was developed further by the early Church. They believed that God had brought to pass what the Jewish faith had borne witness to – that God would send the 'anointed one' (the Messiah or, in Greek, Christ) amongst God's people. Thus, 'Christ' is not like a surname. Rather, as the German theologian Paul Tillich said, we should always understand this doctrine by prefacing it with the definite article, Jesus 'the' Christ, to appreciate fully its significance for the early Church and Christians thereafter.

2.   Truly God and Truly Human

Indeed, Christians went further still than their Jewish inheritance by coming to articulate their belief that, in the human person of Jesus, God's own self was present and active. The complexities of this paradoxical statement need not detain us here. It is worth noting though that it detained the early Church for some centuries until they settled upon the summary explanation of what this means and is now found in the Creed that Christians recite every Sunday (*credo* meaning 'I believe'). Suffice to say here that Christianity believes that Jesus of Nazareth was fully God and fully human.

3.   Salvation and Atonement

The doctrine of the incarnation is crucial to the very business of Christianity – human salvation and atonement with God – re-orienting our path towards communion with God, despite our sinful mistakes and frequent straying. For, as the early Church taught, in going astray, we clouded that share in the being of God which we were granted at birth. So far astray did the human family go from the right path 'home' that God was moved to humble the divine being by becoming human *in order that* human beings might become one with God, might become 'divine'.[4]

4.   God and Love

All of this relates to that earlier mentioned and most essential understanding of the nature of God that Christianity bears witness to – that God is love. For, as the New Testament tells us, God *so loved the world* (Jn 3:16) that he 'gave over' Jesus of Nazareth, God incarnate, the 'Son of God', to the powers of sin and death in order that sin and death would never enjoy the same power again.

CONCLUSION: TAKING LIFE ON FAITH

Christian theology seeks to commend the promise and transformative power of, the very reasonableness of, taking life 'on faith': of living with our limitations, imperfections, unanswered questions, of living without certainties but thereby being released to move towards a greater form of understanding which can really lead us towards greater meaning, purpose and fulfilment in our lives.

In all this, the Christian faith points towards that 'dimension' of existence which brings us out of the ordinary, everyday humdrum concerns of life and points towards what is beyond self, beyond the material, beyond the ordinary mode of existence itself – that which brought us into being and sustains us in that being. This is what Christians refer to as God. In any experience that draws us out of ourselves – such as in appreciating beauty, in coming to understand a significant truth, in witnessing true goodness or in giving or receiving love, we experience the *transcendental* aspect of our being that is the path towards true meaning, purpose and fulfilment. It points us towards God so the path of 'transcendence', towards that limitless horizon, can be glimpsed in every moment where we experience the revelation of the God of love. As theology tells us, we gain glimpses of this even in the everyday experiences of life, wherever we are touched by the good, the true, the beautiful – for these are analogical pathways towards God's own self. They are our lanterns along the journey towards meaning, towards being *fully* human, towards 'going home', where we will find peace for our 'restless hearts'.

Notes

1   Richard P. McBrien, *Catholicism* (2nd ed.) London: Geoffrey Chapman, 1994, p. 571.

2   None of this is to suggest that there is only 'one' correct way of following any particular religious faith. But if some characteristic 'way' of living might be said to represent true Christianity, then perhaps these Ancient Pagans who said, 'Look how these Christians love one another', might provide a clue as to what it would be.

3   Nicholas Lash, *Theology on the Way to Emmaus*, London: SCM, 1986, p. 164.

4   St Athanasius, *De Incarnatione Verbi Dei*, 54, 3:PG, 192B.

CHAPTER 2

CATHOLICISM AND WESTERN CULTURE

Lawrence S. Cunningham

Introduction

This chapter will indicate in broad terms how the rise of Christianity in the West had and continues to have a lasting impact on the common culture of the West. That influence is so pervasive that it is easy to forget that many of today's institutions, ideas and even our language betray that influence. How many of us use the word 'breakfast' and consider that literally we are 'breaking a fast' when we eat in the morning? How many are aware that clocks were first invented by monks who needed to know what time of day it was in order to gather for their common prayer? If you have a friend whose surname is 'Palmer', did you know that one of his ancestors was probably a pilgrim who had gone to the Holy Land and returned with a palm branch tied to his walking staff? Or that the word 'saunter' originally meant 'a saint terre' – to walk to the Holy Land? Or that Christmas originally meant 'Christ's Mass' – the religious celebration that goes back to the fourth century in Rome. In many ways our language, our customs and our habits derive from the profound influence the Catholic faith has had upon our common culture. We cannot, in this brief chapter, even begin to discuss the ways our culture has been shaped by the faith but we can provide some broad outlines of that influence.

Charitable Institutions

Writing in the middle of the second century Justin Martyr described Sunday worship in Rome. At the conclusion of his narrative about the liturgy he says that a collection was taken up and preserved by the head of the community for 'orphans and widows, those who are needy because of sickness or any other reasons, and for captives and strangers in our midst' (*Apology*, 67). In this early period the community provided for all who were in need on a local basis because they were a persecuted community, as they would be until the beginning of the fourth century. Their charity towards the needy was a simple response to the demand of Jesus that the hungry, thirsty, naked, imprisoned were to be helped as if Christ himself was the one being aided; truly, Jesus said, 'just as you did it to one of the least of these who are members of my family, you did it for me' (Mt 25:40).

When Christianity became a tolerated religion in the Roman Empire after the emperor Constantine issued his decree in Milan in 313 CE, the Catholic Church was able to develop more public ways of fulfilling Christ's commands to support and aid those in need. Almost every major charitable institution that one finds in every city in Europe, the United Kingdom and Ireland can trace its origins back to the influence of the Catholic Church's desire to help those in need. It is easy to forget that hospitals, hospices, orphanages, asylums, soup kitchens, shelters and even hotels (originally places for pilgrims to stay as they travelled) are rooted in the Catholic tradition of care for those in need. Between the second and fifth centuries we know that the care centres administered by ordained deacons provided the following: inns for travellers; infirmaries for the sick; foundling homes for abandoned babies; orphanages for those left without family; shelters for women prostitutes (usually under the patronage of Saint Mary Magdalene) and homes for the aged.

As monasticism grew in the West it was also quite common to find, in a period when cities were in decline, granaries for food against the threat of famine and, more importantly, pharmacies for the dispensing of herbs and medicines to the sick. Many of the great hospitals in Europe today began under religious auspices like Saint Bart's in London, the Hotel Dieu in Paris, Holy Spirit (*Santo Spirito*) in Rome and the great hospital (*Ospedale Maggiore*) in Milan. It is true that many such institutions are maintained either under civil or other religious groups but the very notion of such places of care have their remote origins in the Catholic culture of the West.

Education

Even as early as the period of the Roman persecution there were schools for the education of the young. Justin Martyr had a catechetical school in Rome in the middle of the second century; there was another one in Alexandria in

Egypt that flourished in the second century. With the rise of monasteries in the early middle ages, schools and scholars were a feature of all of these institutions. Great scholars in the British Isles like the Venerable Bede, Alcuin and others not only kept learning alive when city life was in decline but Irish monks also did the same in their own country and on the continent. Nuns provided education in their convents for themselves and their lay boarders, and chances are that a female writer in the Middle Ages would have been educated in a convent. Women, alas, had few opportunities for higher education until the modern period.

With the rise of city life local bishops opened cathedral schools to train clerics and literate persons who could serve in the government. Cathedral schools and those connected to monasteries were the organisations from which arose what today we call the university (L. *Universitas*). The story of the university is an interesting one. For our purposes, we will focus on their start in Paris. Towards the end of the twelfth century students flocked to Paris to study with famous teachers attached to the school of the cathedral or the abbey churches of Saint Victor or Saint Genevieve. The teachers formed a corporation like the medieval guilds which they called the *universitas* in order to exert quality control over teaching. In time, they were recognised in law with the power to grant teaching licenses ('masters of arts') and, finally, the right to be called a 'doctor' (L. *docere* – to teach). The *universitas* in Paris was centred on the left bank of the river, soon to be called the 'Latin Quarter', which honoured the language of instruction. One of the colleges for students was endowed by Robert de Sorbon in 1258, which has given the present name of the Sorbonne.

There seems to have been a university at Oxford in the middle of the twelfth century and, due to a quarrel, some scholars left and began a rival school at Cambridge. Many of the colleges of these universities still have names that reflect their ancient Catholic past: Magdalen, Corpus Christi, Christ Church, Trinity, etc. There were similar universities all over Europe, the majority of which followed the Paris model, although the ancient university of Bologna was quite different: the students formed the *universitas* and hired the faculty! By 1500 there were over sixty universities in western Europe, although all did not survive. Those that did have their deep roots in Catholic culture and reflect the Church's mission of education.

Arts

Anyone who has ever strolled through a museum knows quickly that the arts have played a crucial role in the development of western culture. It would not even be possible to list in this chapter the paintings, sculpture, mosaics, frescos and other visual materials which the Church used to instruct the faithful in the mysteries of the Faith (medieval stained glass windows were often called 'the Bible of the Poor') but we can at least call attention to the enormous impact that the Church had on the development of the arts by using one great example: the role of the medieval cathedral.

A cathedral is the church of the local bishop. It gets its name from the *cathedra* – the bishop's chair from which he taught, preached and ruled his local church. Every city had one and some of the finest are to be found in Britain: Canterbury, Christchurch, York, Exeter. First of all, the cathedral was a marvel of architectural technology as artisans learned to create high walls which could be open enough to allow for stained glass. The exterior of the cathedral had elaborate sculptural displays that instructed the faithful in a visual fashion. When one entered the church itself all of the senses were engaged, from the sweet odour of the incense to the music of the liturgy to the visual impact of the sun illuminating the stained glass to the very structure of the cathedral (especially the Gothic cathedral) which drew the eyes upward by the powerful force of the vertical lines. In a sense, the cathedral was designed to help a person experience the sacredness of the place and, by extension, God who was worshiped there. The great cathedrals of Europe were, in essence, a complex interplay of sculpture, painting, music and architecture providing a single experience of God being among us.

When we look at a typical parish church today it is easy to forget that what one finds in such a church is the end result of nearly two thousand years of experiment, tradition and reform shaped by the desire of the church to make the building a place for proclaiming the Gospel. To look closely at the interior of a church is to see a compression of history.

The modern church, like those of ancient times, had two essential elements: a place for the reading of the scriptures and for preaching and an altar for the celebration of the Eucharist: Word and Sacrament. A chapel or an altar for Our Lady and/or a patronal saint came as an early medieval addition. A tabernacle for reserving the Holy Eucharist became common in the high-middle ages; the use of stained glass was also a medieval advancement; Stations of the Cross became common only in the early modern period. Baptismal fonts date from an early period but confessionals came into churches only in the high-middle ages. Candles and lamps, which today are ornamental, were how the church was illuminated until the late nineteenth century. Painting the walls or the sanctuary with sacred scenes goes back into the very early medieval era and perhaps, in the case of mosaics, to the late fourth century. In other words: to look closely at a typical church today is to see a tremendous amount of historical development but, at the centre, there was always a preaching of the Word and celebrating of the Eucharist.

What is true of the visual arts is also true of drama. The earliest plays in the West began in monasteries as monks acted out the coming of the 'Three Marys' discovering the empty tomb of Jesus, done within the church itself. Soon, the dialogue was expanded and the subject matter became more varied with the result that the 'plays' were first performed on the church porch and later on moveable large carts called pageants. By the high-middle ages there were whole cycles of plays performed at various times during the year to coincide with the seasons of the liturgy. When Shakespeare was still a boy he probably saw these so-called 'mystery' or 'miracle' plays performed in or near Stratford. When Hamlet instructs the players not to be too noisy or to show off too much because it 'out Herods Herod' (Act III, Scene II) he is making reference to a stock figure in one of the old religious plays about the Nativity of Jesus. It is from those old plays that all of western drama derives. Shakespeare's own plays are a development of a kind of drama that traces its roots back to the dramatic character of the Catholic liturgy which marries together word and gesture.

It would take volumes to even outline the impact Catholic Christianity has had on the literature of the West but one example might be useful. Saint Augustine wrote his *Confessions* sometime towards the end of the fourth century. Many scholars have named that book as the first real example of autobiography produced in the West. The very idea of charting one's life and, in Augustine's case, seeing it as it unfolds as a search for meaning and significance in the light of God's providence, triggered, in time, a vast literature of such self-reflection. Autobiography, in the deepest sense, is not like a diary which records things as they happen or even a memoir which sees one's life against the background of important historical moments (which is why politicians, actors and military people tend to write memoirs). An autobiography is a recollection of the development of one's own conscious life and intellectual and spiritual development. The best autobiography is a kind of spiritual journey, which explains why the best examples have been such an inspiration for others. Autobiographies like Thomas Merton's *Seven Storey Mountain* or C.S. Lewis's *Surprised by Joy* or the great nineteenth-century *Apologia pro Vita Sua* by John Henry Newman give us a glimpse into the workings of grace upon the intelligence and searching of people who, like pilgrims, move towards a definite end. That is why Dante, at the end of the *Paradiso* in *The Divine Comedy*, could describe himself as being like a pilgrim who has reached his destination. That connection of pilgrimage and discovery is why the Second Vatican Council rightly called the Church the 'Pilgrim People of God'.

Socio-Political Culture

The Christian West has many different forms of political organisation ranging from monarchy to republican representation. All of these forms have behind them a long history. However, the Christian world today shares in certain fundamental values, some of them arrived at after long periods of discernment and struggle, that are characteristic of the world in which we live. Many of these values are enshrined in our body of law (like the English Common Law) while others are located in our national documents. We take it for granted, for example, that individuals have some basic human rights, that persons may not be capriciously punished by the government without evidence of wrongdoing; we resist cruel and unusual punishment of those who do commit crimes, we value the right of family integrity, we think that the most disadvantaged should receive the concern of civil society, and so on.

We need not look back into history but into other parts of the world today to see that these values are not uniformly agreed upon, let alone put into political practice. Now a good case can be made that most of the values we so highly prize in democratic society would be unthinkable if certain ideas, drawn from the teaching of Christianity and its parent religion, Judaism, had not made such a long lasting impact on our common heritage. As the late Pope John Paul II insisted, the fundamental biblical doctrine that all (not just some!) are created 'in the image and likeness of God' (Gen 1:27) has had enormous implications for everything from insisting on basic human rights, to the development of theories of social justice, to the basic right to life, to the insistence that everyone, as a child of God, has the right to decent life, shelter, work, and so on. The very fact that both western governments and independent agencies like Amnesty International, Oxfam and International Red Cross work everywhere in the world is a small indication of how the ancient Christian teaching about care for others has been bred into western consciousness, even though today many of these efforts are only barely conscious of their ancient Christian roots.

These ideas and activities, now commonplace in political talk, are hard-won truths that came about from centuries of reflection by forward-thinking persons, often speaking for the Church, who tried to understand fully the meaning and the imperatives of the Gospel. It should also be said that the Church not only values these hard won values but wants to see them developed for all human beings. It is for this reason that the Church, often to the dismay of the satisfied who already possess the goods of the world, side with the immigrant, the disenfranchised, the persecuted, the unloved, the disabled, the elderly, poor and all others who do not share in the hard-won gifts of our social order.

Conclusion

It would be a mistake to think that everything good in our common culture derives directly from the impact of Catholic Christianity on the West. Anyone who knows history also knows many ugly things have been done in the name of religion. Nonetheless, it is important to understand that for all the failings of individual Catholics and its institutions, the basic idea of love of God and neighbour so insistently preached by Jesus and treasured in the Church has entered into our world in crucial and formative ways.

Jesus himself likened his message to small things – the mustard seed or the leaven in a mass of dough that grows, enlarges and changes. That is a good way of thinking about the Church and its message in culture: small constant efforts to help people, to bring peace, to aid the needy, to allow true human life to flourish free from inhuman conditions. All of those efforts manifest themselves in culture. Some efforts flourish as major movements or institutions while others remain local and hidden. Such efforts have been developed by gifted individuals and others by groups and communities. All of those efforts, small and large, are signs that the Gospel is still alive and still practiced. They are not now nor will they ever be perfect; such perfection will only come in God's good time, which is why we pray always, 'Thy Kingdom come'.

The presence of the Church's influence on our culture, described so briefly in this chapter, is not merely a record of the past; it is, rather, a fact of the present. Whatever the Church has accomplished was brought about by a response to the call of the Gospel and that call is as insistent today as it was when the Twelve began to preach two millennia ago. It is every person's responsibility who bears the name Catholic and it is easy to do. As Peter Maurin, one of the founders of the Catholic Worker Movement, put it so succinctly: 'Step outside the door and begin to do good.'

Further Reading

Cunningham, Lawrence S., The Catholic Heritage, New York: Crossroad, 1983.

O'Collins, Gerald and Farrugia, Mario, Catholicism: The Story of Catholic Christianity, New York and London: Oxford University Press, 2003.

Benedict XVI, Deus caritas est, 2005.

Paul VI, Gaudium et spes, 1965.

SECTION 1

CHRISTIAN FOUNDATIONS

CHAPTER 3

THE HEBREW BIBLE

Martin O'Kane

Introduction

'The Old Testament' is the name traditionally given to the first part of the Christian Bible and conveys the idea, held by Christians, that much of its history, beliefs and theology are fulfilled in 'The New Testament', centred around the person of Christ. Frequently, however, this first section of the Bible is now referred to as 'The Hebrew Bible', reflecting the more neutral and inclusive view that its stories, characters and values are not only important for an understanding of the New Testament and Christianity but also lie at the very heart of Judaism. Additionally many of its themes and events are also reflected in the Koran so that, in a very real sense, we can say that the Hebrew Bible is immensely significant for an understanding of the world's three monotheistic faiths: Judaism, Christianity and Islam.

For many scholars and commentators, however, the terms 'Old Testament' and 'Hebrew Bible' are quite interchangeable and readers should use whatever term they feel most comfortable with. My own preference is to use 'Hebrew Bible' because it underlines yet another factor – and an absolutely crucial one – that although we read it in translation, the original language of this part of the Bible is Hebrew. There is probably no other language, ancient or modern, that can so powerfully and vividly express the dilemmas and ambiguities of the human condition or explore the perceived presences and absences of God, known as Yahweh, in the world. The Hebrew authors, through a subtle use of language, excel in creating tantalising plots, storylines and characters to convey how Yahweh is the force that directs the destinies of humans – sometimes quietly and unobtrusively as in the stories of the early patriarchs of Genesis, Abraham, Isaac and Jacob, but at other times dramatically and flamboyantly as in the stories associated with Moses and the events of the Exodus. These grandiose narratives – in which the reader may sometimes feel a powerless outsider – are balanced elsewhere in the Hebrew Bible by intensely personal poetry often expressing the joys, sorrows and emotions of the individual (particularly in the Psalms) with which the reader might more readily identify. The Hebrew Bible is, then, first and foremost inspirational literature, made up of narrative and poetry and we should approach it as such if we are to draw out effectively its meaning and richness.

Unlike the Greek language (in which the New Testament is written), Hebrew is concerned not with the abstract and conceptual but rather with the immediate, the earthy, the tangible and the visual. No wonder then, that it is the Hebrew Bible that has had the most profound influence on the arts in our western culture. Writers, musicians, artists and film-makers have all succumbed to the potential of the biblical story and have explored its subtleties and nuances through many different artistic forms. Often what we know about the Hebrew Bible comes not from the text itself but from a visual expression of it, in a church, art gallery or film. This can be a really wonderful way to enter the world of the Bible and to learn to ask challenging questions of it in the same way that the artist has done. Frequently we find that, in addition to depicting what is expressed in the biblical story, the artist (for example, Rembrandt or Caravaggio) will draw attention to those characters deliberately silenced or marginalised by the biblical author and, through their painting, give a voice to the voiceless – particularly in the case of women in the Hebrew Bible, as feminist biblical critics have amply demonstrated. Contemporary biblical scholars value the contribution of artists and musicians in illuminating the biblical text and in helping us see how texts can be read in a whole range of original and imaginative ways.

The literature of the Hebrew Bible operates within specific geographical and historical parameters. Its world is bordered on the west by the River Nile in Egypt and on the east by the Tigris and Euphrates rivers running through ancient Mesopotamia, in what is today Iraq. Jerusalem, capital of the kingdom of Judah and the location of the Temple, the dwelling place of God, was situated more or less at the crossroads between two major empires, Egypt and Mesopotamia, and its fate was frequently in the hands of one or other of these major powers. This is reflected in the movement of individuals and groups throughout the

Hebrew Bible and is responsible for providing that nomadic flavour we associate with the ancient Near East. At the command of God, Abraham travels from Ur in Mesopotamia to Canaan (today's Israel and the occupied territories) and later Joseph settles in Egypt and consolidates the Hebrew people there. Subsequently, under Moses, the Israelites travel through Sinai to the 'Promised Land', graphically described in the Book of Exodus, which they now re-name Israel (in the same way that their ancestor Jacob had been re-named 'Israel' in Genesis). Later, when Jerusalem falls to the Assyrians in 587 BCE, the people are taken into exile in Babylon. Quite apart from these massive upheavals and movements of people that punctuate the narrative, the literature of the Hebrew Bible seems to consist of a never-ending series of unrelated arrivals and departures, comings and goings, beginning with the expulsion of Adam and Eve from the garden. This, as we shall see, is quite deliberate.

Scholars trace the first editions of our Hebrew Bible to the period of exile in Babylon to 587 BCE. At this time the Hebrew editors collected in one edition earlier literary material that had existed independently. As they edited the material, they were keen to create an impressive 'history' that would serve as a record preserving the ancient heritage of the Jewish people. In many ways, this is specifically a 'theological' history rather than 'history' as we might define it today, in the sense that the editors were keen to document the relationship between God and his chosen people rather than provide a mere political or social history. The purpose was to trace their heritage right back to illustrious ancestors in ancient times – to the patriarchs Abraham, Isaac and Jacob, through a line of powerful kings such as David and Solomon and guided by the strong moral voices of the different prophets. Most importantly, however, the editors sought to identify and comment on the causes of their exile in the first place. How could God, who had selected the Israelites as his chosen people and who chose Jerusalem as his dwelling place in the Temple, abandon them in their hour of need? It is these two aspects, the providing of an illustrious 'history' for the Jewish people and a justification for the exile within that history, that really shaped the Hebrew Bible and gave it its essential form and structure that we still have today. Although some significant additions were subsequently made to this, even a superficial reading of the text shows that it is the theme of exile and expulsion that haunts the Hebrew Bible from the very beginning –

starting with the story of the exile of the first man and woman from the presence of God in the Garden of Eden.

Structure

The structure of the Hebrew Bible can be loosely divided into five sections: (a) the Pentateuch (Gk *five*) which consists of the first five books of the Bible starting from the story of creation in Genesis and concluding with the death of Moses in Deuteronomy; (b) the 'historical' books, starting from Joshua's entry into the Promised Land in the Book of Joshua and ending in 2 Kings with the fall of Jerusalem and the exile to Babylon; (c) prophetic literature that expresses the ethical and moral concerns of the ancient Hebrew world; (d) the Psalms, sometimes described as the 'hymnbook of the temple'; (e) wisdom literature which concerns itself with reflecting, sometimes in a philosophical way, on the meaning of life, for example the Books of Job and Ecclesiastes. Scholars today emphasise the importance of engaging with each of these sections as *literature* rather than attempting to use them *chronologically* to create an accurate and continuous history of an ancient past – something that the texts do not really allow us to do. So briefly, I want to outline the most significant literary aspects to look out for in each of the five sections.

(a) The Pentateuch

The first five books of the Bible are the most important and authoritative of the entire Bible for Judaism and are called the *Torah* (meaning Law) since they relate the processes by which God gave the Jewish law to the Israelites through Moses, culminating with the issuing of the ten commandments in Exodus 20. In fact, the entire Book of Deuteronomy purports to be the last words of Moses before he dies and in which he details the value and purposes of the Law for posterity. However, the Pentateuch is much more than that. The reader is swept along from the initial and dramatic creation of the world by God in Genesis 1 (wonderfully expressed in so many works of art), through the fall of Adam and Eve (Genesis 3), to an exploration of how evil inclinations came into the world, through the early ancestry of the patriarchs Abraham, Isaac and Jacob and concluding with the story of Joseph in Egypt at the end of the Book of Genesis. It is in the superb storytelling and through the creation of such wonderful characters (and not through abstract theology) that the author communicates to us how God acts in the world. God is presented in a variety of ways: he is creator, he is given human characteristics, he is protective, he punishes, he saves, and in the story of Isaac he rewards the deviousness and deceit of Rebeccah and Jacob. The many different aspects of God are explored in such a way that he is presented as perhaps the most controversial and ambiguous character in the entire narrative. The author elicits sympathy for some characters but antipathy for others: Abraham is presented in a very good light although he acts as a dysfunctional father to both his sons, Isaac and Ishmael. While Isaac is presented as a weak, ineffective patriarch, his wife Rebeccah is presented as powerful and manipulative. Within the Pentateuch, one of the most moving and most brilliantly constructed narratives, is the story of Joseph, and the reader who is not familiar with the Book of Genesis could do no better than to read his story (Genesis 37-50). Other important passages to start with are the dismissal of Hagar and Ishmael (Genesis 21); the sacrifice of Isaac (Genesis 22); the deception of Isaac (Genesis 27). These are all superbly created narratives and will give the reader an appreciation of the skill of the Hebrew authors and the timeless issues with which they wrestle.

(b) The Historical Books

The block of narrative running from Joshua through to 2 Kings gives the impression of a history of sorts but it is really a contrived history, the focus of which is to offer an explanation as to why the people and their leaders were taken into exile in Babylon. The idea of a land promised specifically to the Israelites is clearly laid out in the book of Joshua as well as the choice of Jerusalem as the capital of this land and God's choice to build the Temple, his dwelling place, there. The Book of Judges contains an account of how the early leaders, called *Judges*, protected the land against their perpetual enemy, the Philistines. One particularly excellent account concerns how Samson fulfils his role as judge with God's direction. It is a wonderfully constructed narrative and ends with the death of Samson, brought about by Delilah (Judges 13-16). This is one of the most painted subjects in the entire history of art and typical treatments of the subject by Reubens or van Eyck will help the reader explore some of the darker sides to the story, in particular the role given to Delilah's seductive sexuality in Samson's downfall. The Books of Samuel and Kings critique the moral character of the kings of the land who succeeded the Judges. The fact that many are judged to be inadequate by both God and the author is the main reason for the punishment of exile. The most famous of all kings in Hebrew literature is, of course, David and his story takes up a very large part of this section. David is presented as someone torn between his public duty as king and his private passions and emotions; his affections, both sexual and familial, often get in the way of his royal duties as the narrative 2 Samuel 11 through to 1 Kings 2 amply demonstrates. The reader might wish to reflect on the rights and wrongs of David's actions in relation to Bathsheba in 2 Samuel 11 (and ponder on Rembrandt's *Bathsheba,* hanging in the Louvre) and his grief-stricken reaction to the news of his son Absalom's death, so poignantly related in 2 Samuel 18.

(c) Prophetic Literature

In addition to the three 'major' prophets, Isaiah, Jeremiah and Ezekiel (so called because the books named after them are the longest in the prophetic literature), there are twelve minor prophets. Unlike our meaning of the word today which suggests someone who can see into the future, by 'prophet' in the Hebrew Bible we mean someone who speaks on behalf of God and addresses the concrete social and political situation in which the prophet lived. We really do not know very much for certain about the identity of the prophets (or whether indeed they ever existed) but we do know that much of the literature called after them addresses the theological questions raised by the catastrophe of the exile and explores why such a devastating experience should happen to God's chosen people. For the reader not familiar with prophetic literature, the best place to start is the Book of Isaiah – frequently referred to as 'the finest poetry in all antiquity' – and chapters 40–66 specifically. It is generally agreed that these chapters were written during the period of exile in Babylon where the poet encourages the exiles to return to Jerusalem – God has completed the punishment of his people. The chapters contain exquisite poetry which abounds in exaggerated similes and metaphors that reassure and encourage the people. Uniquely, here too God is imaged as a woman – a woman in labour (Isa 42:14). The Book of Isaiah is extremely important for the New Testament because it is regarded as containing many passages that refer to Christ; for example, 7:14 (the

Emmanuel reference) and especially the image of the famous 'Suffering Servant' (Isa 53) that the early Christians identified as Christ (and Vincent van Gogh as himself). For this reason, the text of Handel's *Messiah* derives almost exclusively from the Book of Isaiah since its purpose is to pick up messianic references from the Hebrew Bible and apply them to Christ.

(d) The Psalms

The Psalms are poems (many of which were composed as songs – the word comes from the Greek verb *psallo*, meaning 'to sing to the accompaniment of the harp') that express a wide variety of sentiment and emotion. Collectively, they are attributed to King David the musician but, despite this traditional association, it is now agreed that they were written over a period of centuries – some to be performed at sacred events in the Temple in Jerusalem, others for individual use. Many of the Psalms were composed simply to praise God, evident in the abundant use of the term *Hallelujah!* (meaning 'Praise God!'); for example, Psalms 8 and 104 emphasise the works of God's creation. Others are poems of thanksgiving, for example, Psalm 92, while others express individual anguish and distress, for example, Psalm 3 and 5–7. Many of the Psalms reflect the superb skill of the Hebrew poet, and the reader unfamiliar with this literature might like to start with the beautiful, intimate and immediately accessible sentiments expressed in Psalm 139. Another Psalm that may be familiar to the reader is Psalm 51, the so-called *Miserere* (L. 'have mercy on'). Traditionally ascribed to David after his union with Bathsheba in 2 Samuel 11, it has had a most illustrious history in the musical traditions of Judaism and Christianity for over two millennia, for example, in Allegri's famous version *Miserere*, as well as a multitude of other musical settings in Hebrew, Greek and Latin.

(e) Wisdom Literature

Wisdom literature is distinctive from any Hebrew literature discussed so far. It is so called because of the number of times 'wisdom' and 'foolishness' occur. The literature has a timeless flavour and suggests that advice it offers is relevant for all times and places. In the Book of Proverbs, the figure of Wisdom is often personified as a woman. Indeed, female figures tend to play a significant part in this literature – even in ways that today we might consider irrelevant or inappropriate – for example, the advice to the male on how to procure a good, wise and virtuous wife (Proverbs 31). King Solomon, son of King David, is the figure most associated with wisdom. Traditionally King Solomon was viewed as the author of the Books of Proverbs and Ecclesiastes. For the reader who wishes to explore this literature, one of the best places to begin is with the Book of Ecclesiastes: it tries to figure out the meaning and purpose of life not from a specifically religious point of view but from the evidence of the cycles of nature and from human experience, both pleasurable and painful.

Terminology

There is some terminology that occurs repetitively in biblical commentaries that needs a word of explanation. *Canon* is a term frequently used in connection with the Hebrew Bible. Essentially it refers to the official list of books that have been accepted as constituting the Hebrew Bible in Judaism and Christianity. For Jews, only books originally written in Hebrew carry authority and therefore only those are included in the Jewish canon, while for Christians some books originally written in Greek (the commonly used language of the early Church) are also included, for example, Tobit, Judith and 1-2 Maccabees. To complicate matters, at the time of the Reformation, Protestant Churches made the decision to retain, as in Judaism, only those books written in Hebrew as authoritative while the Catholic and Orthodox traditions continued to include several books in Greek. In most English versions of the Bible today, the complete list of Greek books can be found under the heading of *Apocryphal* or *Deuterocanonical*. Issues associated with the biblical canon are complex and those engaging with the literature of the Hebrew Bible for the first time need not be overly concerned about them, apart from recognising the terms and understanding why the Hebrew Bible in the Catholic tradition is considerably longer than in Protestant versions. Two other terms should also be mentioned here: the *Septuagint* refers to the Greek translation of the Hebrew Bible (from the Greek word for 'seventy', since tradition has it that seventy translators were involved) and the *Vulgate* refers to the Latin translation (from the Latin word meaning 'common' or 'popular' version), undertaken by St Jerome and used in the Catholic Church right up until the Second Vatican Council in the 1960s. There are, of course, very many English translations of the Hebrew Bible and the one generally recommended as being most sensitive to the nuances of the

Hebrew is the *New Revised Standard Version* (NRSV). For the beginner, it is much more important to read and engage with the actual narrative itself rather than involving oneself in the history of the transmission of the Hebrew Bible through its various translations, which is a task more suited to advanced study.

Conclusion

The most important activity for the person who wants to become more familiar with the Hebrew Bible is to begin by reading specific passages from the text itself rather than commentaries. There is no better starting place than the colourful and entertaining stories of Genesis or the vibrant and passionate poetry of Isaiah 40-66. Remember, too, that it is only right to ask questions of the texts and their authors: how can God treat characters in the way he does? Is the author's explanation of the origins of evil in Genesis too naïve and simplistic? Has the authors' bias towards women, foreigners, specific classes, helped create the concept of the Other, the Outsider, that has been part of western culture and thought for so many centuries? A short bibliography is appended but remember that paintings, sculpture, music and films also act as excellent commentaries on the biblical stories they depict; they too often ask the hard questions of the text that we must continue to ask in every age.

Further Reading

Barton, John and Muddiman, John (eds) *The Oxford Bible Commentary*, Oxford: Oxford University Press, 2001.

Collins, John J., *Introduction to the Hebrew Bible*, Minneapolis: Fortress Press, 2004.

Sawyer, John F. A. (ed.) *The Blackwell Companion to the Bible and Culture*, Oxford: Blackwells, 2006.

CHAPTER 4

THE CHRISTIAN BIBLE

Anne O'Leary

Introduction

The Christian Bible is made up of two parts: the first and larger part consists of the books of the Hebrew Bible (Old Testament); the second and smaller part consists of the New Testament (NT), which tells us much about Jesus of Nazareth. The NT records his pre-existence with God since the beginning of time and how at a point in history he is born of Mary in Bethlehem through the power of God's Holy Spirit (c. 4 CE). It records how, in his life, death and resurrection, he reveals himself to be the Messiah whom the people called 'the Christ' ('Anointed'), 'the Son of God' and 'Saviour of the world', and it records that, subsequent to the resurrection, he promises that his spiritual presence will be with those who believe in him and in the community that forms the Church (Gk *ekklesia*).

The Hebrew Bible provides a record of the Israelites' experience of God's involvement with them in the geographical and spiritual journeys that they make throughout their history. The NT provides a record of how God becomes involved in the history of the world in an utterly new way through the Incarnation that happens when God becomes flesh in Jesus (Jn 1:14). In his adult life (c. early thirties), Jesus begins to live out publicly his unique mission of bringing good news (or God's news) to individuals and communities that he meets along the roads, in the towns and villages, the length and breadth of Israel and sometimes even beyond its boundaries. It is a mission that he shares with those who come to believe in him and which he entrusts to his disciples down through the ages up until now.

What is the 'good news' that Jesus, the Christ, brings? The good news is that he continues God's mission of bringing about reversals, which ultimately bring about goodness and justice in the world, in the whole of creation and the cosmos. The NT records that just as in the past the Jewish people had seen how God 'brought down the powerful from their thrones, and lifted up the lowly'; 'he filled the hungry with good things, and sent the rich away empty' (Lk 1:52; cf. 1 Kings 17:8-16), so now they see how Jesus does the same. Jesus sets about reversing every kind of suffering and injustice that he encounters – physical, social, moral and/or spiritual (Mt 25:31-46). Sometimes 'a reversal' happens when he shares in a meal with people at their homes (cf. Lk 7:36-50); sometimes, it happens out of doors when people go to him (cf. Mk 3:7-12); sometimes he causes it to happen at a distance from where he is (cf. Jn 4:46-54).

Often it is the poor and suffering ones who become the heroes and heroines in Jesus' eyes. Their vulnerability opens the way to receiving him (cf. Mt 9:20-22 pars; Mk 12:41-44 pars; Lk 19:1-10; Jn 9). Always he celebrates the new life given to each one he encounters and he tells those that have 'ears to hear' (i.e. come with faith in him) that God rejoices with them too. Moreover, the people who come to recognise who Jesus truly is celebrate his presence among them (cf. Lk 15).

Jesus challenges powerful people and groups (e.g. the Scribes and the Pharisees) who place unjust economic, political, social and/or religious burdens on others, especially vulnerable people. He goes about addressing the root causes of these realities. He challenges and empowers his followers to do the same. When he sends his disciples out to continue his mission, he tells them that it may cost them economically, socially and spiritually. They may lose their wealth, their worldly status and even their lives. In doing so they inherit the cross and gain eternal life. However, he assures them that, 'those who lose their life for my sake will find it' (Mt 10:39).

Jesus' mission leads ultimately to his being nailed to a cross in Israel's capital city, Jerusalem, by the nation's authorities who are threatened by the kind of kingdom that he is bringing about. Those who are open to it come to understand that it changes how they live their lives. When people query Jesus as to what the most important principles or commandments for life are, he gives them only two:

> This is the first … 'The Lord, our God, the Lord is one;
> [therefore] you shall love the Lord your God with all your heart,
> and with all your soul, and with all your mind, and with all your

strength'. The second is this, 'You shall love your neighbour as yourself.' There is no other commandment greater than these.' (Mk 12:30-31)

All that Jesus says and does points believers to recognise his true identity as the Messiah whose coming inaugurates the messianic age of peace, harmony and right relationships. According to the Hebrew Bible, the Jewish people had longed for this. Jesus wishes each one 'to see' (i.e. to believe) that the origin and end of everything lies ultimately in God and in him, who is the Son of God. Such is the impact that Jesus makes on the people of his day that one NT author, having written a gospel (old English word for 'good news') about him, enthuses: 'But there are also many other things that Jesus did; if every one of them were written down, I suppose that the world itself could not contain the books that would be written' (Jn 21:25).

Perhaps the last and most extra-ordinary reversal that God brings about which is recorded in the NT happens when Jesus is risen from the dead and appears to some of his disciples (the first appearance is to women, cf. Mt 28; Mk 16; Lk 24; Jn 20). After this he commissions them to continue to live like him, loving God and neighbour (which they understand to include not only other people but the whole of creation; cf. Mk 16:15; Rom 8:18-27).

Remembering and Recording the Good News

We do not have any text that was written by Jesus. After his resurrection, people began to spread the good news about him orally for a number of decades ('oral tradition'). Most likely, this news was passed on in Aramaic (a dialect of Hebrew), the language that Jesus spoke, but also in the other linguistic currencies of the Near East of his day – Hebrew (the language of the Jews), Greek (the language of trade and commerce), and perhaps even Latin (the first language of the Romans who ruled at this time). Early on, some believers were inspired through the power of the Holy Spirit of God (often termed 'the theory of Inspiration') to begin to record in Greek the apostles' memories of Jesus ('apostle' is the term used of the twelve chosen disciples of Jesus and others, like Mary from Magdala and Paul, who had seen the risen Jesus). Others composed hymns and prayers for use in their teaching about (Gk *parenesis*) and worship (Gk *leitourgia*) of him as 'the Christ' and 'Son of God', and in their remembrance of him at their eucharistic celebrations as 'the Lamb of God who takes away the sin of the world!' (Jn 1:29).

Paul, a Hellenistic Jew (i.e. of Greek culture but Jewish race), had once persecuted believers whom he called followers of 'the Way' until his dramatic conversion to faith in Jesus Christ whom he came to know as his 'Lord' (cf. Acts 9). After his conversion he became a zealous apostle. He made three great journeys around the Mediterranean area and found a number of Christian communities. He continued to support and challenge these communities to grow in their faith through the medium of correspondence by letter. His subject is always a proclamation (Gk *kerygma*) of some aspect of the significance of Jesus Christ and its implications for how believers are to live and worship in community. Seven such theological letters are extant, dating from between 50 and 70 CE. These include the Letters to the Romans, 1 and 2 Corinthians, Galatians, Philippians, 1 Thessalonians and Philemon. It is understood that these letters or copies of them would have been passed on to other communities and read in public for the same purpose, namely, to strengthen their faith in Jesus Christ. Later, between c. 70 and 110 CE, others wrote letters in the same style as Paul, which today are called 'Deutero-Pauline letters', to provide theological and pastoral advice to believers and communities. Six of these are extant – the Letters to the Ephesians, Colossians and 2 Thessalonians, as well as what are termed 'the Pastoral Letters', namely, 1 and 2 Timothy and Titus.

In between these two periods of letter writing, some among the early communities set about recording a narrative account of Jesus' life, death and resurrection and its significance. They did so using the genre of ancient *historical bioi* (biographies; Gk sing. *bios*), giving us what we now know to be the four Gospels, as well as a theological history of early Christianity in the Acts of the Apostles ('Acts'). The evidence suggests that they did this for several reasons: first, they realised that the immanent return of Jesus that they had anticipated (Gk *parousia*) appeared unlikely; second, that the memories about Jesus could die with the first eyewitnesses, the apostles; third, that they needed written accounts for the purpose of evangelisation, that is, spreading the good news in fresh territories; fourth, to guard against false teachings about Jesus or heresies.

Each of the four Gospels and Acts are attributed to a final author-cum-editor (often termed 'evangelist'), whose names are, according to tradition, Mark, Matthew, Luke (also author of Acts), and John. All are composed between the late sixties and early nineties CE. The first three evangelists give such similar accounts that together the three gospels form what is called the 'Synoptics' (Gk *Syn*, meaning 'together' and *opsis*, meaning 'appearance').

At the time of the writing of the gospels until the turn of the second century (c. 70–110 CE), several others wrote catholic (or universal) letters about matters which are of concern to some of the believers and churches. Seven such letters are included in the NT: Letters to James, Jude, 1 and 2 Peter, 1, 2 and 3 John, plus one other called the Letter to the Hebrews. The latter is more an exercise in Christology (the study of the person of Jesus Christ) than a letter proper. The last book of the Bible, called the Book of Revelation (c. 95 CE), is apocalyptic in genre and dates from a period when Christians are being persecuted under Roman rule. Its author records a message of hope, namely that in the end good triumphs over evil through the power of Jesus Christ. Traditionally it is attributed to the same author as the fourth gospel, John.

Spreading the Good News

All of the gospels are written in codex format (the notebook format used by merchants and produced in first-century Rome), rather than in the form of bulky scrolls as the books of the Hebrew Bible had been. This enabled the texts to be carried easily over long distances. In the first century CE, there was much travel and trade between the countries and cities that circled the Mediterranean Sea. It is worth tracing the stages of Paul's three great missionary journeys, the outline of which is usually found in the map section at the back of most study editions of the Bible. The availability of codices and relative ease of travel, along with the fact that there existed already a network of communication among the diaspora Jews of the first century, facilitated well the missionary zeal of Paul and others to spread the good news of Jesus Christ in the Gentile (non-Jewish) world.

Forming the Canon of the New Testament

Just as some believers were inspired to write a record about Jesus Christ and his significance for believers and the Church, so too over the first four centuries CE the early communities were inspired to establish a fixed list or canon (Gk *kanon*, 'yardstick') of writings according to which all believers and communities could measure their growth into faith in Jesus Christ. They selected and set in order the twenty-seven writings listed above which together provide an authentic account and interpretation of who Jesus is and what his life, death and resurrection mean for humanity and the whole of creation. During this time it also became necessary to standardise a list of books which would be authoritative for all Christians for their prayer, worship and instruction. Further, it served as a defense (Gk *apologia*) against some false teachings or heresies about Jesus Christ that began to be preached and recorded in writing by groups such as the Gnostics, who denied that Jesus Christ was fully human. The Jewish community also set about establishing a fixed canon, which became what we now know as the Hebrew Bible.

An Overview of the New Testament and its Message

In bibles or editions of the NT, the books are included in a fixed order. Similar type books are placed together. First, we find the four Gospels; second, the Acts of the Apostles; third, the Letters, and fourth, the Book of Revelation. Let us examine briefly each section in turn.

1.   *The Gospels: Matthew, Mark, Luke and John*
The question of the chronological order of the Synoptic Gospels and the use of sources by the Synoptists is often termed 'the Synoptic Problem'. It appears that the Gospel of Mark (c. 68 CE, Rome) is used as a source for the gospels of Matthew (c. 80s CE, Antioch, Syria) and Luke (c. 80s CE, Antioch, Syria). Matthew and Luke also appear to have drawn from another common source for their respective gospels called 'Q' (Ger. *Quelle*, meaning 'source') as they share much material in common that does not appear either in the Gospel of Mark or John.

The fourth Gospel, John (c. 90 CE, Ephesus), differs from the first three. It has less narrative material about Jesus and more discourse material than the Synoptics. Over all, it provides a more spiritual account of Jesus Christ. Hence, there is less consensus about the issue of John's use of the Synoptic Gospels as sources (often referred to as the 'Johannine Problem'), than the issue of Matthew and Luke's use of Mark as a source.

Mark begins with an account of the preparation made by John the Baptiser for the coming of his cousin Jesus, who is Christ and Son of God (Mk 1:1-8). Matthew and Luke, however, provide distinct narrative accounts of the Infancy of Jesus (cf. Mt 1-2; Lk 1-2). John omits the account of Jesus' infancy and includes instead an opening hymn as a prologue, which speaks of Jesus as the Word (Gk *Logos*) who has been with God since the beginning (Jn 1:1-14).

All of the gospels record much of the words and deeds of Jesus. Today, it is the work of scripture scholars to draw out the appropriate meaning of these records (Gk *exegesis*) in order to instruct people who are separated by more than two millennia from the people written about in the NT, and whose lives are socially, culturally and geographically very different.

In the Synoptics, Jesus uses wisdom sayings such as similitudes, parables, exemplary stories, blessings and woes when speaking of the Kingdom of God or the Kingdom of Heaven.

(i) *Similitudes* are concise statements that compare the Kingdom of God/heaven (or the supernatural world) to something or some event in the natural world. This helps the hearer/reader to understand some of the characteristics of the former. Luke often introduces these with a question: 'Which one of you …?' For example: 'Which one of you, having a hundred sheep and losing one of them, does not leave the ninety-nine in the wilderness and go after the one that is lost until he finds it?' (Lk 11:4; cf. 11:5; 14:28, 31). Matthew and Mark prefer to use more explicit comparisons: 'The Kingdom of God/heaven is like …'. For example: 'The Kingdom of heaven is like treasure hidden in a field, which someone found and hid; then in his joy he goes and sells all that he has and buys that field' (Mt 13:44; cf. Mk 4:26, 30-31).

(ii) *Parables* are true-to-life stories that are vivid in detail, narrated in the past tense and persuasive. The point of each is to instruct the reader/hearer on some aspect(s) of the nature of the Kingdom of God/heaven. All three Synoptic Gospels include the parable of the Sower and Seed where God is compared to a Sower who sows seeds of faith in Jesus as the Christ, and people are compared to various types of soil. The seeds grow if the conditions are right. Where there is openness to God, faith can grow (cf. Mk 4:3-8; Mt 13:1-8; Lk 8:5-8). In the parable of the Lost Sheep, God is compared to a good shepherd, and people, to sheep. When the sheep stray, the shepherd seeks them out and brings them home. This is an example of a parable taken from Q (Mt 18:12-14; Lk 15:3-7).

(iii) *Exemplary Stories* provide a true-to-life account of an event that instructs the hearer/reader about the second of Jesus' two commandments – how to love one's neighbour as oneself. Thus, the point or lesson has to do with morality. The best known of this genre is the story of the Good Samaritan (cf. Lk 10:30-35).

(iv) *Beatitudes and Woes* are blessings and curses which reflect God's mission of reversals. They belong to the special teaching of Jesus, found in Q. Blessings are the gifts brought to others by people who facilitate God's mission. Woes are the challenges given to those who impede this mission in any way. Both, when meditated upon, tell us about the kind of spirituality that those who listen to Jesus are called to live. Matthew provides eight beatitudes in Jesus' famous Sermon on the Mount (5:1-12). Luke records four beatitudes and four woes as part of Jesus' Sermon on the Plain (6:20-26).

In the gospels, Jesus demonstrates what the Kingdom of God/heaven is like through his deeds as well as his words. Again and again he reveals his true identity through working miracles or, in Johannine terminology, by doing 'signs'. Jesus' extra-ordinary power over illness and natural calamities affirms that he is truly the Son of God. The Synoptists record many healing miracles and several nature miracles. In all three Synoptics we find an account of Jesus' Healing a Paralytic at Capernaum (cf. Mk 2:1-12; Lk 5:17-26; Mt 9:1-8), and an account of Jesus' Calming a Storm at Sea (cf. Mt 14:22-33; Mk 6:45-52; Lk 8:22-25).

All gospels carry extended accounts of the passion, death and resurrection of Jesus (cf. Mk 14-16; Mt 26-28; Lk 22-24; Jn 18-21). The accounts do not agree on all details. However, together they provide us with an extremely rich basis for understanding further Paul's earlier accounts in his letters of the necessity of Jesus' death upon a cross in the story of human and cosmic salvation (cf. 1 Cor 1:18-31).

2.   *Acts of the Apostles*
In the Acts of the Apostles, Luke presents an account of the early Church, beginning with the coming of God's Holy Spirit at Pentecost (cf. Acts 2:1-13), and of its expansion in the Roman Empire. He tells of the preaching done by Peter (cf. Acts 2:14-36; 3:11-26; 10:34-43) and Paul (cf. Acts 13:16-

41), and of the witness and martyrdom of Stephen for the faith (Acts 7). All three disciples outline how the coming of Jesus Christ had been foretold in the Hebrew Bible.

3.   *Letters*

The Letters are the primary communication mechanism between the early churches. They usually follow the standard format of the day: (i) Opening formula or greeting from the sender to the addressee (cf. 1 Thess 1:1); (ii) Thanksgiving to God for some blessing (cf. 1 Thess 1:2-10); (iii) Body or main message(s) (cf. 1 Thess 2:1-5:22); (iv) Concluding Formula or farewell wish (cf. 1 Thess 5:23-28).

4.   *The Book of Revelation*

The Book of Revelation is a two-part apocalyptic work which is addressed to seven churches in the Roman province of Asia Minor (part 1:1:4-3:22; part 2:4:1-22:15). The author structures the matter (disputes about doctrine, persecution by the civil authorities, struggles with Judaism and complacency) in a series of seven parts which are framed between a Prologue (foreword, 1:1-3) and Epilogue (final word, 22:16-21). He assures the disciples, especially those facing persecution and martyrdom, that their experience under the Roman emperor, Domitian (51–96 CE), will be ultimately reversed. At a future time, they will experience only goodness, which has been won for them by the death of Jesus Christ on the cross. He records some of the hymns used to celebrate this belief at the liturgies of this time. It is interesting to note that this book contains the largest number of early Christian liturgical hymns of any book in the NT (cf. Rev 5:9-10; 15:3-4).

Conclusion: Receiving the Good News

The fundamental elements of the remembering and recording, the spreading and forming, and the message of the Christian Scriptures (NT) have been outlined above.

Toward receiving the message of the NT, it is always fruitful to first read and reflect upon smaller units or *pericopae* (Gk sing. *Pericope*, e.g. the texts given in brackets above, or the texts that form the Liturgy of the Word at weekday or Sunday Liturgies of the Eucharist); and then, to begin to read entire books from beginning to end. It is also highly profitable to use in tandem a recommended bible study guide on the NT (such as those cited at the end) and to discuss the fruits of your research with others. A fascinating exercise is to explore the reception of characters or themes of the NT (e.g. the Magi, the Samaritan Woman, the Infancy or Passion narratives, the Last Supper, etc.) as they have been interpreted and communicated during one or more period of Christianity in different parts of the world, in extra-biblical media such as painting, literature, sculpting, drama, music, film and information technology.

The ultimate goal of the authors of the NT reflects the goal of the chief subject of their writings, Jesus Christ, which is that all would come to faith in him and in his mission. Having come to faith, they are called to witness to it through good words and good deeds in their life situations. Jesus Christ, the true Light (cf. Jn 1:9), both challenges and inspires his disciples and would-be disciples thus:

> You are [to be] the light of world. No one after lighting a lamp puts it under the bushel basket, but on the lamp stand, and it gives light to all in the house. In the same way, let your light shine before others, so that they may see your good works and give glory to [God] your Father in heaven. (Mt 5:14-15)

Further Reading

Brown, Raymond E., *An Introduction to the New Testament*, London: Anchor Bible Reference Library, Doubleday, 1997.

Karris, Robert J. (ed.) *Collegeville Bible Commentary New Testament Set*, Collegeville, Minn.: The Liturgical Press, 1980–2006.

CHAPTER 5

A GOD 'EMBARRASSED AT THE PROSPECT OF POSSESSION': EXPLORING DIVINE REVELATION

Eamonn Conway

I give thanks
To the giver of images,
The reticent god who goes about his work
Determined to hold on to nothing.
Embarrassed at the prospect of possession
He distributes leaves to the wind
And lets them pitch and leap like boys
Capering out of their skin.
Pictures are thrown behind hedges,
Poems skitter backwards over cliffs,
There is a loaf of bread on Derek's threshold
And we will never know who put it there.

'A Giving', Brendan Kennelly[1]

Introduction

Divine revelation is the term Christians use to express the process whereby God discloses God's self in history, a process that begins with creation and climaxes in the person of Jesus Christ. Christians understand God not only to have created the world, but, from the very beginning, to have freely chosen to relate to that world. According to Christians, God freely enters into a self-giving relationship with the whole of creation, and more profoundly and personally with humankind.

The purpose of this chapter is to try to understand something of the nature and dynamics of divine revelation and of the process whereby humans experience it and seek to respond to it. I will begin by discussing the nature of the God who reveals, and then proceed to sketch how some theologians have attempted to speak of divine revelation.

Searching for Language

The closer we get to what lies at the heart of Christian faith, the more inarticulate we seem to become. Even when we are trying to speak of relationships between human beings, of deep feelings we have for each other, for example, of love, joy, and so on, words tend to let us down.

The challenge to express meaning is multiplied when it comes to speaking of our relationship with God. It is all the more vital, then, that when we seek to discuss divine revelation, we acknowledge the poverty of our language. Words will, at best, be ever only 'short-hand'. Over the centuries, theologians have acknowledged the limited nature of the language at their disposal by reminding us that all language about God is essentially analogical. This means that whatever we assert of God we must at the same time hold in our minds the radical inadequacy of what we have just said.[2]

Poetry is a less inadequate form of language with which to speak of the divine and so I begin with the Irish poet, Brendan Kennelly, who, in his poem 'A Giving', provides us with a good starting-point for reflecting upon the nature of God.

The 'Reticent' God

In Kennelly's poem, the word 'reticent' stands out. At first glance it seems to ruin the image otherwise being put forward of a generous and self-giving God. Why then should we think of God as 'reticent' in relating with humankind?

The strict meaning of 'reticence' is a certain reserve in self-expression, an avoidance of saying all one knows or feels. However, God's hesitancy does not originate in a desire to hold back or to hold out on us. It is not because of a selfish desire to cling to divine dignity. Rather, God's 'reticence' springs from deep respect for the dignity of creation and especially for the gift of freedom already bestowed on human creatures. Conscious of how easy it would be to overpower, to impinge on fragile human freedom, God's approach is by way of invitation, not ultimatum. This is echoed in the Old Testament where we find a God who is encountered more in the gentle breeze than in the raging storm; who, eventually, is recognised as to be less like a king commanding than a shepherd gently beckoning to his weary and somewhat wary flock.

Thus, the first important point we need to understand about the Christian notion of divine revelation is that it is a *freely chosen act* of God, a movement by God towards creation and especially towards humans, motivated entirely by love, to which the only adequate response is one of *free loving acceptance*. As with all instances of love, freedom, on both sides, is required.

The Christian tradition has always been anxious to emphasise God's freedom in revealing God's self. This has led to an important debate which we can only touch on here. It is the issue of whether or not humans, left to their own devices, so to speak, could have any knowledge or understanding of God.

The Church has always been anxious to teach that, in principle, in a purely 'natural' state, God 'can be known with certainty from the created world, by the natural light of human reason'.[3] Affirming this point brings home the fact that God could, in principle, have created us without having had any *special* plan or intention to reveal God's self to us in the *fullest* sense, that is, to communicate God's self to us. And so it emphasises that this divine self-communication is in no way owed to us by virtue of the fact that God created us. It is pure gift.

At the same time, the Judaeo-Christian tradition has never believed that it is dealing only with a *deus absconditus*, a god who creates and then abandons God's creatures. Theologians argue that a purely 'natural' state never arises in reality as we encounter it because, as the Second Vatican Council's decree on divine revelation, *Dei Verbum*, states, God 'manifested himself to our first parents from the very beginning ... and he has never ceased to take care of the human race'.[4] Theologians speak of a kind of 'general' or 'universal' revelation of God that begins with creation and is 'the ongoing outpouring of God's creative, formative love into the entire world', as well as of a 'special', 'exceptional', 'historical' divine revelation 'in the history of Israel and in the person of Jesus of Nazareth'.[5] We will deal with the former type, 'general' or 'universal' revelation towards the end of the essay. We will explore the event of revelation in history first.

In no way 'needy' of relationship or friendship with creation, God freely chooses to enter into intimate relationship with us from the very beginning. In fact, it is for such a relationship that we are created. We humans, in turn,

EXPLORING THEOLOGY

are free to accept or reject God's loving invitation to relationship. At the same time our freedom is a creaturely freedom, and so, limited, in the sense that it is not a capacity to do whatever we like with our lives as though our free acts lacked consequences. Freedom is a particular capacity we humans have to enable us to reach our full potential as human beings; a capacity to enable us to 'become' the people we are called to be. It is, as Karl Rahner says, a capacity we have 'for the eternal'. By exercising our freedom we determine who we wish to be for ever.

So a free movement in love towards creation and human creatures characterises divine revelation. Similarly, free love must also characterise the human response to God's self-revelation. We must reckon with the possibility that we can, and sometimes do, say no to God and thus play our own part in obscuring God's revelation.

Two points follow from what has been said above. The first is that a negative response to God's divine revelation on our part does not leave us in a kind of 'neutral' situation. As Augustine put it, we are made for relationship with God. A deliberate refusal of such a relationship not only puts us in contradiction with God but with our deepest selves as well, since it is precisely for such a relationship that we are made.

The second point is that there is no contradiction between our own deepest desires for ourselves, and God's deepest desire for us. Sometimes one hears in popular spirituality the view that people must set aside their 'selfish' desires for themselves to follow or do God's will. But if we are made for communion with God then God's will, our own deepest will and our most mature desires for ourselves coincide.

There is another aspect to God's 'reticence' to which we can draw attention. This is an aspect that Enda Lyons, in his aptly titled *Jesus: Self-portrait by God*, helps us to understand.[6] When any of us seek to be creative we are limited by the means at our disposal. An author is limited, for example, by language and vocabulary; a painter, by canvas and oils, and so on. God, too, is limited when God seeks to 'ex-press' God's self, that is, 'press out' the divine self into the realm of that which is not God. It is not so much that God avoids saying all God knows or feels but rather that God's speech, God's Word, is limited not by God's self but by the means at God's disposal. Creation, so to speak, provides the infinite God with a finite 'canvas' upon which to express God's self.

Among creatures, human beings provide God with the least limited 'canvas'. Among human beings, Christians believe that Jesus of Nazareth, being the most fully human of human beings, whose humanity is in no way diminished or distorted by sin, is the most perfect self-expression of God's nature possible in created reality. The *Preface of Christmas 1* used in the Catholic Liturgy captures this well:

> In the wonder of the incarnation your eternal Word has brought to the eyes of faith a new and radiant vision of your glory. In him we see our God made visible and so are caught up in love of the God we cannot see.

Jesus of Nazareth is the Word of God in flesh, the 'sum total of revelation' as the Second Vatican Council put it.[7] Yet even though Jesus provides us with the most radiant vision of God possible in this order of reality, nonetheless it is true to say that God still remains hidden.

This brings us to one final aspect of God's reticence upon which we should remark before moving on: the *persisting* hiddenness of God. When we speak of a certain reserve on God's part in terms of God's self-revelation, it brings to mind, for instance, that our experience of God can at times seem to be far from revelatory. In fact sometimes it can seem ambiguous, confusing and even disappointing. Faced, for example, with the reality of evil and suffering, God's presence may seem very reticent indeed. Curiously, even the most devout believers and those who invest most in coming to know and love God seem to have this experience of God's hiddenness. It is not something that recedes with love and knowledge of God but rather seems to be characteristic of the human-divine relationship at its most intimate and intense, as the lives of many of those we recognise as saints testify.

The Judaeo-Christian tradition has always emphasised that God's self-revelation is characterised by incomprehensibility. St Augustine noted this dimension to our experience of God when he said, *Si comprehendis, non est Deus*,[8] meaning 'if you understand, then it is not God'. Karl Rahner, especially towards the end of his theological life's work, also emphasised the mysterious nature of God's self-revelation. He stressed that while approaching us as 'self-giving nearness', God nonetheless remains God and is thus shrouded in mystery.

It is important to clarify what we mean when we use the term 'mystery' as it is fundamental to the Christian understanding of God. Theologically speaking, mystery does not designate as yet unanswered or even apparently unanswerable questions. It is not about questions and answers as such. Nor is mystery, theologically speaking, susceptible to resolution. Rather, it refers to the hidden depth that is characteristic of life. The more we come to know and understand, this hidden depth does not seem to 'bottom out' as we might expect, but rather seems to get deeper and more mysterious. Interestingly, even Albert Einstein recognised and accepted this:

> The most beautiful experience we can have is of the mysterious. Whoever does not know it and can no longer wonder, no longer marvel, is as good as dead, and his eyes are dimmed. It is this knowledge and this emotion that constitutes true religiosity.[9]

Mystery defies resolution. But it invites surrender. By surrender I do not mean 'giving up' but rather 'giving in' trustfully; perhaps even delightfully letting go into the wonder of life and even of one's own life. What has been said here about the mysterious hiddenness of God we also experience about ourselves. Active acceptance of the mysterious nature of our own lives and of life itself is, according to Karl Rahner, already an implicit acceptance of God as the origin and giver of life.

Faced with the mysterious and incomprehensible nature of something as painful and life-defying as suffering and evil, Rahner urges us to turn such experiences into moments when we school ourselves in acceptance of God's incomprehensibility. Thus, he says,

> If there is not ... acceptance of the incomprehensibility of suffering then all that can really happen is the affirmation of our own idea of God and not the affirmation of God himself.[10]

For Rahner, the fundamental challenge facing humans is to allow God to be God. It is to respect God's freedom just as God respects ours. This means not imposing upon God our notions of how God should be and resisting the temptation to evacuate the mysterious nature of God with facile if consoling answers.

When we reflect upon it, we realise that mystery characterises the most intimate of human relationships. As Hans Urs Von Balthasar notes:

> The moment I think I have *understood* the love of another person for me … then this love is radically misused and inadequate, and there is no possibility of a response. True love is always incomprehensible and only so is it gratuitous.[11]

Ultimately it is useless to try to ask or answer the question as to why someone loves us or why we love someone. Similarly, divine-human love is shrouded by an incomprehensibility to which there is only one 'answer': gracious letting-self-go.

To summarise then: we have noted that our perception of a certain 'reticence' or reserve on God's part, God's hiddenness, can be understood in a number of ways. It can be understood in terms of the unavoidable limits finite reality places upon God's self-expression. It can also be understood in terms of the respect which the Creator has for creatureliness and especially for fragile human freedom. We have also noted the distorting effects of human sinfulness which dim and obscure our ability to perceive divine revelation.

Fundamentally, however, God's reticence must be understood in terms of mystery. Though God communicates God's self in absolute self-communication, nonetheless this same God remains eternally a mystery, infinite, incomprehensible and inexpressible.

We will now probe this mystery a little further.

Embarrassed at the Prospect of Possession

One of the songs often sung at the Jewish celebration of the Passover, the *Dayenu*, goes as follows:

> Had he brought us out of Egypt and not fed us in the desert, we'd be satisfied …
> Had he fed us the manna, and not then ordained the Sabbath, we'd be satisfied …
> Had he then ordained the Sabbath, and not brought us to Mount Sinai, we'd be satisfied,

Had he brought us to Mount Sinai, and not given us the Torah, we'd be satisfied …

Had he given us the Torah and not led us into Israel, we'd be satisfied …

The Old Testament tells the story of a people first chosen and then prepared over time to receive the Good News about God's stance towards Creation and especially towards the human race. Quoting the Letter to the Hebrews, *Dei Verbum* notes, through the centuries from the call of Abraham to the coming of Jesus Christ, God spoke 'many times and in various ways'.[12] In terms of naming God and defining God they never really got beyond the encounter of Moses in the burning bush: 'I am who am.'[13]

At another level, however, perhaps the most important one, the Jewish people became aware that this unnameable God is revealed in deeds more than in concepts. They became aware of God's journeying with them in and through their history as a people. They became aware of God's fidelity towards them and forgiveness of them. They had a sense of being rescued and shepherded by God again and again and it is this experience that formed them and gave them their identity as a people.

The Jews found that one of the reasons God seemed to defy definition was that with God there was always 'more'. Too often they thought that the same limitations that marked their response, the infidelity that curbed or foiled their generosity towards God, was also characteristic of God's stance towards them. It took some time for them to recognise that the 'eye for an eye' reciprocity characteristic of human relations did not apply to relationship with God.

Christians add another verse to the *Dayenu* cited above, and in addition hold that the coming of Christ completes and perfects all that has gone before.[14] In Jesus, in the words of the *Preface* mentioned earlier, we have 'a new and radiant vision of God's glory'.

Sometimes we forget just how dependent we are on Jesus of Nazareth for an insight into God's nature. The familiarity with which we speak *of* God, for example, calling God *Abba*, meaning 'Father', and the familiarity with which we speak *with* God in prayer, we owe to Jesus of Nazareth. In fact, Christians believe that they can only speak of and with God 'through him [Christ], with him and in him'. Christians believe that everything known about and experienced of God is radically transformed in the Christ event.

In the suffering and death of Christ on the cross, God is rendered present to, transforms and heals humankind and human history. At the same time, human history becomes part of God's 'history', so to speak; it becomes part of the inner life of God and thus is given eternal value. In the first centuries of the Church the maxim emerged: 'that which is not assumed, is not redeemed.' Christians believe that in Christ all things are assumed; taken up, into the mysterious love of God. The suffering of Jesus and his death determine the course of human history.

The effect of the Christ event, according to Julian of Norwich, is that even our sins will be placed on the heavenly display shelf as trophies of the triumph of God's grace. Similarly, Balthasar brings out the radical depths of the incarnation when he speaks of Jesus even descending into hell, where he suffers an agony of incredible loneliness with those who may have definitively chosen 'to put their I in place of God's selfless love'.[15] Balthasar speculates that the sinner who chooses to be separated from God finds God in the weakness of crucified love, and that even hell can be understood as a Christological place. Thus, human sinfulness, instead of frustrating divine revelation, brings out its radical depths.

Christians believe that in an important sense Jesus Christ 'closes' revelation.[16] But this is, as Rahner insists, a positive statement, not a negative one. It is, as he says, 'a pure Amen'.[17] What has come to an end is the 'holding back' of God's self. In Jesus, God and God's creation have become irrevocably one, 'forever without confusion, but forever undivided'.[18] The 'more' of God is eternally in our midst, an ever-replenishing plenitude of love.

We conclude this section by returning to consideration of the nature of God's love. As Balthasar observes, we have nothing with which to compare the love of God:

> The love of God is great beyond comparison. It has no ground except itself and always comes from farther away and leads still farther on than I could have thought and imagined. In my limitation, therefore, I must unceasingly add an 'and'; but what I thus bring about has already long ago been brought about by the love of God.[19]

This is an important reminder: when we think of God's love we tend to do so in human terms. But God, as theologians in more recent times have been very keen to point out, is not simply one being among other beings, and certainly not a kind of 'super' human being. For the Anglican theologian, John Macquarrie, God is better understood as Being rather than 'a being', if even the most supreme and powerful one. For Macquarrie, Being includes 'becoming' and has as its essence the dynamic act of 'letting-be'.[20] Just one word of caution here. By 'letting-be' is not meant, in any sense, a 'laid-back' approach to life, a kind of 'letting it all hang out'! Letting-be, in Macquarrie's sense, means dynamic engagement and passionate commitment but with a detachment founded on love which respects freedom.

There is, of course, no 'proof' that this aptly describes the nature of God, if by proof we mean scientific evidence. But science does not answer all our questions, or even perhaps the most important ones. However, there is evidence I find persuasive. We humans experience ourselves as most alive, most truly ourselves, when we are being generous. We are happiest when we are 'letting-go', perhaps painfully surrendering to the mystery of life and our own lives. In contrast, we are least happy when we find ourselves calculating, possessive, fearfully clinging, anxious, controlling and slow to trust.

If, as the Christian tradition has consistently claimed, humans are in the image of God, the *imago Dei*, and if we humans are most truly ourselves, most fully alive when we are graciously letting-be, does this not reveal to us something of the nature of God, accepting, of course, that our 'letting-be' is infinitesimal compared to that of God? In addition, when we look at the life of Jesus Christ, the one whom Christians believe to have lived a fully human life, that is, one undiminished by sin, do we not find a gracious letting-be in the sense described above? The Gospels recall that his very touch seemed to enable people bent double to stand up straight and they tell countless other stories of people being restored by him to the fullness of life.[21] But apart from deeds as recorded, his entire life story seems to have been one of active self-giving surrender, overcoming darkness, sin and evil by trusting in the power of goodness and truth. The Gospels emphasise how he let himself go into the mystery of God, not always understanding but clearly trusting and graciously surrendering to the will of the one he called 'Abba'. Among human beings Jesus is most perfectly the *imago Dei*. Thus, in him is revealed not only God's nature, but ours as well.

Finally we can make the point that emphasises just how much God dispossesses God's self. Although at times in the history of the Church God has been portrayed as harsh and demanding, the Christian tradition has consistently taught that God seeks friendship with us. This is recalled again in *Dei Verbum*:

> Through this revelation, therefore, the invisible God (see Col 1:15; 1 Tim 1:17) out of the abundance of His love speaks to men as friends (see Ex 33:11; Jn 15:14-15) and lives among them (see Bar 3:38), so that He may invite and take them into fellowship with Himself.[22]

Genuine friendship is difficult: it is an invitation to share one's life through a love that is on the one hand passionately caring and involved, on the other, detached and selfless. It means self-emptying, vulnerability, openness, letting-go; it means actively intending the good of another for his/her own sake. Friendship requires freedom; it implies equality and mutuality. How can such a relationship exist between creatures and their Creator?

St Thomas Aquinas (1225–1274) is our best guide here.[23] He stresses that it is the incarnation that makes possible the equality and mutuality necessary for friendship between God and the human race. In the incarnation a divine 'condescension' takes place: the Word of God 'collapses naked and bare into our narrow creaturliness'[24] and assumes all the weakness and vulnerability of the human condition. This is captured by the Letter to the Philippians when it speaks of Jesus not regarding equality with God something to be 'exploited' or 'grasped' but instead taking the form of a human being subject to death.[25]

The Word of God stoops down to us but not just to join us in the messiness and at times the misery of the human condition. The incarnation marks not just divine condescension but also human elevation. Through Jesus Christ the human race is made worthy of God's friendship. We are restored to the dignity God had intended for us from the beginning. Thus, it is not just Christ who is exalted by God but the whole human race. Gerard Manley Hopkins puts this beautifully:

I am all at once what Christ is, since he was what I am, and
This Jack, joke, poor potsherd, patch, matchwood, immortal diamond,
Is immortal diamond.[26]

The Christian tradition has understood the incarnation as an invitation to *koinonia*. This Greek term gives us 'community' and 'communion'. Thus, we can see how it is God's invitation to friendship that provides the basis for the Christian community and why the Eucharist, in which we celebrate our friendship with God in the most intimate act of table-fellowship, is central to the life of the Church.

Now that we have explored something of the nature of the God that is revealed through Jesus Christ we need to consider how and in what way God is encountered.

A Loaf of Bread on Derek's Threshold

At the outset we spoke of two kinds of revelation: 'general' or 'universal' revelation that begins with creation, and the 'special', 'exceptional', 'historical' divine revelation 'in the history of Israel and in the person of Jesus of Nazareth'.[27] We now need to explore what is meant by 'general' or 'universal' revelation.

As we saw, the Second Vatican Council taught that from the very beginning, that is, long before the call of Abraham, and so before God's 'special' revelation commenced, God manifested God's self. God did not just create the world but also communicated God's self to that world. The dilemma facing theologians is to try to understand and explain this without on the one hand implying that God, in creating us, *had* to reveal God's self and give God's self to us. Such an implication would compromise the free, gratuitous, gifted nature of revelation, and so undermine it as a loving act entirely initiated by God out of the fullness of God's love.

On the other hand, if insufficient emphasis is laid on some kind of 'general' revelation, then there are also difficulties. One difficulty is that it is then hard to explain how people who have never had the opportunity to hear of 'special' revelation can respond to God and thereby freely accept God's offer of friendship. Remember that we are speaking here of the vast majority of humanity; all those born before the call of Abraham; all those since who, for whatever reason, have not come to recognise and accept Christ as God's ultimate self-communication in history. Does God ignore them? Are they 'damned', through no fault of their own? Or does God save them despite themselves, but in so doing vitiate and compromise their freedom? [28]

A second difficulty is that unless we acknowledge some kind of 'general' revelation, then 'special' revelation seems to come to us entirely as something incongruent, extrinsic to our everyday experience. Would we even be able to recognise God's 'special' revelation in Jesus Christ if God had not already sown in us the seeds of such a revelation, so to speak; if we had not already been formed in such a way that we 'knew', however vaguely, to anticipate and to yearn for such a revelation? According to Avery Dulles:

> From Augustine to Karl Rahner theologians of stature have repeatedly affirmed that if we did not somehow know God in our experience we could not even raise the question of God. Before we begin to search for God, we already apprehend him obscurely and implicitly in the restlessness of our own hearts, in which grace is operative ... When we do find in Christ – or elsewhere – the appearance of God our Saviour, we spontaneously feel that we are recognising what we already know in an obscure anticipatory way. [29]

If we did not already experience God in our everyday lives then we would not be able to raise a question about God in the first place, or recognise as true the claims made explicitly about God by Christianity.

The verse we cited from Kennelly at the beginning of this chapter suggests the ordinary nature of encounter with God. For Kennelly, God is met in the ordinariness of everyday experiences such as leaves stirred up by the wind or the gift of a loaf of bread.

Key to understanding this is to stop thinking of God as one being 'out there' to be met and encountered just like we meet and encounter people and things. As we noted with Macquarrie, God is more like the gracious letting be of being, rather than a particular being, however great, however magnanimous, standing alone among other beings. [30] God is not encountered in isolation from God's creatures.

St Ignatius of Loyola (1491–1556) stressed that God is to be found in all things. Influenced by him, but also by Thomas Aquinas, Rahner is the theologian who, in recent times, has most emphasised what he called 'the mysticism of everyday life'. Rahner prefers to speak of God being 'co-experienced' rather than 'experienced' as such. By this Rahner does *not* mean that we do *not* experience God directly, but rather that our immediate experience of God occurs in our experience of ordinary everyday moments and events. Human experience, according to Rahner, is the platform for God's self-revelation. In our experience of ourselves, others and creation, we experience God. In accepting, responding to and loving our deepest selves, others and creation, we accept, love and respond to God.

Rahner's way of speaking of experiencing God overcomes a number of difficulties. In particular, it enables people to integrate experiences of God in 'the bits and pieces of Everyday'[31] with the God as proclaimed in the Christian community and encountered in the Church's worship and sacraments. It intrinsically connects our experience both of 'general' and 'special' revelation.

At the same time an emphasis on experience creates difficulties of its own. In trying to avoid extrinsicism, we run the risk of subjectivism. We can forget that our subjective experience is a limited enough prism from which to view and to judge reality. According subjective experience primacy, making it the measure of everything that is important to and valued by us, can diminish our capacity to encounter God as God is; to let God be God.

In addition, it is very difficult today, especially in a postmodern context marked by fracture and fragmentation of shared categories for understanding and interpreting human experience, to speak of human experience in any monolithic or undifferentiated sense. Perhaps the most serious difficulty has been alluded to by Balthasar. Balthasar is concerned that an emphasis on human experience as the 'locus' of the most fundamental revelation of God effectively relativises the 'special' revelation that takes place in the history of Israel, and in the life, death and resurrection of Christ. Thus such an emphasis also undermines the sacramental life of the Church as the representation of Christ's saving work. An over-privileging of subjective human experience 'reduces' the saving event of Christ to mere fulfilment of a well-anticipated human need by a God who, in the very act of creation, had already committed God's self to loving and rescuing humankind. For this reason, Balthasar argues that:

It might be true that from the very beginning man was created to be disposed towards God's revelation, so that with God's grace even the sinner can accept all revelation ... But when God sends his own living Word to his creatures, he does so, not to instruct them about the mysteries of the world, nor primarily to fulfil their deepest needs and yearnings. Rather he communicates and actively demonstrates such unheard-of things that man feels not satisfied but awestruck by a love which he never could have hoped to experience. For who would dare to have described God as love, without having first received the revelation of the Trinity in the acceptance of the cross by the Son.[32]

The difference of emphasis between Rahner and Balthasar on this point has led Rowan Williams to refer to Rahner's Christ as the answer to the human question and Balthasar's as a question to all human answers.[33] Kennelly's description of pictures being thrown behind hedges and an unexpected loaf of bread appearing on Derek's threshold captures both the ordinariness and extraordinariness of divine revelation.

It seems to me that the surprising, wonder-inducing, category-defying love of God as revealed in Jesus Christ does not need to be protected and is, in fact, ill-served by playing down the reality that God,

wishing to open the way to heavenly salvation ... manifested himself to our first parents from the very beginning ... and he has never ceased to take care of the human race, in order to give eternal life to all those who seek salvation by perseverance in doing good.[34]

Perhaps an image that can help us here, one that is not as trivial as it might seem in that we find it in the Gospels,[35] is that of salt that transforms the flavour of food. Jesus told his disciples that they are to be to the 'salt of the earth'. This can only be the case, however, if he, the one they are to follow, is understood as such himself. The 'special' revelation of God's love that takes place in the history of Israel and climaxes in Jesus Christ can thus be

EXPLORING THEOLOGY

understood as drawing forth, intensifying and transforming the 'general' revelation of God that, through a free act of God, has accompanied God's creation from the very beginning.

Conclusion

Further systematic study of the concept of divine revelation is necessary, to which this chapter should only be taken as an introduction. Such a systematic approach one finds, for example, with Alister McGrath, who details revelation in terms of doctrine, presence, history and experience.[36] Along similar lines, Avery Dulles speaks of revelation in terms of five 'models': Doctrine; Revelation as History; Revelation as Inner Experience; Revelation as Dialectical Presence; Revelation as New Awareness.[37]

A close reading of *Dei Verbum* is also essential. In particular one should look out for the Council's emphasis on revelation as a personal self-disclosure by God, inviting a personal response; the Church as the 'servant' of revelation, not its master; revelation taking place in history and therefore in human experience; the re-emphasising of the biblical and Trinitarian dimensions to revelation; and, finally, the main point: that a person, Jesus Christ, rather than an institution, is at the centre of divine revelation and human history.

Understanding divine revelation is one thing, graciously accepting God's gracious acceptance of us is another. This chapter began with the phrase, 'I give thanks'. Eucharist means thanksgiving, and giving thanks is the most fundamental Christian prayer, and therefore the most appropriate response to a God 'embarrassed at the prospect of possession' in whose image we are made.

Notes

1   Brendan Kennelly, 'A Giving', *A Time for Voices*, Newcastle upon Tyne: Bloodaxe Books, 1990, p. 106.
2   See Karl Rahner, 'Experiences of a Catholic Theologian' in Declan Marmion and Mary E. Hines (eds) *The Cambridge Companion to Karl Rahner*, Cambridge: University Press, 2005, p. 299.
3   'Dogmatic Constitution on Divine Revelation' *Dei Verbum*, n. 6, 99–100 in Austin Flannery (ed.) *Vatican Council II, The Basic Sixteen Documents*, Dublin: Dominican Publications, pp. 97–116. [hereafter DV]
4   DV 3.

5   See Gerald O'Collins, 'Revelation' in Joseph Komonchak, Mary Collins and Dermot Lane (eds) *The New Dictionary of Theology*, Minnesota: Glazier, 1995, p. 884.

6   Enda Lyons, *Jesus: Self-Portrait by God*, Dublin: Columba, 1994.

7   DV 3.

8   *Sermo* 52, 16: PL 38, 360. See also Benedict XVI, *Deus caritas est*, n. 38.

9   Albert Einstein, *Ideas and Opinions*, New York: Crown Publishers, 1954, p. 11.

10   Karl Rahner, 'Why does God allows us to suffer?', *Theological Investigations* 19, London; DLT, 1983, pp. 207–208.

11   Hans Urs Von Balthasar, *Love Alone: The Way of Revelation*, London & Dublin: Sheed & Ward and Veritas, 1968, p. 44.

12   DV 3. See also Chapter 4.

13   Exodus 3:14.

14   DV 4.

15   Medard Kehl and Werner Löser (eds) Hans Urs Von Balthasar, *The Von Balthasar Reader*, Edinburgh: T & T Clark, 1982, p. 153.

16   DV 4.

17   Karl Rahner, 'The Development of Dogma', *Theological Investigations 1*, London: DLT, 1974, p. 49.

18   See the Symbol of Chalcedon (451) in Joseph Neuner and Jacques Dupuis (eds) *The Christian Faith*, London: Collins, 1983, pp. 153–154.

19   See Hans Urs Von Balthasar, *The Von Balthasar Reader*, p. 111.

20   John Macquarrie, *Principles of Christian Theology*, London: SCM Press, 1966, p. 110

21   Luke 13:10-17.

22   DV 2.

23   See *Summa* (IIa IIae, qq. 23- 46); See also Eberhard Schockenhoff, 'The Theological Virtue of Charity (IIa IIae, q. 23- 46)' in Stephen J. Pope (ed.) *The Ethics of Aquinas*, Washington: Georgetown University Press, 2002, pp. 244–258.

24   Karl Rahner, 'Erfahrung eines katholischen Theologen' in Albert Raffelt (ed.) *Karl Rahner in Erinnerung*, Düsseldorf: Patmos, 1994, p. 148.

25   Philippians 2:5-11.

26   Hopkins, *That Nature is a Heraclitean Fire and of the Comfort of the Resurrection*, from Norman H. MacKenzie (ed.) *The Later Poetic Manuscripts of Gerard Manley Hopkins in Facsimile*, New York and London: Garland Publishing, 1991, pp. 330–331.

27   See note 5.

28   See Eamonn Conway, *The Anonymous Christian – A Relativised Christianity?*, Frankfurt: Peter Lang, 1993; Eamonn Conway, 'So as not to despise God's grace' in *The Courage to Risk Everything … Essays Marking the Centenary of Karl Rahner's Birth*, Eamonn Conway (ed.) *Louvain Studies*, Vol. 29, Spring-Summer 2004, pp. 107–131.

29   Avery Dulles, *The Survival of Dogma*, 49. Cited in G. Donald Maloney SJ, 'Revelation and Experience', *Doctrine & Life*, March 1975, p. 196.

30   Karl Rahner, *Foundations of Christian Faith*, London: DLT, 1978, 54ff.

31   Patrick Kavanagh, 'The Great Hunger', *The Complete Poems*, Newbridge: Goldsmith Press, 1972, p. 88.

32   Hans Urs Von Balthasar, 'Current trends in Catholic theology and the Responsibility of the Christian', *Communio* 5, Spring 1978, p. 80.

33   Rowan Williams, 'Balthasar and Rahner' in John Riches, *The Analogy of Beauty*, Edinburgh: T & T Clark, 1986, p. 34.

34   DV, 3. See also Eamonn Conway, 'A Constant Word in a Changing World: Recognising and Resolving Tenisons and Tendencies in a Post-Modern Context', *New Blackfriars*, Vol. 87, No. 1008, March 2006, pp. 110–121.

35   Matt 5:13; Mk 9:80; Lk 14:34.

36   Alister McGrath, *Christian Theology: An Introduction*, Oxford: Blackwell, 1994, pp. 151–158.

37   Avery Dulles, *Models of Revelation*, Garden City, NY: Doubleday & Co., 1983.

CHAPTER 6

TRADITION

Brendán Leahy

Introduction

What does Tradition mean in Catholic theology? A simple working definition runs: Tradition is both the process of 'handing on' the Gospel and the contents of the Good News itself that is handed on. It is the life of the Church that gives life. To delve a little deeper into this, perhaps a useful exercise is to imagine yourself in different moments of the Church's two thousand years of existence.

Communicating What We Are

First, imagine you are an official of the Roman Empire in the year 80 CE. You have been sent to draw up a report on a new movement that has come to life ever since Jesus of Nazareth was put to death under Pontius Pilate in c. 30 CE. You've had to book several travel tickets because the investigation has taken you to a number of cities of the Roman Empire – Jerusalem, Antioch, Ephesus, Alexandria and Rome.

The first thing you note for your report is how much these 'Christians' focus on love and love for one another. Yes, of course, they have their difficulties, but yet they really believe in a love that has lit up their lives. It is a new kind of love – they call it *agape*-love. In fact, they say because of Jesus' life, death and resurrection, this new love is God's very own love poured into their hearts and lived out among them. They talk of the Holy Spirit as the great protagonist of their new history.

They are so taken up with their new experience that they are very keen to hand it on to all they meet. (If you have been in love yourself, you know how much you want to share yourself and all about yourself – from the smallest details to the greatest – with the person you love.) They communicate it in all kinds of ways – both by word of mouth and in writing.

And they are all involved, men and women, in all kinds of ways – apostles, evangelisers, preachers, teachers, prophets, administrators, helpers etc. The means of handing it on are dynamic. They recall episodes and sayings from Jesus' life as well as the meaning of his death and resurrection. They share experiences of how it impacts on their lives, narrating especially the original *kergyma* (preaching) of the apostles. They write letters, compose songs and summary formulae. They gather together instructions on how to live their new community life. The most important moment for them each week is the Eucharist. It is the culmination as it contains everything.

More recently, gospels have been written. And certain letters are beginning to stand out as key foundational texts for the new community. These gospels and letters are like a mirror reflecting the lively exchange of 'handing on' (in Latin, *tradere*, hence 'tradition' in English) among them. Increasingly, there is a sense that the 'Tradition' with all its traditions (all that has been shared and handed on from the apostles who in turn handed on the words, examples and deeds of Jesus) needs to be guarded faithfully (see 2 Thess 2:15; Rom 6:17). In the letters to Timothy and Titus you read that the Gospel (with a capital 'G'), the Good News, the preaching of the apostles and the instructions about how to live the communitarian life, are like a sacred 'deposit'? (1 Tim 6:20; 2 Tim 1:14).

It is not so easy to get across in a report, but you can see that 'Tradition/handing on' is not merely a technical operation for these first Christians. In fact, they use the word 'Tradition' (to hand over, to give over) also in recalling how God gave his Son for us (Rom 8:32), and how Jesus gave up his Spirit as he was dying on the cross (Jn 19:30), and how the apostles and those who founded church communities transmitted what they had received (1 Cor 15:3), especially the rite of the Eucharist. Paul of Tarsus wrote that the narrative about the Eucharist was handed on to him and he in turn has handed it on to others (1 Cor 11:23). In short, it seems the origin of Tradition as the 'handing on' process goes right back to God who gave himself to us in Jesus Christ and the Holy Spirit.

A definite quote for your report has to be an extract from one of the letters written by John. It is a succinct description of just how important the first Christians viewed Tradition. It tells us they experienced it as a lively dynamic that introduced them into the new life in God that opened up in Jesus Christ:

That which was from the beginning, which we have heard, which we have seen with our eyes, which we have looked upon and touched with our hands, concerning the word of life – this life was made manifest, and we saw it, and testify to it, and proclaim to you the eternal life which was with the Father ... so that you may have fellowship with us, and our fellowship is with the Father and with his Son Jesus Christ. And we are writing this that our joy may be complete. (1 Jn 1:1-4)

Your report has to get the balance. On the one hand, when the Christians are talking about Tradition, they are referring to the gospels, other writings, doctrinal summaries and prayers, instructions in community life and essential institutional aspects of their community, creedal formulae as well as catechetical summaries and hymns. But they also focus on the communion of life, love, joy and sharing in God that is to be communicated. That is the whole point of Tradition. It is the living transmission, accomplished in the Holy Spirit who is Light, of God's Love-Revelation in Jesus that opens up deeper and deeper understandings of life, outreach to your neighbour and hope for the future.

Faith has a Shape to it

Imagine yourself now in another moment of history. You are a recently converted Christian soldier writing around 170 CE. You are stationed in Gaul (modern day France) where Blandina, one of the first Christian women martyrs, died, and your local bishop of Lyons is the famous Christian leader, Irenaeus. By now Christianity has spread. Merchants, mercenaries, soldiers moving from one end of the Roman Empire to another (and beyond) have been real 'apostles'.

It never ceases to amaze you just how the now very extensive Christian family keeps going without falling apart. Christians have had to face persecutions. But what's more (and perhaps a more subtle challenge), they have had to face new cultural mindsets and, in particular, the challenge of *gnosticism*, a mishmash of religion, philosophy, astrology and bits of Christian vision thrown in to form a 'secret knowledge' for only 'the enlightened'. Some people have started to confuse this with Christianity!

It took Irenaeus to set down benchmarks to clarify things. That is why you are proud of him. He has written a famous work, *Against Heresies*. In this work, Irenaeus gathered all the doctrinal elements settled up until then and showed how in the Christian religion there is a solid and coherent vision in which all the elements refer to and strengthen each other. Above all, Irenaeus emphasised how much Jesus, the Son of God, was really human and how, through his death and resurrection, we have been brought to share in the dynamic of God's Trinitarian life, that is, the life of mutual love that exists between the Father, Son and Holy Spirit.

As a recent convert, you know the followers of Jesus Christ aren't confused people with vague ideas or syncretistic notions. No, they are united in what Irenaeus called a 'rule of faith'. That is, the Christian life is one whose doctrine has a shape to it: it is structured around our faith in God the Father as *Creator* of all, Jesus Christ the Son who is *Redeemer* and the Holy Spirit, the *Sanctifier,* who pours love into our hearts. That is our real 'homeland'. This simple summary structure explains our Christian 'living space', as it were, and is like a roadmap to help people read, contemplate and make new discoveries in scriptures.

Irenaeus is also the one who pointed out that the bishops succeeded the apostles in guaranteeing the faithful transmission of the Christian Tradition. If Christians want to make sure they don't miss the mark, they need to stay in communion with the bishops, and these bishops, in turn, view the Church of Rome (where Peter and Paul lived and were martyred) as a touchstone of that Tradition. If you want to know if something fits in to the general Tradition of the Church, the bishop of Rome, the Pope, has a special charism to ensure unity among Christians in being faithful to the Tradition.

The most astounding fact, as Irenaeus put it, is that although the people that make up the Church are scattered throughout the whole world, it is as if they are living in one house, having one soul and heart and handing on the Gospel Tradition as if they had only one mouth: 'For though languages differ throughout the world, the content of the Tradition is one and the same. The churches established in Germany have no other faith or Tradition, nor do those of the Iberians, nor those of the Celts, nor those of the East, of Egypt, of Libya …' (*Against Heresies*, I, 1).

We Need the Church

This time imagine you are a theologian who has attended a large council of bishops held in Trent, Northern Italy. It lasted from 1545–1563 and one of the thorny issues was the topic of Church and Tradition. Your background research on this council has focused on the Protestant Reformation.

On the one hand, for centuries the Church's teachings, sacraments, rituals, stories of martyrs and saints, creeds, prayers and instructions on community life as well as devotions and practices were taken for granted. There was a sense that to be born into the life of the Church was like being born into a paradise of spiritual life that communicated the Tradition that came from Christ and the apostles. And this in a number of ways – the Gospel proclaimed every week at Mass, the Mass itself, the example and company of great gospel people. Tradition has been channelled through the existence of monasteries, the fraternity and preaching of the Mendicant Orders, the stories of the saints, the beautiful cathedrals and churches, church music, the various rituals and customs, the writings of theologians and mystics. Tradition is like a maternal atmosphere you live in; it is the life that forms you in holiness and love, it gives you a sense of belonging, it provides you with a world view, it is something you experience day to day in all kinds of ways.

But Martin Luther of Germany has pointed out that the picture has not always been rosy. From 1517 onwards Luther has been highlighting abuses, saying we need to return to the Gospel and reform our ways. People picked up the impression that he was calling on the Church to leave aside much of what for centuries was considered really important. It seemed he was saying there was no need for Church to come between believers and their interpretation of scripture.

For Luther, doctrines and practices that weren't directly found in scripture should not be obligatory. What he had in mind were some of the sacraments (confirmation, marriage, holy orders, penance and anointing of the sick), purgatory, praying for the dead, the doctrine of transubstantiation. Instead, Luther said 'scripture alone' is necessary and it has its own hermeneutical (interpreting) principle based on the key biblical concepts such as sin and justification.

All of this has unleashed a big debate. Huge confusion arose on all sides – not to mention a great lack of *agape*-love all round! As a theologian you appreciate why this Council of Trent wants to sort things out and draw a line in the sand so that everyone can move on. Of course, it re-affirms the importance of the Church in how we read Scripture. It is the Church as a community of faith, sacrament and ministry that provides the context for doctrinal and moral interpretation of Scripture. The Church always had the task of judging the interpretation of Scripture. In fact, when it came to deciding the precise number of gospels and other writings in the New Testament, it was the Church as a community with a living Tradition that clarified the issue. At this Council, it is also said that there are some traditions that were not written down but have come down to us from the apostolic era.

Tradition is something Dynamic

Imagine now you are a journalist just as the Second Vatican Council (1962–1965) is beginning – the biggest council to date! To adequately report on it, you are going to have to know something of what happened in the past four hundred years.

You see, following the Council of Trent, some of its teachings were not well presented. You know how it is – teachers try to synopsise too much for students! In their teaching and books, some theologians gave the impression there were two separate sources of revelation – Scripture and traditions that Catholics have, whereas Protestants don't. As the centuries went on, the caricature grew that Protestants believed in Scripture alone (with no Tradition) while Catholics believed in Tradition (which contained Scripture but had much more than what was to be found in Scripture). A 'quantitative' perspective of Tradition began to take hold.

So in the nineteenth century, some theologians, such as Roschini from Germany's Tübingen Catholic School of Theology and Scheeben from the Roman Universities, began to address this issue and present a renewed sense of Tradition as something 'living'.

In England, Cardinal Newman proposed rediscovering the organic sense of Tradition. He wrote:

> I think I am right in saying that the Tradition of the apostles, committed to the whole Church in its various constituents and functions ... manifests itself variously at various times: sometimes by the mouth of the episcopacy, sometimes by the doctors, sometimes by the people, sometimes by liturgies, rites, ceremonies, and customs, by events, disputes, movements, and all those other phenomena which are comprised under the name of history.[1]

Newman distinguished Episcopal Tradition, that is, handed on along the apostolic line of bishops (church teaching, sacraments and community guidance) from prophetical Tradition, that is, that of the prophets who are interpreters of revelation (founders, mystics, saints). He also emphasised how all the baptised have an 'instinct' of faith and they work together in handing on the one Tradition.

Coming closer to the Council, in the twentieth century, biblical scholars opened up many discoveries about Scripture that hadn't always been appreciated before. The Catholic Church underwent a whole renewed study and love of Scripture. In this context too, Tradition was re-discovered as the living communitarian dynamic that accompanies Scripture as its home. The 1950 definition of the Marian doctrine of the Assumption (Mary assumed body and soul into heaven) also gave rise to discussions between Catholics and Protestants about Tradition.

Maybe you have read the French Dominican theologian Yves Congar's book called *Tradition and Traditions*. You have noticed Congar's distinction between Tradition with a capital 'T' and 'traditions' with a small 't'. His point was that there is a need to distinguish Apostolic Tradition, the steady core of church life, from smaller traditions that might change. In other words, not every single thing we do in the Church is part of the great Tradition of the Church. No, traditions change. For instance, once Mass was said in Latin; now it is said it in the languages of the world. The Mass is essential to Tradition, the language it is celebrated in is a 'tradition'. Likewise, dipping our finger into the water font on the way into a church is a tradition. It points to the heart of Tradition: the fact that we are united through baptism to Jesus Christ who has brought us into a relationship with God the Father and the Holy Spirit, the Giver of Life.

Congar pointed to Mary as a good example for understanding what Tradition is in the Church. She pondered on the Word in her heart and her insight into it grew deeper throughout her life. Like Mary, as the Church journeys along history, with new things happening and through believers studying, contemplating and putting the Gospel into practice, the Church guards her Tradition but also gains new windows of insight into its meaning. In this way, the Church engages in a loving dialogue, guided by the Holy Spirit, with God.

You have done your research. Now you can look forward to the Council.

Revelation and its Transmission

Finally, imagine you are at the press conference the day they release the Vatican Council's document on Divine Revelation (18 November 1965).

You know there was difficulty in drafting it. But you discover it to be reasonably easy to read. You would recommend it! You notice the title, *Dei Verbum*, Word of God. And Chapter 2 zeroes in on Tradition as the transmission of revelation. It is such a short chapter, but really full of clarifications so that it needs to be read carefully.

You notice, first, in *Dei Verbum*, paragraph 7, how it speaks of the one Gospel of salvation that comes to us from Jesus and the apostles and the bishops who succeeded them. Tradition and Scripture are described as a mirror in which the Church can contemplate God. Paragraph 8 of *Dei Verbum* is a gem. It lists the ways the Tradition process goes on in the Church: 'In this way the Church, in her doctrine, life and worship, perpetuates and transmits to every generation all that she herself is, all that she believes …' This is no static dead process. The document states: 'The Tradition … makes progress in the Church, with the help of the Holy Spirit. There is growth in insight … This comes about in various ways. It comes through contemplation and study of believers … from spiritual … experience …' Charisms are sent to help us. Of course, those entrusted with the 'sure charism of truth' (the bishops) have a specific and essential role to play in this process. Tradition makes sure that the Word of God continues not as a dead book but as alive, opening us up to the continuing dialogue between God and God's people.

In *Dei Verbum*, paragraph 9, you notice how the Council underlines the interrelationship between Scripture and Tradition. It doesn't get into whether or not there are parts of the Good News in Scripture and other parts in Tradition. But it does say that both Scripture and Tradition come from the one source, fusing in some fashion to form one thing and move towards the same goal. There is a profound interdependence between Scripture and Tradition.

But there is more. Scripture and Tradition on their own are not the full story. You read in *Dei Verbum*, paragraph 10, that the 'authentic interpretation' of the Word of God, whether 'in its written form or in the form of Tradition', has been entrusted to the living teaching office of the Church alone. It is as if there is a tripod upon which the communication of God's self-revelation is set: 'it is clear, therefore, that, in the supremely wise arrangement of God, sacred Tradition, sacred Scripture and the Magisterium of the Church are so connected and associated that one of them cannot stand without the others.'

Conclusion

So, what is Tradition? It is what the Church community, as a Mother, hands on, all that she is and has (doctrine, sacramental celebration and community life practices and institutions). The more there is mutual love in the Church, the more our Tradition comes alive because its deepest roots are in the life of God who is mutual love.

Catholics view Tradition as very important. It informs the Church's teachings on a wide range of issues. While the relationship of Scripture and Tradition remains a point of tension between the churches, thankfully, there have been good developments such as the 1963 Montreal World Conference on Faith and Order's statement on Scripture, Tradition and Traditions. The *Catechism of the Catholic Church* reminds us that:

> Tradition is to be distinguished from the various theological, disciplinary, liturgical or devotional traditions ... These are the particular forms, adapted to different places and times, in which the great Tradition is expressed. (n. 83)

Scripture is Tradition written down. Scripture is the 'norm' against which to measure Tradition. Tradition, however, is Scripture lived. It is the life that gives life, making us Christians who are fully alive, with a sense of belonging, a worldview, an 'atmosphere' where we are at 'home' but always outward bound in love.

Note

1   John Coulson (ed.) *On Consulting the Faithful in Matters of Doctrine*, London, 1961, p. 63.

Further Reading

Dei Verbum (Vatican II, 1965).

Catechism of the Catholic Church, Part 1, Chapter 2, Article 2 on the Transmission of Divine Revelation.

Congar, Yves, *Tradition and Traditions*, London: ET, 1966.

O'Collins, Gerald, 'Finding the Tradition within the Traditions' in *Fundamental Theology*, Mahwah, NJ: Paulist Press, 1981, pp. 208–224.

Rahner, Karl and Ratzinger, Joseph, *Revelation and Tradition*, NY: Herder and Herder, 1966.

SECTION II

Christian Creed

CHAPTER 7

JESUS, THE CHRIST

Fachtna McCarthy

Introduction

Christian faith rests on what we believe about the person of Jesus Christ, its founder two thousand years ago. The life of Jesus, a Palestinian Jew of the first century, has had an enormous impact on human history ever since. One quarter of the world's population today professes to be Christian. Every age asks the central question Jesus put to his apostles in the gospels: 'Who do you say I am' (Mk 8:29). We ask today: Who was this Jesus in history? What was he about? What did he really say or do? What did he claim to be? Why was he put to death?

The study of Jesus Christ, who he is, what he said and did, is vital for Christian faith. That is so for three reasons: Jesus reveals who God is, who we are and what the Church is all about. Firstly, our Christian understanding of God is rooted in the story of Jesus of Nazareth. God is the Almighty Creator of heaven and earth who is hidden in mystery from us, his limited creatures. The central claim of Christian faith is that God reveals God's true self in the historical person of Jesus. 'God has made himself visible: in Jesus we are able to see the Father.'[1] To tell the story of Jesus is to tell the story of God with us. He is the eternal Son of the Father who has entered human history to reveal God as the loving and saving Father of all humankind. 'The Word became flesh and dwelt among us' (Jn 1:14). The Son of God (Word) became incarnate; that is, he took on a human nature in order to save us. 'Belief in the true Incarnation of the Son of God is the distinctive sign of the Christian faith.'[2]

The question about Jesus is also about our identity: saying who we think Jesus is tells us who we think human beings are. Jesus lived a fully human life as one of us. He was born of Mary and grew into adulthood with the full range of human experiences, except sin. In complete solidarity with us he speaks to our deepest questions about the meaning of our lives, our joys and sorrows, our loves and losses and the realities of evil, suffering and death.

Finally, the Christian Church was founded in Jesus' name to carry on his mission in the world at all times and in all places. What we believe the Church to be about today depends on what we believe Jesus Christ to be about in the past. Our most important Church festivals, such as Easter and Christmas, and our great celebrations like the Eucharist re-present crucial parts of the story of Jesus. The heart of Christian faith is a relationship to a person, Jesus Christ, who lives now and forever as the risen Lord. For Catholics, to be a follower of Jesus means to be a member of the church community.

Christianity then is not a set of timeless truths or ideas, a lofty theory about the way things are in the world. It is an historical religion, a narrative or story about particular events that happened to a particular people at a particular place and time. Certain past events have an essential importance for the present: the person, life, preaching and above all the death and resurrection of Jesus of Nazareth. What Christians believe today is very much shaped by these crucial events of the past.

Jesus never wrote a book; his followers wrote about him in the Gospels of Matthew, Mark, Luke and John. The gospels are not biography, a complete account of the life of Jesus from cradle to grave. They are 'faith-documents': they tell the story of Jesus viewed through the eyes of his disciples who have come to believe in him after his resurrection. We know hardly anything about the 'hidden years', the first thirty years of his life. He was born of Mary in Bethlehem about 4 BCE and lived quietly as a carpenter in Nazareth. The gospels concentrate on Jesus' public ministry, which lasted anywhere between one and three years. The story of Jesus in the gospels has three important moments: his ministry, death and resurrection.

The Ministry of Jesus

Jesus, the observant Jew, belonged to the social and cultural world of first-century Palestine. It was a time of crisis for the Jews who lived under Roman colonial occupation. The Roman legal system, heavy taxation and pagan religion were alien and oppressive to their ancient Jewish faith. That faith was based on fidelity to the Torah, the Covenant law found in the Hebrew

Scriptures (Old Testament), the central plank being the Ten Commandments. Jews believed that keeping the law in all its smallest detail would bring God's blessing. As a matter of survival and to preserve the purity of their faith, the Jews separated themselves from all that was unclean, especially non-Jews or pagans. This code of separation also ensured that those Jews who broke the law were branded unclean; as sinners they were excluded from community life and the synagogue.

Jesus of Nazareth emerged from this background to begin his public ministry when he was baptised by John the Baptist at the River Jordan. There he experienced God's call to mission and was filled with the Holy Spirit. As a wandering preacher and healer, he began to proclaim the coming Kingdom of God. He gathered a small group of disciples around him who came to believe he was the Messiah (the Christ), the promised Saviour of his Jewish people. Crowds flocked to him because he was preaching Good News (Gospel), especially to the poor, people on the edge of society, the sick and suffering.

At the heart of Jesus' preaching was the theme of the coming reign of God or the 'Kingdom of God'. Linked to this was the idea of Messiah, the Anointed One, who would bring the kingdom about. 'The time has come. The Kingdom of God is at hand. Repent and believe in the Gospel' (Mk 1:15). There is a sense of urgency and excitement about Jesus' message. Kingdom is an ancient Hebrew image about God's saving action on behalf of his people. God would act decisively for his people, blessing them, giving them *shalom* (peace) and well being, protecting them from enemies and bringing justice and peace for all. The Jews believed that God's kingdom would come only at the end of history, on the last day when God would judge the living and the dead. However, Jesus proclaimed that the kingdom is very near; it is already breaking into history with his coming. God's reign was already at work in Jesus' life, preaching and healing. The compassionate and loving God is coming close to heal and save, bringing about justice and peace for all. That hope is the focal point of Jesus' preaching and guides all his actions.

All are called to enter the kingdom, but it belongs especially to the 'the little ones'. Jesus reached out to people on the margins, the oppressed poor, the sick and suffering and public sinners, all of whom were excluded from Jewish community life. He sought their company as they were the special concern of God's compassion and love. Jesus' 'option for the poor' expresses his concern for social justice, his desire to free people from all that oppressed them and to restore their dignity within the community. He was tough on the self-indulgent rich and powerful who exploited the poor and imposed unjust, heavy burdens on them.

Jesus' distinctive actions included miracles of healing. He restored to wholeness those who were wounded by life or who were broken by sin or guilt. His great freeing acts of healing were expressions of God's compassion for the suffering of the world and it left a deep impression on the movement he left behind. They were a sign and a promise of God's future salvation, people were being made whole again and evil was being defeated. The power of God working through Jesus cured many physical ailments, but more significantly, he healed them in spirit when he lifted their burden of guilt by forgiving their sins. In a typical action he shared his table with public sinners, challenging the accepted view that sickness was a punishment for sin. Table-fellowship with Jesus was experienced as a pledge of their reconciliation with God and an invitation to turn away from sin. This controversial action of eating with sinners scandalised the religious authorities who demanded the separation of the 'clean' observant Jews from the 'unclean' public sinners.

The preaching of the Kingdom of God challenged people 'to repent and believe in the Gospel'. Jesus asked people to be open to the good news, to be converted to the gospel message. Conversion meant throwing off the old sinful way of life, a change of mind and heart and a new relationship with God and others. Jesus taught about God's kingdom in striking stories and parables, his own distinct way of challenging the old ways of seeing things. The parables of the Lost Sheep, the Lost Coin and the Prodigal Son (Lk 15) express God's solidarity with sinners and his joy in their return to the fold. Jesus called disciples to follow him. He called an inner group, twelve apostles who represented the twelve tribes, the whole people of Israel, and he gave Peter a unique leadership role. They left everything, homes, jobs and families, for the sake of the kingdom. He taught them to imitate his life, his love of God and his compassion for the poor and needy. A wider group of men and women travelled with him, they listened to his teaching and were sent out on mission by him. Jesus formed a new kind of family, not based on clan or blood ties, but on acceptance of the message of the kingdom. This new community was founded on equality and inclusion, a 'discipleship of equals'. It was not restricted to pious religious observers or men only. Jesus was a boundary breaker who invited the unclean, outcasts and sinners. Men and women shared in discipleship, with the women followers of Jesus playing a central part at the cross and resurrection of Jesus. If Jesus lived his life in the service of others, then loving and forgiving service of neighbour was the mark of his community. 'Be compassionate as your heavenly Father is compassionate' (Lk 6:36).

Jesus' aim was not to found a new religion but to reform his own Jewish faith. He was faithful to the core of the Torah, the Covenant Law, and yet he felt free to reinterpret it on his own authority. 'I have not come to abolish but to fulfil the law' (Mt 5:17). Union with God and service of others were the guiding traits of his life. He summed up his teaching in the twin commandments, love of God with one's whole heart and love of neighbour as oneself. Both were at the heart of the kingdom. Love was understood as the giving of self on behalf of the neighbour in need. Neighbour included not only family and fellow-Jews but strangers, outcasts, sinners and even enemies. No group or individual was excluded. Taking revenge on your enemies was no longer acceptable. 'But I say to you, love your enemies' (Mt 5:32). He was critical of the Jewish concern with the tiny matters of the law while neglecting the big issues, like mercy for sinners or compassion for the suffering. Jesus put the cause of the sick, the hungry and the suffering before the heavy burdens of the law. 'You ignore the commandments of God and hold fast to your human traditions' (Mk 7:8). The well-being and care of people was more important than the rigorous demands of the Sabbath, food laws or laws of ritual purity.

The centre of Jesus' life is the strength of his relationship with God, whom he calls Abba, a child's babble-word for his/her father. Abba expresses the very unique, close and intimate experience Jesus has of God, his heavenly Father. Jesus lives with and for his Father. The full implications of how close Jesus was to God would emerge only after the Resurrection and the sending of the Holy Spirit. His whole ministry was rooted in prayer to his Father, in tuning in to his Father's wishes and in doing everything in obedience to his will. Jesus teaches his disciples to pray for the coming of his Father's reign in the 'Our Father' and so to call God, Abba, Father also. He encourages them to trust God the way little children trust a loving parent to look after them with great care and affection. For Jesus every person is a beloved child of God and is completely and unconditionally accepted by his heavenly Father.

Death and Resurrection

The gospels portray the ministry of Jesus in two phases. Jesus began in his native Galilee as a dynamic preacher of the reign of God and as a charismatic healer. People flocked to him as he was 'Good News', especially for the poor, the sick and the rejected. Many saw him not only as a great prophet but the promised Messiah, the saviour of his people. They had hopes Jesus would save his people from their Roman enemies, but became disillusioned when he refused the way of violence. God's kingdom was not based on political power or military might. His quarrel was not with the political powers but with the destructive forces of evil. It was a spiritual kingdom, an inner kingdom of the human heart. His challenge to the religious laws of Judaism and his radical preaching led to a growing conflict with the religious authorities. From the outset Jesus' own religious vision was very different from that of his contemporaries. He challenged the pattern of separation and exclusion because he viewed God as compassionate and merciful to all, especially sinners. His message that God loved sinners offended their sense of the holiness and righteousness of God. His ministry divided people: some were enthusiastic followers and others were bitterly opposed to him.

In spite of increasing hostility Jesus went up to Jerusalem, the home of his enemies. The incident of the 'cleansing in the Temple' sealed his fate. The Temple in Jerusalem was the centre of Jewish religious and cultural life. Jesus causes a riot when he attacks the buyers and sellers in the Temple, his 'Father's house', and threatens to destroy it. The Temple priests feel threatened, they plot to kill him and he goes into hiding. In the context of a Passover meal, Jesus institutes the Eucharist at the Last Supper, the gift of his body and blood to be given on Good Friday for the life of the world. Jesus saw his death coming at some distance, knowing the fate of prophets before him. In the Garden of Gethsemane he is in fear and dread and yet submits to the Father's will being done. He is arrested and put on trial by the Romans and unjustly condemned to death by Pontius Pilate on criminal charges of stirring up revolt against Rome, refusing to pay tribute to Caesar and making himself king of the Jews (Lk 23:2). He is interrogated, scourged and crucified on Good Friday outside the walls of Jerusalem, an inhuman and degrading form of execution. His body is placed in the tomb of Joseph of Arimathea and the entrance sealed. His shocked disciples desert him, and even his beloved Father appears to have abandoned him to his fate. To his followers Jesus' life had ended in failure and they were left in crisis to mourn their dead leader and a lost cause. Nobody expected the Messiah to die, to become the victim and not the conqueror of his enemies.

The death of Jesus was not a tragic accident; it was the price he paid for his ministry, for living out the demands of love. His death was his final act of love, a gift of himself to God and to his followers, in laying down his life for his friends. He showed how to bear suffering with dignity and hope. After the Resurrection, his disciples saw his death as a perfect sacrifice offered to God which would make up for the sins of the rest of us (1 Jn 2:2). God 'shows his love for us in that while we were still sinners, Christ died for us' (Rom 5:8). While not denying its devastation, the Cross of Jesus was not seen as a defeat but as a victory by which human beings were reconciled with God (2 Cor 5:14-21). Jesus 'gave his life as a ransom for many' (Mt 20:28). The symbol of the Sacred Heart of Jesus in Catholic devotion points to the generous, loving heart of Jesus wounded in love for us in atoning for our sins.

The shameful death of Jesus on the cross was not the end. Against this bleak horizon the news of resurrection dawns: God has raised his son Jesus from the dead. The women disciples go to the tomb to embalm the body but find it empty. At first the disciples are sceptical but their unbelief turns to belief after more and more witnesses report meeting the risen Lord. Their discouragement and sense of loss is turned into a joyful celebration – the Lord has triumphed over death and is risen indeed! The gospels struggle to describe this unique event and the new reality of the risen Jesus. It is the same Jesus who died on the cross as he still bears the marks of crucifixion. Yet it is not a return to the old earthly life, like the raising of Lazarus. Jesus has been transformed, raised up into glory and now shares forever the life of God. The Resurrection vindicates who Jesus is, what he said and what he did. God is truly the loving and compassionate Father, about whom Jesus witnessed with his life and the Resurrection is a sure sign that God's kingdom is coming about. The Resurrection makes plain who the earthly Jesus is, the divine Son of God his Father, now coming in power through the

Holy Spirit. St Paul makes the Resurrection the central belief of the Christian Church: 'If Jesus Christ is not risen then our faith is in vain' (1 Cor 15:14).

The death and resurrection of Jesus are two sides of one event: the Paschal mystery, the great events of Easter that bring about our salvation. 'By his death, Christ liberates us from sin: by his Resurrection, he opens for us the way to new life.'[3] The resurrection means that Jesus' new spiritual way of being is no longer limited by space and time and so he is able to be present now to people everywhere. 'Jesus is Lord' and 'Jesus is the Christ' summed up the post-resurrection belief. He is truly the Lord, given the sacred name of God in the Hebrew scriptures, a statement of his divinity. To proclaim Jesus is Lord as the only Son of the Father, who alone is worthy of worship, is to reject all other so-called gods as idols. To proclaim him the Christ (Messiah) is to proclaim him the Saviour of his people, who brings freedom from the evil forces that would enslave us.

The resurrection is not something that happened to Jesus alone. The disciples experienced the power of the Risen Lord through his gift of the Holy Spirit at Pentecost. The Spirit transformed them from demoralised followers into fearless witnesses and preachers of the Risen Lord. The raising of Jesus is decisive in the battle against evil. Jesus has conquered our great enemies, sin and death. To become a Christian by being baptised is to share in the risen life of Jesus, to become a new creature filled with the new life of the Spirit. If God raised Jesus, so we can also hope in the promise of our future resurrection. Our suffering and dying are not final but are a passage to a new and eternal life with God.

Christian faith spread rapidly from Palestine into the greater world of Roman and Greek culture, even in the face of periodic persecution from the pagan Roman emperors. The Christian Church of the first few centuries defined its central beliefs about Jesus in church councils, which were put in creeds like the Nicene Creed or the Apostles' Creed. Jesus is truly God and truly human. In the first few centuries the Church had to defend this central teaching about Jesus. There was much misunderstanding as the early Church tried to clarify its belief and to exclude false views or heresies. The Council of Nicea 325 CE proclaimed that Jesus Christ, the Son of God, is of the same being, equal to God the Father. In 451 CE the Council of Chalcedon used technical language to pronounce that the one person Jesus Christ has a divine nature and a human nature in the unity of one person. That stands for equal emphasis on the divinity and humanity of Jesus Christ, fully human and fully divine in the integrity of one undivided person. The Council sought to protect the conviction of the New Testament about the identity of Jesus and this teaching became the norm for Catholic faith ever since. But we can never fully grasp the reality and the uniqueness of Jesus Christ in words. The mystery of his person, the depth of his love, his relationship with the Father, his saving death and victorious resurrection, will always elude our best efforts.

Conclusion

The task of Christian teaching is to bridge the gap between the past and the present, to link the story of Jesus in history with the story of his followers in the Christian community today. The challenge of the Church is to be about the reign of God. We are to tell and retell the story of Jesus as the story of God with us and to walk in his footsteps. As his followers we are to celebrate the presence of the living Lord in our midst and to live the values of the Gospel in the world.

Notes

1   Benedict XVI, *Deus caritas est*, Dublin: Veritas, 2006, 17.
2   CCC 462.
3   CCC 654.

Further Reading

Catechism of the Catholic Church, Dublin: Veritas, 1994.
O'Collins, Gerald, *Interpreting Jesus*, New Jersey: Paulist Press, 1983.
Lane, Dermot, *The Reality of Jesus*, Dublin: Veritas, 1975.
Senior, Donald, *A Gospel Portrait of Jesus*, New York, Paulist Press, 1992.
Johnson, Elizabeth A., *Consider Jesus*, New York: Crossroad, 1990.
Lyons, Enda, *Jesus: Self-portrait by God*, Dublin: Columba, 1994.

CHAPTER 8

TRINITY

Carol Barry

Introduction

Before even learning how to say their prayers, most Christian children are
first taught how to bless themselves in the name of the Father, and of the Son,
and of the Holy Spirit. Generally speaking, people are also familiar with the
use of this Trinitarian formula in the rite of Baptism. Over the years, many of
us have listened on 'Trinity Sunday' to various attempts to shed light on this
mystery of the Trinity. Often we found ourselves confused about the possible
relevance of this doctrine for our daily lives. Indeed, it is probably fair to say
that for the most part, when it comes to how we view ourselves, our work, our
world, and how we live and act, this doctrine appears to hold very little
significance. Consequently, the doctrine of the Trinity makes no real impact
on our lives. The philosopher, Immanuel Kant, went so far as to dismiss the
doctrine of the Trinity as 'a piece of useless speculation, from which nothing
whatsoever can be gained for practical purposes'.[1]

According to Church teaching, however, this doctrine, far from being a
piece of useless speculation, is in fact the central mystery of Christian faith
and life. Trinity is the central Christian doctrine because Jesus is truly God.
Furthermore, Christianity teaches that the innate dignity of human beings
derives from the fact that we are made in the image and likeness of God
(Gen 1:28). Therefore, the ideas we hold in relation to God have a direct
bearing on how we view *ourselves*. Consequently, this chapter will address
two related questions. First, what does the doctrine of the Trinity tell us
about God? Second, what does the doctrine of the Trinity tell us about
ourselves, about what it means to be a human being? An exploration of these
two questions will enable us to understand the centrality of the doctrine of
the Trinity for the Christian life.

Naming God – Trinity

Names matter. The meaning and stories behind names matter a great deal. I recall being deeply honoured when some Kenyan women 'named' me after I had spent some time amongst them. They explained that, based on their experience of me, they were trying to capture in my African name some essential characteristics of who I am as a person. They also commented, 'but this name is not the whole of you, Carol. No name captures the whole of you. You will have to come back and we will learn more of you!'

When we speak of and name God, who as totally 'Other' transcends humankind, it is even more important to acknowledge the inadequacy of our words, ideas and images, for 'our human words always fall short of the mystery of God' (CCC 42).

The Trinity is the specifically Christian way of naming God. The name 'Trinity' emerged to express a distinct experience of God. This experience of God is rooted in the saving words and deeds of the Judeo-Christian tradition, culminating in the life, death and resurrection of Christ. The story of Christianity is rooted in the story of Judaism, a monotheistic religion. Judaism, Christianity and Islam all share in the belief in one God. However, because of the revelatory events of the life, death and resurrection of Jesus, Christianity goes beyond its Jewish roots. It confesses that 'this one God involves a threeness, a Trinity. This God is a triune God'.[2]

Doctrine of the Trinity

The theology of the Trinity is an attempt to understand this Christian mystery of one God in three distinct persons; Father, Son and Holy Spirit. Christian doctrine and the formulation of doctrine do not emerge 'out of thin air'. Doctrine has a history. Clarity of thought and language in relation to the Trinity developed amidst a maze of controversies, heresies and theological debates that dominated early Church life. The early Christian community engaged in a genuine and difficult search for rules of speech that would best articulate their experience of God. The word 'Trinity' is associated in particular with the work of a lay theologian, Tertullian (d. 220), and while not a biblical word, reflects biblical revelation of God. The experience of God revealed as Father, Son and Holy Spirit came first; language used to faithfully express this revelatory experience came later.[3]

The development of the doctrine of the Trinity and its elucidation is intrinsically linked with the history and teaching of early Church councils. The decisions made in defence of the divinity of Jesus and of the Holy Spirit at Nicea (325 CE), and Constantinople (381 CE) and the definitive Christological Council of Chalcedon (451 CE), played a major role in the development of the doctrine.[4] The central truths about God affirmed in this doctrine are outlined here.

Unity in the Trinity

In naming God as Father, Son and Holy Spirit, Christianity is not suggesting that there are three 'Gods'. The Christian belief is that while there is only one God, God is not solitary. God is the loving communion of Father, Son and Holy Spirit. In other words, God's being is relational. Father, Son and Holy Spirit are fully and equally God sharing the one divine nature. Human beings refer to our common human nature. We all share equally in human nature, despite our unique individuality. The three divine persons are fully and equally God sharing the one divine nature. No one of the three divine persons is more or less divine than the other two. There is no hierarchy in the Trinity: Father, Son and Holy Spirit are equal and one.

In the development of the doctrine, a number of words came to prominence in order to articulate the unity of the three persons: substance, essence and nature. We speak of the divine nature of Father, Son and Holy Spirit, who share the one divine essence or substance (Gk *ousia*). The three divine persons do so, not in the sense of each having a 'bit' of divinity or being 'part' of God: rather, 'the Father is that which the Son is, the Son is that which the Father is, the Father that which the Spirit is, i.e. by nature, one God' (CCC 253). Accordingly, in the creed, Christians confess that Jesus is 'of one being with the Father' and the Holy Spirit is worshipped and glorified together 'with the Father and the Son'.

Distinction in the Trinity

While Father, Son and Holy Spirit are of the one divine essence, each one is unique within the relationships of the Trinity. This distinction is affirmed in the Catechism: 'He is not the Father who is the Son, nor is the Son he who is the Father, nor is the Holy Spirit he who is the Father or the Son' (CCC 254). The unity of the Trinity is unique in that it embraces the distinction of the three divine persons. Diversity in the Trinity does not negate the unity of the Trinity; the divine unity exists because Father, Son and Holy Spirit are distinctly unique.

The word 'person' (Gk *hypostasis*) is used to try and designate what is distinct about Father, Son and Holy Spirit. It also allows us to speak of relations in the Trinity and thus draws us deeper into the mystery of personal loving communion that is God.

Relations in the Trinity

The idea of 'person' is used to express the distinct relations within the Trinity. Today, the word 'person' tends to convey the sense of a separate, self-contained individual. Person, however, is also a relational word: it speaks of *someone*, not *something*. The fact that *we* are persons means we have the potential to enter into relationships. We can love and be loved by other people. We can also choose to cut off from other people and to reject relationships. While it is true that our journey into an authentic sense of self involves how we relate to and with others, our relationships do not define who we are, nor do they constitute the whole identity of our personhood. When we use the word 'person' of the Trinity though, this is not the case. The three divine persons *are* their relations to one another. Their relation to one another defines each person's identity. We *have* relationships. God *is* the relationships of Father, Son and Holy Spirit.

In the Greek culture and language, which played such a significant role in the formulation of Christian doctrine, the word 'person' stood for someone in relationship. It carried with it the sense of coming to be through relationship. Being a person in God is defined solely in and through relationship with the others. The name or title 'Father' does not reveal the essence of God, but relation to the Son. Father, Son and Spirit are persons *in and through* their relations. As Michael Downey explains:

> The term person when used of God is a way of saying that God is always toward and for the other in self-giving which is constitutive of love. To say there are three persons in God is to say that God is not an in-and-of itself, a for-itself or a by-itself.[5]

In other words, self-gift is at the heart of who and how God is; God is a tri-personal mystery of love. The Father, Son and Holy Spirit so love one another that they are ever united in the loving communion that is God. Saint John sums this truth up concisely in the biblical proposition, 'God is love' (1 Jn 4:8).

Drawing on this proposition, St Augustine used the analogy of the Father as lover, the Son as the beloved and the Holy Spirit as the love between the two to speak of unity, distinctions and relations in the Trinity. Michael J. Himes summarises Augustine's thinking rather beautifully when he writes, 'From all eternity God is the lover who gives Godself away perfectly; and the beloved who accepts being loved and returns it perfectly; and the endless perfect bond of mutual self-gift uniting the lover and the beloved'.[6] This profound truth about God is not something we human beings could discover by ourselves. We are able to catch glimpses of the 'inner life' or essence of God because God chooses to reveal something of who God is through God's outreach to humanity.

Divine Revelation

Catholic tradition has always upheld the belief that human beings, by the use of reason, can affirm the existence of God (Rom 1:20). It suggests that the wonder of creation, the order of the universe, human experience and conscience are all possible departure points for such a conviction. However, believing that God exists is one thing: knowing what God is like, or what God wills for human beings is another matter altogether. Christianity contends that human beings, by the use of their reason alone, cannot discover who God is, or how God wants to relate with us. Indeed, why would we even think God wants to relate with humanity? A relationship with God is not something that is ours by right or demand. It is only by God's own outreach to us in the words and deeds named 'salvation history' that God reveals who God is and what God wills for humanity. The realisation that God freely chose to do so helps us appreciate the pure gift of divine revelation.

Jewish Roots

Saint Paul reminds Christians that Judaism is the root which sustains them (Rom 11:8). Through the sacred texts of the Hebrew Scriptures we learn of a people who were open to and experienced God's self disclosure. For the Israelites, the work of creation, their personal and communal story, as well

114

as significant historical events, all contained revelatory importance in relation to God. God's saving activity on their behalf revealed something of who God is.[7] The central saving act of God for the Jewish people is the Exodus event in which they were saved from slavery in Egypt. For Christians, this dramatic event is the forerunner of the central saving act of Jesus whose life, death and resurrection delivered the world from the slavery of sin and death.

The theological term 'Economic Trinity' is used to denote all of God's actions in creating, redeeming and sanctifying humanity. The term 'Immanent Trinity' speaks for the very *being*, essence, or *inner life* of God. From our own experience, we know that how we treat ourselves and others reveals a great deal about who we are. We often say 'actions speak louder than words'. Similarly, we learn about God through God's actions on our behalf. God's outreach to us in turn becomes God's own self-disclosure. Through the events of our salvation of which the cross and resurrection are central (Gal 3:1; 6:14) the love of God is revealed and manifested. What God did and does for us cannot be separated from who God is: the Economic Trinity reveals the Immanent Trinity. The story of who God is culminates in the incarnation of the Son of God.

Love made Visible: The Incarnation

Hans Urs von Balthasar describes the incarnation as 'the stepping forth into visibility of the love of God'.[8] With the incarnation God enters our human story in a very visible and tangible way. The love that is God finds human expression in the person of Jesus. The 'word made flesh' (Jn 1:14) who is the image of God and who is intimate with the Father is the one who fully and finally reveals God. Jesus tells Philip, 'If you know me, you will know my Father too' (Jn 14:7). God is made accessible to humankind in the attitudes, actions, teaching and ministry of Jesus. Jesus' self-gift and loving surrender to death on the cross encapsulates his life's message and mission. What we see in Jesus – his compassion, love, healing touch, concern for the marginalised, his merciful outreach to sinners – is a true reflection of who God is. As Herbert McCabe states: 'The story of Jesus is nothing other than the triune life of God projected onto our history.'[9]

Trinity: Revelation of Who We Are

Jesus tells us who God is, what God desires and how God acts. But Jesus also models a way of life that reveals what it means to be truly human. He calls and challenges human beings to follow his journey of self-giving love. His message is simple: 'Love one another as I have loved you. There is no greater love than this: to lay down one's life for one's friends' (Jn 15:12-13). Living this call to love as Jesus did is not simply an ethical or social issue. It is about discovering who we really are as human beings and as *children* of God.

Christianity asserts that our innate dignity as human beings derives from the fact that we are made in the image of God. The God in whose image we are made is a Triune God. As God is a relational communion of love, it follows that we human beings are made for relationships; in giving and receiving love we too come to be. The Trinity is the ultimate paradigm of all our personal relationships: in the sincere gift of ourselves to and for the other we discover our true selves.[10] God is not solitary; hence we are not created to be solitary. We are called to communion with ourselves, others and God.

In fulfilling that call we become who we truly are. God reaches out to us and includes us in his community of love; the Father is our Father, the Son is our brother, the Spirit lives in our hearts. Jesus taught us, and died for us, to draw us all together in the love of God. The presence of the Spirit is the presence of God in our lives today! God is to be found in our hearts, yes; but God also dwells in the heart of our lives. Our relationships, the joy and pain of falling and growing in love, all these realities become holy ground, the place where God is revealed. God is not 'out there' waiting to be found in some extraordinary experience. God is present in the ordinary everyday experiences and relationships that make up our lives. The teaching of Saint John tells us not only that 'God is love': it tells us 'where love is, God is' (1 Jn 4:8).

Holy Spirit – Gift Given

Jesus revealed the face of God. In our call to Christian discipleship (one who is intimate with and follows Christ), we, in turn, are called to reveal the face of God to others. How can we fulfil the command to love as Jesus loved? How can we image and witness to the mystery of self-gift which is at the heart of God in whose image we are made? As Pope John Paul II wrote, 'To imitate and live out the love of Christ is not possible for man by his own strength alone. He becomes capable of this love only by virtue of a gift received'.[11] In Baptism, we are filled with the gift of the Holy Spirit, who draws us into and empowers us to live the mission of Jesus.

Jesus promised his disciples the gift of the Holy Spirit who would empower them to understand and live the love he revealed (Jn 14-16). The risen Christ's gift is the Holy Spirit whose first fruit is love. This outpouring of the Holy Spirit, the third person of the Trinity, flows from and is intimately linked to the saving death of Jesus. As Saint Paul puts it, 'God's love has been poured into our hearts through the Holy Spirit which has been given to us' (Rom 5:5). Through the Holy Spirit, we are drawn into the mystery of love that is the Trinity and given a share in the life of God. The Holy Spirit is accessible to us in the Word of God, in the sacraments, in the Church community, in creation, in all people of good will and in the depth of our own hearts.

Conclusion: Contemporary Theology

In recent decades, certain issues have become prominent in theological reflection and debate on the Trinity. Within the scope given here we cannot delve deeply into these matters. But we need to at least acknowledge the importance of these issues.[12]

Many theologians believe a deeper appreciation of the Trinity would lead to a different kind of culture and a different shape to society. Trinitarian life speaks for love, community, mutuality, unity that embraces diversity and self-giving that does not involve self-annihilation. The Trinity could and does inspire people to work for a society and model of Church that is more communal than hierarchical; that appreciates diversity as a gift, not as a threat; and where God's love and concern for the poor and marginalised is reflected in efforts that seek their liberation and empowerment.[13]

Feminists critique the use of sexist language in relation to God. Exclusive use of masculine language (Father, Son, God-as-He) is a direct contradiction of the inclusivity of God revealed in Jesus Christ. Whether we can substitute other terms for God than the traditional ones enshrined in doctrine is a matter of lively debate. Feminist theologians also highlight the significance of relations in the Trinity as a source of inspiration for living faith and developing self-understanding.[14]

Modern interpretation and usage of Trinitarian terms such as *person* and *nature* also give rise to theological debate. Whether these terms are still valid in conveying the true meaning of Trinitarian doctrine is seriously questioned. These and other issues have contributed to a welcome and renewed interest in, and reflection on, the central mystery of Christian faith and life.

An ancient writer offers this wisdom: 'Life begins with the Trinity, and its end and aim is the Trinity.' 'Life begins with the Trinity' means we are baptised in the name of the Father, Son and Holy Spirit. 'Life ends with the Trinity' means that our future and final home is in heaven, in the threefold presence of God.

Notes

1 Immanuel Kant, *Der Streit Der Fakultaten*, Leipzig; Philosophische Bibliothek, IP34.

2 Thomas Marsh, *The Triune God*, Dublin: Columba, 1994 (Chapter 2). Herein the author explores the development of the doctrine in relation to the Judaic understanding of God.

3 Revelation (L. *revelare*: to remove the veil) refers to the reality that God chose to make Godself known to humanity. This disclosure is a gift to humanity.

4 Within the limits of this work we cannot give due attention to these important councils, their history and teaching. For clear and helpful treatments of their significant role in the development of the doctrine, see Mary Ann Fatula, *The Triune God of Christian Faith*, Collegeville, Minn.: The Liturgical Press, 1990, pp. 55–81. Also Thomas Marsh, op. cit. pp. 95–128.

5 Michael Downey, *Altogether Gift: A Trinitarian Spirituality*, Dublin: Dominican Publications, 2000, pp. 53–55.

6 Michael J. Himes, *The Mystery of Faith*, Cinncinnati, Ohio: St Anthony Messenger Press, 2004, p. 8.

7 We derive the word 'salvation' from the Latin *salvus* (Gk *Sotero*, from *Sozo*, to save, rescue), connoting healing, wholeness, restoration. It speaks of deliverance or rescue from that which imprisons. Salvation is being delivered from personal or collective suffering and evil. It carries with it the sense that we are saved 'from' something that is destructive, but we are also saved 'for' something. We are saved 'from' sin and 'for' love.

8 Hans Urs Von Balthasar, *Mysterium Paschale*, Edinburgh: T & T Clark, 1993, p. 111.

9 Herbert McCabe, *God Matters*, London: Mowbray, 2000, p. 48.

10 GS 24.

11 VS 22.

12 Thomas Marsh gives a summary of these issues in *The Triune God*, op. cit., pp. 174–191.

13 Leonardo Boff examines this theme and argues that the Trinity is a source of inspiration for a critical attitude to personhood, community, society and Church. See Leonardo Boff, *Trinity and Society*, London: Burns & Oates, 1988, pp. 148–155.

14   Catherine Mowry La Cugna, *God for Us: The Trinity and Christian Life*, New York: San Francisco, 1991. See also Anne Hunt, *The Trinity and the Paschal Mystery*, Collegeville, Minn: The Liturgical Press, 1997; Elizabeth A. Johnson, *She Who Is: The Mystery of God in Feminist Theological Discourse*, New York: Crossroad, 1993.

Further Reading

Downey, Michael, *Altogether Gift: A Trinitarian Spirituality*, Dublin: Dominican Publications, 2000.

Fatula, Mary Ann, *The Triune God of Christian Faith*, Collegeville, Minn.: The Liturgical Press, 1990.

Hellwig, Monika, *Understanding Catholicism*, New York: Paulist Press, 1984.

Himes, Michael J., *The Mystery of Faith: An Introduction to Catholicism*, St Anthony Press, 2004.

Marsh, Thomas, *The Triune God: A Biblical, Historical and Theological Study*, Dublin: Columba, 1994.

Marthaler, Bernard, *The Creed*, Mystic, Conn.: 23rd Publications, 1987.

CHAPTER 9

THE HOLY SPIRIT

Pat Mullins

Introduction

Catholics bless themselves in the name of the Father, the Son, and the Holy Spirit and the Creed is divided into three sections, one for each of the three persons of the Trinity. The stories about Jesus in the gospels make it easy to imagine the Son and the one he called *Abba* (Father) but many people find it more difficult to imagine or relate to the Holy Spirit.

This chapter is about the principal means by which Jesus the Christ ('Christ' means 'the One anointed' by the Father with the Holy Spirit) has redeemed and saved us: his gift to us of his own Holy and Sanctifying Spirit. Christ did not come to give us good example and then leave us without the power and help we need to follow that example, like giving someone a car but no means to fill it with petrol, or giving a child a train set and not enough batteries to make it work! By giving us the very same Holy Spirit who had guided his own life on earth, and by enabling us to have the same personal relationship with the Spirit that he enjoyed, he transformed us interiorly and gave us the power, the strength and the gifts of grace that we need to follow him, and to love God and our neighbour as he did.

The Old Testament tends to focus on *what* the Spirit does rather than on *who* the Spirit is. In Hebrew, the word for 'Spirit' is *ruach*, a feminine noun with a variety of meanings, including 'breath' and 'wind'. Just as a trumpet does not sound a note unless someone blows into it, so too can we not live or breathe without God's breath of life in us (see Job 34:14-15). Like a powerful storm, the divine Breath can make people capable of extraordinary things. Joshua, who led the people of Israel after the death of Moses, is described as 'a man in whom is the *ruach*-Spirit' (Num 27:18). The *ruach*-Spirit of God turned the newly anointed king Saul 'into another man' and enabled him to prophesy (1 Sam 10:6). In time to come, this mysterious *ruach*-Spirit of God would be poured out on the whole of Israel, on daughters and on sons, on both 'maidservants' and 'menservants' (see Joel 2:28-29).

We do not experience the Spirit of God in the same way that we experience, say, a cup of coffee or a walk in the park. God is not one experience among many others. People often become aware of God's presence and power when they reflect on the common thread uniting the moments of self-transcendence that we all experience. Like the taken-for-granted process of breathing, the birth of a new baby, or the signs of new growth when spring comes round, there is something mysterious and wonderful about the gift of life itself. It is not entirely within our control. There are also moments in our everyday lives when we recognise with renewed wonder the gift of another's love, the joy of being forgiven, the amazing beauty that surrounds us, or the liberating power of truth.

No matter what it is that we are experiencing, including our dreams, we are also always conscious that it is we, and not other people, who are having that particular experience. Our experience of God's Spirit is similar in that it always accompanies the experience of something else. As we learn to pay attention to this dimension of living, loving and being loved, we gradually become more familiar with the particular characteristics that are the hallmark of God's Spirit.

Do you 'believe' in electricity? Electricity is a power – an impersonal force – that has always been there but that has only been understood and harnessed in the last few centuries. Although we cannot, as such, see it or touch it, we can experience the effects of electricity when there is a bolt of lightning or, simply, when we turn on an electric light. The same could be said about our breathing, which is also invisible but which can become visible as warm, moist breath turns to ice crystals on a frosty morning. John's gospel says that the wind 'blows where it wills and you hear the sound of it but you do not know where it comes from or where it is going. So it is with anyone who is born of the Spirit' (Jn 3:8). We cannot see or touch the Spirit but the Spirit, too, is a powerful force in our lives. Unlike electricity and unlike the wind, however, Christ has revealed to us that the Holy Spirit is a person who 'dwells with you and will be in you' (Jn 14:17).

One of the best ways to explore what it means to live in a close relationship with the Holy Spirit is to examine the way in which the Gospels present the role of the Spirit in the conception and birth of Jesus, the outpouring of the Spirit on Jesus at his baptism in the Jordan, the ongoing relationship between Jesus and the Spirit and his outpouring of the Spirit on his disciples at Pentecost following his death and resurrection.

The Holy Spirit and Jesus

The Gospels of Matthew and Luke attribute the conception of Jesus to the Holy Spirit (see Mt 1:18-20; Lk 1:35) in a way that invites us to recognise the role of the Spirit in our own spiritual rebirth thanks to baptism and confirmation. In Luke, the public ministry of Jesus begins with his baptism, after which, while he was praying, 'the heaven was opened and the Holy Spirit descended upon him in bodily form, as a dove, and a voice came from heaven, "You are my beloved Son; with you I am well pleased"' (Lk 3:21-22). It is the Holy Spirit who led Jesus into the wilderness so that he could overcome the temptations of the devil (see Lk 4:1-2), after which Jesus returned to Galilee 'in the power of the Spirit' (Lk 4:14). Quoting the prophet Isaiah, Matthew says that Jesus was anointed with the Holy Spirit so that he would 'proclaim justice to the Gentiles' (Mt 12:18-21). Matthew closely associates the sanctifying power of the Spirit with the coming of the Kingdom of God (Mt 12:22-27): 'But if it is by the Spirit of God that I cast out demons, then the kingdom of God has come upon you.' Mark distinguishes John the Baptist, who 'baptised with,' or immersed people in, water, from Jesus, who baptises with the Holy Spirit (Mk 1:8).

John's gospel puts particular emphasis on the fact that the Spirit not only descended on Jesus at his baptism but also remained on him throughout his public life (see Jn 1:32-34). It was because the Spirit 'remained on' or 'dwelt in' Jesus that he could 'give the Spirit without measure' (Jn 3:34). The evangelist probably intended his readers to recognise their own initiation as Christians in terms of the Spirit descending and remaining on them in a way that also gave them the power to overcome all that threatened their lives and relationships.

John's gospel also highlighted the personal nature of the pneuma-Spirit, a neuter noun in Greek. Jesus promises that, when he returned to the Father, he would ask the Father to give us 'another Paraclete/Advocate, to be with you for ever' (Jn 14:16). So important for us was the gift of the Spirit that Jesus insisted that it was ultimately to our advantage that he left us to return to the Father: 'For if I do not go away, the Paraclete will not come to you; but if I do go, I will send him to you' (Jn 16:7).

In his conversation with Nicodemus, Jesus teaches us that the process of coming to share in God's own life demands a spiritual rebirth, a radical break with the past to embrace a new way of life. So important is this rebirth that it is only those who have been born anew (i.e. born 'from above' of water and the Spirit) that can enter the Kingdom of God (see Jn 3:1-15). The necessity of the gift of the Spirit and the fact that humanity devoid of God's help ('flesh') cannot achieve eternal life is emphasised in Jn 6:63: 'It is the Spirit that gives life, the flesh is of no avail; the words that I have spoken to you are Spirit and life' (i.e. Spirit- and life-bearing).

The Holy Spirit: Christ's Gift to the Church

In describing the death of Jesus, John's gospel does not use Mark's expression 'to expire' (Mk 15:37), or Matthew's 'to give up the Spirit' (the origin of the expression 'to give up the ghost', Mt 27:50). Instead, he coins a new phrase, 'to hand over the Spirit' (Jn 19:30), implying that Jesus did not merely 'breathe his last breath' but that he also handed over the Holy Spirit /Breath to the Father.

John notes that blood and water came out of Jesus' side when it was pierced with a spear (see Jn 19:34). This probably refers back to the 'rivers of living water' flowing out of the heart of Jesus (see Jn 7:37-39), which the evangelist specifically identifies with the Spirit. John seems to be suggesting that we are renewed and invigorated by the experience of being immersed/baptised in the Spirit in the same way that we would be by bathing in a river of living/flowing water. The reference to both 'blood and water' flowing out of the side of Jesus on the cross suggests that the life-giving gift of the Spirit (water) is necessarily linked to the life-giving death of Jesus (blood).

On the evening of the day of the Resurrection, Jesus appeared to the disciples saying, 'Peace be with you. As the Father has sent me, even so I sent you'. He 'breathed on' them and said to them: 'Receive the Holy Spirit. If you forgive the sins of any, they are forgiven; if you retain the sins of any they are retained' (see Jn 20:19-23). Just as the gift of forgiveness by someone we have wronged can provide a radical 'new beginning' for the relationship, the reference to Jesus 'breathing onto' his disciples (see the gift of the breath/Spirit as the source of life at creation in Gen 2:7 and Ezek 37:9; Wis 15:11) suggests that the Evangelist regarded this experience as a Pentecostal 'new creation' for humanity. Jesus breathes his Holy Spirit onto the disciples so that they would be able to fulfil their mission of forgiving sins through the power of the Holy Spirit.

If we compare the two books attributed to 'Luke', the Gospel of Luke and the Acts of the Apostles, we see that the account of the coming of the Holy Spirit at Pentecost (Acts 2:1-4) occupies the same key place in Acts which Jesus' baptism has in Luke (Lk 3:21-22). Just as the descent of the Spirit on Jesus marked the whole of his subsequent mission and ministry, so too the descent of the Spirit on the disciples marks the whole subsequent mission and ministry of the Church. Luke's account of Pentecost emphasises four distinct but related aspects. He highlights the fact that the Holy Spirit who came at Pentecost was poured out by the risen Christ (see Acts 2:33). He presents the Pentecost gift of the Spirit as fulfilling the promise of the Father (see Lk 24:29; Acts 1:4). The outpouring of the Spirit was received communally (see Acts 1:14; 2:1). It was also received by people of different races and languages (see Acts 2:6, 11). Luke probably intended that these four elements should also characterise any genuinely Spirit-filled person or group.

The Spirit is closely associated with the work of the ministers of the Church. It is the Spirit who tells Philip to approach the Ethiopian eunuch and who leads him to other work once the eunuch had been baptised (see Acts 8:29, 39). The Spirit alerts Peter about the three pagan men sent by the centurion Cornelius, thus opening up the Church to pagans (see Acts 10:19). The Spirit sets aside Saul (Paul) and Barnabas for their missionary work (Acts 13:2, 4) and appoints the guardians of the flock (Acts 13:28). The decisions of the meeting of the apostles and elders at Jerusalem are described as being made jointly by the Holy Spirit and the Apostles: 'It has seemed good to the Holy Spirit and to us' (Acts 15:28).

The Spirit does not work only in and through the formal office holders; ministers of the Church and the communities founded by Paul were notable for their 'charismatic' richness (see Gal 3:2-5; Rom 15:18-19; 1 Cor 1:5). Paul recognised, however, that the various charismatic gifts enjoyed by the members of the Christian communities were the work of one and the same Spirit (1 Cor 12:11) and that they were given for the common good (literally, 'to the profiting', see 1 Cor 12:7) and to provide the various services necessary in the one body of Christ (see 1 Cor 12:12-27).

For Paul, the three principal operations of the Spirit in the Church are to give life, to build up the Church and to unify the Church. The Holy Spirit is 'the Spirit of him who raised Jesus from the dead' and if this Spirit dwells in us we can hope that the Father will give life to our mortal bodies also 'through his Spirit which dwells' in us (Rom 8:10-12). The Spirit builds up the Church in Christ so that it becomes a dwelling place of God in the Spirit (Eph 2:22) and so that it can be called the 'temple of the Holy Spirit' (1 Cor 3:16). The Spirit also unifies the Church in such a way that all believers are one in Christ Jesus (Gal 3:18) and that the one Spirit makes the whole Body one (Eph 4:4; 1 Cor 12:8-9; Rom 12:6-7).

In Romans 5:3-5 Paul attributes the outpouring of love in our hearts to the Spirit 'who has been given to us'. Together with faith and hope, this gift of divinely enabled loving constitutes the basis of the Christian life. Paul is nevertheless aware that, in this present life, we have only the 'first fruits of the Spirit' (Rom 8:23).

Believing in God the Holy Spirit

The Creed that is usually said at Mass has three parts, one for each person of the Blessed Trinity. The third section is centred on the Holy Spirit who, like the Father and the Son, is 'Lord' and is 'worshipped and glorified'.

It begins with the words: 'We believe in the Holy Spirit, the Lord, the giver of life, who proceeds from the Father and the Son.' We believe in the Holy Spirit as the one who gives us access to eternal life in Christ and who is therefore Lord of life. Sent from the Father and breathed out onto his disciples by Christ, the Spirit comes both from the Father and from the Son.

'With the Father and the Son he is worshipped and glorified. He has spoken through the Prophets.' Together with the Father and the Son, we worship and glorify the Spirit as equally divine with them. It was the Holy Spirit who spoke through the Old Testament prophets, foretelling the coming of Jesus as the Messiah. It was the Spirit who enabled the New Testament writers to give a continuing powerful testimony to the life, death and resurrection of Christ.

'We believe in one holy catholic and apostolic Church.' We believe that the community who live in communion with Christ's Sanctifying Spirit were intended to form the one People of God. We are the fruit of the common work of the three divine persons and we are called to unity despite our diversity. Vatican II's *Gaudium et spes* 22 recognises that the Holy and Sanctifying Spirit offers to all people the possibility of being made partners, in a way known to God, in the paschal mystery. In other words, all people are called, through his sanctifying Spirit, to unite their lives with the life of the resurrected Christ. It is because the Spirit is poured out on the People of God that the Church is 'catholic', sharing fully in the means through which Christ is made present among us and capable of integrating into itself the diverse gifts and talents of the whole human race. The Spirit also ensures the apostolicity of God's People, giving us all a share in the mission that Christ gave to the apostles and enabling us to remain faithful to the Good News that Christ entrusted to the apostles.

'We acknowledge one baptism for the forgiveness of sins. We look for the resurrection of the dead, and the life of the world to come. Amen.' The sacrament of baptism is the principal means through which the Spirit brings about forgiveness and reconciliation and it is thanks to the life-giving Spirit that we can hope to share Christ's resurrection and eternal communion with him in heaven.

Conclusion

Metropolitan Ignatios of Latakia sums up the difference that the Holy Spirit makes, or should make, in the life of the Church and in the life of each Christian, in the following way:

> Without the Holy Spirit, God is far away, Christ stays in the past, the Gospel is a dead letter, the Church is simply an organisation, authority a matter of domination, mission a matter of propaganda, the liturgy is no more than an invocation, Christian living a slave morality, but in the Holy Spirit, the cosmos is resurrected and groans with the birth-pangs of the Kingdom, the risen Christ is present, the Gospel is the power of life, the Church shows forth the communion of the Trinity, authority is a liberating service, mission is a Pentecost, the liturgy is both memorial and anticipation, human activity is deified.

Further Reading

Congar, Yves, *I Believe in the Holy Spirit* (3 Vols), New York: The Seabury Press; London: Geoffrey Chapman, 1983.

Gaybba, Brian, *The Spirit of Love: Theology of the Holy Spirit*, London: Geoffrey Chapman, 1987.

Groppe, Elizabeth Teresa, *Yves Congar's Theology of the Holy Spirit*, American Academy of Religion Academy Series, Oxford: Oxford University Press, 2003.

Harrington, Wilfrid, *Spirit of the Living God*, Wilmington, Delaware: Michael Glazier Inc., 1977.

O'Carroll, Michael, *Veni Creator Spiritus: A Theological Encyclopedia of the Holy Spirit*, Collegeville, Minn.: The Liturgical Press, 1990.

CHAPTER 10

THE CHURCH,
A COMMUNITY OF DISCIPLES

David McLoughlin

Introduction

The Church exists to point to what happens when God draws near, what Jesus calls the Kingdom. As such, the Church exists to continue the reconciling work of Christ by reconciling humanity to God, and men and women to each other. Jesus leaves his disciples with enormous freedom to realise this work. This inevitably leads to choices, decisions and so at times disagreements and tensions. This essay will look at some of the key responses of Jesus' disciples to the challenge of being Church in our time.

Jesus goes into the villages and towns and eventually to Jerusalem itself to meet people in their everyday world. He speaks of God in everyday terms, addressing the transcendent Lord of History with a child's name for a loving parent – *Abba*. He chooses the twelve, an unlikely bunch of religious reformers. They included Matthew, a traitorous tax collector, Simon, a nationalist Zealot, a group of fishermen, and so on (Lk 6:12-16; Mt 10:1-4; Mk 3:13-19). Apart from the brothers Peter and Andrew and James and John, they had little in common, but as a group of twelve they had symbolic significance echoing the twelve original tribes of Israel. He called them 'apostles', literally people sent to speak on behalf of another. Very early on he sent them out to speak in his name of the coming of God's kingdom and to call men and women to prepare for that coming.

In this simple beginning we have the origin of the Church. The twelve are a sign of what can happen when God comes close. They and those who support them and gather round them are an alternative community in embryo, a symbolic new Israel. They are counter-cultural, bearing witness to values different to those of the Roman Empire or the religious power elite in Jerusalem. At the heart of these values are forgiveness and reconciliation, and the essential worth of every woman, child and powerless person. Around Jesus a different style of community emerges where the weak and the frail and the marginal are at the centre. In Jesus' teaching human need takes precedence over religious precept. In the face of those who criticise his approach to religion he says: 'The Sabbath was made for humans, not humans for the Sabbath' (Mk 2:27).

One, Holy, Catholic and Apostolic

In this simple outline is found the essentials that make up what it is to be Church, the community of those who gather together to follow Jesus. The twelve are called apostles, the sent ones, and forever after the community will remember them and remodel their witness and so will call itself *apostolic*. It is sent out into the world to bear witness to the same message that the apostles lived and died for. This message was first taught and lived by the original sent one, the Word of God, the Son of the Father, Jesus.

The experience of God as Abba is the basis of the community's claim to a *catholic* or whole vision. Abba is the creator and the Father of all. In Jesus' vision all men, women and children are called to be children of God. Jesus will underline this with his teaching on the family of God which stretches far beyond the ties of blood or class or race. In doing this he evokes the freedom of God to be called Yahweh, 'I am who I am', or 'I will be who I will be', or even 'I will be where I will be' (Ex 3:13 ff.). This God of sovereign freedom cannot be limited by religious structures or definitions. The community of Jesus' disciples prays each day that the rule of this free God will become ever more real in our world – 'on earth as it is in heaven'. So this community is catholic and apostolic.

The life it is called to live is based on its own experience of forgiveness and reconciliation. The rock on which Jesus built his community, Peter, was pretty wobbly. He consistently misunderstood Jesus' intentions during the ministry and he abandoned him when it came to the crunch (Lk 22:57-62). Yet the risen Jesus again meets him in that wonderful encounter on the side of the Sea of Galilee (Jn 21) and reminds Peter of the good times they shared, the meals they ate in common and the miracles. Then beyond failure and weakness he commissions Peter to feed his sheep and lambs – to care for the young community. The rock on which the Church is to be built is a forgiven sinner.

This becomes a pattern. The greatest preacher of the good news is its forgiven former enemy, Paul of Tarsus. The community of Jesus is primarily holy not because of the holiness of its members but because the Holy Spirit of God comes close to confront, convict in faith, reconcile and empower. So the community is *universal* or *catholic*, *apostolic* and *holy*. And across time and history it is *one*. A strange thing to say to anyone who knows anything about church history with its internecine early struggles to define a shared faith, its split east and west, and its tragic Reformation fragmentation. Yet the centre of Christian life and faith is singular. Paul refers to this essential unity in three ways: 'The grace of our Lord Jesus Christ, and the Love of God and the Fellowship of the Holy Spirit' (1 Cor 13:13).

The unity of the disciples of Jesus is not to be found perfected in any human community but in the very life of the one God. Those baptised in the name of the Father, the Son and the Holy Spirit always have more in common than any differences of denomination or theology might imply.

Church as the Community for the Kingdom

Jesus proclaimed the Kingdom of God and the apostles experienced that kingdom happening around Jesus. They saw it renewed again beyond the despair of the cross when Abba raised Jesus to new risen life. They felt the continuity of that reign in the outpouring of the Spirit of Jesus at Pentecost. Jesus promised this community would happen – 'When two or three are gathered in my name' (Mt 18:20). When Jesus faced his inevitable death in Jerusalem he entrusted his mission to his apostles. He gave them no structural blueprint but did provide a model for the leadership they would need to face the future. He washed their feet, normally the role of a wife for a husband or a slave for a master or mistress. 'No servant is greater than his master ...', Jesus says, 'Now that you know all this, happiness will be yours, if you behave accordingly' (Jn 13:16-17). Whatever the community would become over the centuries it had a clear picture of what to expect of its leaders – a servant leadership. This model remains a critique of all deviant alternatives.

A Community of Active Remembering

Jesus gave a model of leadership and a meal to remember him by. He had used meals to open up a shared space for those who were normally excluded. However, this final meal was also a Passover meal, Israel's great annual remembrance of the liberating God of Exodus. Jesus takes this memory of God's sovereign free choice of nobodies, twelve gangs of migrant workers, and links it with the future of this bereft group of twelve individuals. Then he takes the symbols of the Exodus – the blood of the lamb that signed and protected the Hebrews, the unleavened bread of the pilgrim people and the wine of delight and ultimate celebration, and he reinterprets his own life with these symbols. Whenever they remember this meal together in the same spirit of faith he shared with them, then the reconciled and liberating life of God would flow through their community to the world. 'This is my body … this is my blood', he says as he takes and blesses the bread and wine. In other words, this is his life. To this day the meal of thanksgiving is the heart of the community of Jesus' disciples and is the means of that community's growth and flourishing. The Eucharist (from the Greek meaning 'thanksgiving') makes the Church and the Church enables Eucharist to happen.

Without a shared memory we lose any sense of solidarity and of the possibilities of collective social transformation for ourselves, for those who come after us, but also for those victims of what went before. In the Church's Eucharist we bring our remembrance of our time and the remembrance of the story of God in Christ together. In this dual remembering, his story and ours merge and mutually interpenetrate one another, provoking us to find renewed shared meaning now. In this shared vision, constantly struggled for and always in need of renewal, men and women freely cooperate with God's Spirit in the incarnating of Christ's freedom in every era.

As we look back at Jesus' life and ministry it can seem amazing that he would entrust his life and message to these twelve with so little emphasis on structure or institution. He entrusts the project to those who have followed him and have shared his lifestyle. They remembered his clear challenging stories, the wonderful encounters with unlikely and unloved people, significant events and a few key teachings but the structure of what we call Church was left to them. It is an amazing freedom allowing great creativity and inevitable struggles.

A Time of Struggle: Vatican II and its Aftermath

We live in an age of Church renewal. This renewal is the fruit of a great struggle to remember and re-imagine the community of disciples in faithfulness to Jesus' life and teaching. In 1963 Pope John XXIII called the world's bishops to the Second Vatican Council (1962–1965) to discuss the Church in the modern world. They self-consciously returned to the scriptures and the pattern of the early Church. The result of this creative remembering was to imagine the Church as the *People of God*, on a journey in history, pointing to the Kingdom of God and its signs wherever they might be found, whether in other churches, other faiths, or even in the journey of integrity of the convinced atheist. The Church began to see itself less as an embattled institution and more as a multifaceted mystery to be explored. Yet underneath this new openness there was and is a battle for hearts and minds, a struggle to find an identity that can be owned and shared in the modern world.

Images of Church

In Vatican II the three images that the bishops focused on out of the ninety-five available in the New Testament were 'People of God', 'Body of Christ' and 'Temple of the Holy Spirit'. The first reminds us that our identity is tied up with the original people of God – Israel. It builds on Paul's refusal to develop a unique Christian identity without Israel. It reaffirms the Jewish scriptures and Israel's history as uniquely revelatory and necessary for our understanding of Jesus and his Gospel. This is a return to a more inclusive model of religious history capable of dealing with the freedom of God's involvement with creation. The use of a collective term 'People of God' had the further effect of countering any sense of the Church as a primarily hierarchical reality. An egalitarian note is sounded; we are all sons and daughters of God in baptism, all brothers and sisters in Christ.

The second chosen image of the Council was 'the Body of Christ'. This image had received a powerful push in Pius XII's 1943 encyclical, *Mystici Corporis*. Pius tried to balance the emphasis on the institutional hierarchical Church with a reflection on the inner divine aspect of the Church. However, the benefits of this were reduced by the exclusive identification of the body of Christ with the Roman Catholic Church. Vatican II used the same image with a different spin. The risen Christ is now present to the world in his body, the Church, which participates in his Spirit poured out on the original community of disciples at Pentecost. This post-resurrection presence is now potentially global. Jesus is no longer bound by time and space but moves within the limitless reality of the divine life and so offers a global, indeed cosmic, relationship. This echoes the Christ of Ephesians and

Colossians, the Word in the prologue of the fourth gospel and Christ the High Priest in Hebrews.

However, the image when applied to Church has a tension in it. If the reality of Church is primarily to incarnate the Spirit of Christ and bear witness to it, then it is clear that not all that has been and is Church always serves this end. The contemporary Church is a fractured mirror reflecting the Christ she bears witness to in fragments. No one model of Church or even collection of models is adequate. The New Testament itself is like a series of mirrors whose images complement one another but never to the point of one dominating the others. We are the body of Christ, not the head. The pentecostal Spirit of the risen Christ, like the kingdom which Jesus lived to bring into being, is a bigger concept capable of being partially realised and mirrored but never encapsulated in some definable religious or social structure.

The Church in its various forms comprises the variety of communities that have responded to God's call in Christ and the Spirit. And for all the abiding fragility and at times bloody-minded stubbornness of its leaders and members, like the Israel of old, it remains still the Spirit-endowed body that actively remembers the living God in history and time. It enacts this memory in the murkiness and mixed motives of contemporary politics and economics within which it is variously entangled, like the wheat and the weeds, till the Lord comes.

The Council's third image of 'Temple of the Holy Spirit' sought again to balance the western Church's traditional and perhaps too exclusively Christ-centred view of Church. The recent opening to the Spirit in the Charismatic Renewal movement and the phenomenon of worldwide Christian Pentecostalism made it possible to speak of a new age of the Spirit in the Church. However, it is to the eastern Church's faithful remembering of the Spirit that Catholicism has turned in recent years to refresh its own remembering. Pope John Paul II called this 'breathing with both lungs'. If Christ institutes the Church, it is the Spirit who constitutes it.

The Spirit indwells the living community of disciples as a life-giving presence, enabling the life of the risen Christ to be effective through this community, at this time, in this world. The gift of the Spirit is for the world, in the service of God's reign. The impulse of Pentecost is outward, not inward. The first Spirit-inspired mission was into a real world of violence and corruption, of fear and hate. A world of brutal Empire, the logic of whose rule and very particular mechanisms (the manipulation of need and greed, of fear and insecurity) Jesus had challenged with his practice of the kingdom. The disciples are still led by the Spirit into the world's suffering in solidarity with their crucified and now risen Lord, alongside the 'little ones' whose cause he had made his own.

Office and Charism and Inevitable Tension

As in any institution there is always a tension between individual liberty and corporate solidarity. The tradition we have inherited has an exaggerated dependence on office, on hierarchy, on defined doctrine, on clerical authority and power at the expense of the universal expectation of the Spirit's presence. Yet, office in the Church is the charismatic first gift of the Spirit on Easter Sunday when the not-yet ascended Lord breathes on the disciples and says, 'Receive the Holy Spirit. If you forgive the sins of any they are forgiven: if you retain the sins of any they are retained' (Jn 20:22-23).

The apostles are called to the particular ministry of reconciliation, which will eventually become the role above all of the ordained. However, there is a further second gift of the Spirit which is given to all the redeemed (Acts 2ff.). From then on, all disciples of Christ are seen as 'Spirit-bearers'. In the words of John's first letter, 'you have been anointed by the holy one, and you all know' (1 Jn 2:20).

This model of Church as Temple of the Spirit points to the presence of the unimagined and unexpected God of Exodus – 'Yahweh'. In this model God is not precisely located in a place where it is convenient for us to situate God. A renewed sense of a Spirit-led community does not allow a withdrawal into beautiful liturgy away from the harshness of the world. Jesus' revealing of the kingdom brought healing and reconciliation but also opposition, hate, fear and death. The solidarity that we have in the Spirit as Church draws us into just such complexity.

Church serving Kingdom

Vatican II (GS, 3, 92) speaks of the Church's role in the world as one of service, in particular the service of unity among humanity. The perspective is outward looking and the Church is seen as working alongside others to build a better world. As it proclaims the Gospel and celebrates the sacraments, the Church is called to a service that includes the struggle for a new social order. The kingdom is transformative of all reality and the Church is to serve this transformation. However, at present there is considerable debate between groups in the Church about the relationship between Church and Kingdom of God.

Vatican II places the Church in a clear relation of subordination to the kingdom (LG, 5; GS, 45). Whether it aids the world or whether it benefits from it, the Church has but one sole purpose – that the Kingdom of God may come and the salvation of the human race be accomplished (GS, 45).

Any simple identification of Church and kingdom leads to a triumphalistic model of the Church, which Vatican II rejected. Salvation in the scriptures comes from the little ones: a sterile old woman, the liberated Hebrew slaves, a marginal Jewish craft worker from a village that never appeared on a map. The Church as sign and pointer of the kingdom is called to be a space where the stories of the word's victims are remembered above all in the great act of remembering that makes the Church – the Eucharist.

Central or Local?

For most of the first millennium the Church was primarily the people gathered around their local bishop. The universal Church was the total community of local churches. However, the second millennium has seen the growth of two differing tendencies. The first leans towards a federalist model with the local church as the real Church of Christ in a particular place. The second offers a more centralist view where the local is a manifestation of the universal.

Taking the local church seriously has been one of the most difficult tasks since Vatican II. If the participatory nature of the local church is to be truly respected then the appointment of bishops needs to be more clearly a joint act of the local church, the local bishops' conference, in discussion with the Pope and his advisors as head of the universal college. Bishops are called to the God-given ministry of drawing the disciples into a unity of faith and service. This is a ministry of unity but not of uniformity. They are called to enable communities in which fresh models of ministries and service can be discerned and affirmed and nourished. Something of this can be seen in some of the new movements and models from South America, Africa and Asia. The Church is being challenged to develop new ways of working and speaking together which serve the Spirit's capacity, as at Pentecost, to communicate without demanding we all speak the same language or share the same customs or even gender.

Conclusion: Post-Vatican II *Communio* Models of Church

The three models of 'People of God', 'Body of Christ' and 'Temple of the Spirit' form a reference grid for a Trinitarian and Spirit-based vision of the mystery of the Church. This is picked up in contemporary *Communio* or Fellowship models of Church, which recognise that the differences of function, ministry and service are secondary to the common gifting with the Spirit.

The unity of the Church is ultimately rooted in the life of God, revealed as Abba, through the work of the Son and Spirit. The mystery of communion, which the Church is sent out into the world to reveal, is the unity of the mysterious Tri-une God revealed in the scandalous particularity of the life of a craftsman, Jesus of Nazareth, and in the work of the all-permeating Spirit who networks and draws into relation seeming dispirited voices, as in the first Pentecost. Real unity (*communio* or fellowship) comes through reconciled diversity, not institutional mergers.

The community of disciples finds its deepest reality united in the Spirit with the Son, responding to the depth of God, revealed as compassionate Abba. This Trinitarian communion is opened up in the world through the Eucharist, seen as one body of Christ in many members (1 Cor 10:15-17). This is the Church as a living symbol of a reconciled world. In the Eucharist and in what flows into and from it, the real God is revealed anew, and our own mystery is renewed. The challenge in every age is to develop structures, institutions and rites to ever more clearly manifest this.

Further Reading

Comblin, Jose, *People of God*, New York: Orbis Books, 2004.

Doyle, Dennis M., *Communion Ecclesiology*, New York: Orbis Books, 2000.

Dulles, Avery, *Models of the Church* (2nd edn) London: Gill and Macmillan, 1987.

Fuellenbach, John, *Church Community of the Kingdom*, New York: Orbis Books, 2002.

Phan, Peter C. (ed.) *The Gift of the Church: A Textbook on Ecclesiology*, Collegeville, Minn.: The Liturgical Press, 2000.

Sullivan, Francis A., *The Church We Believe In*, New York: Paulist Press, 1988.

CHAPTER 11

MARY OF NAZARETH

Caroline Renehan

Introduction: Mary of Nazareth: Lost in Images

Throughout the past two thousand years Christians have found ways to discover, re-discover and understand Mary of Nazareth. For this reason, images and icons of Mary have abounded. Some of these images eventually contributed to doctrines about her, ranging from the most complex to the most simple in form. Among the most complex are Theotokos (the God-bearer), Virgin and Mother, Mediatrix, the Immaculate Conception and the Assumption. Among the simpler are Mother of Jesus, Handmaid of the Lord and the Perfect Disciple. The list is endless. From around the 1950s to the early 1980s, if most Catholic Christians were asked to whom the following images referred, 'Mirror of Justice', 'Seat of Wisdom', 'Mystical Rose', 'Tower of Ivory', 'Vessel of Honour', 'Queen of Patriarchs', 'Virgin Most Powerful', 'Morning Star', they would have been likely to reply that it was 'Our Lady', 'Mary, the Mother of God' or 'The Madonna'. Ten years ago, if the question were asked, 'who is The Madonna?' the answer might have been, 'she's the material girl living in a material world'. The response, of course, would have been a reference to the singer Madonna, who has an album interestingly entitled, 'The Immaculate Collection'.

The myriad images of Mary that stood fast for so long now sometimes appear archaic and are also often misunderstood. For example, they have contributed, albeit unwittingly, to difficult relations between the Catholic and the Protestant traditions. On the one hand, Catholic (and Orthodox) teaching exaggerated and multiplied Mary's images, bestowing on her personage a legacy of superhuman proportions. On the other hand, Protestant teaching in the post-reformation era went in the opposite direction.[1] From the end of the sixteenth century, particularly in the

Lutheran and Reformed churches, teachings on Mary had either shrunk or become non-existent. It is a shame that these two extremes in both traditions have been a source of division. Mary belongs to all believers of Christianity, not excluding Judaism and Islam. Shades of her female characteristics can also be found in Hinduism and Buddhism, but because of the complexity of her images and our general inability to assimilate them, we are in danger of losing her. Of this woman who has stood the test of time, Warner has claimed, '… the Virgin's legend will endure in its splendour and lyricism, but it will be emptied of moral significance, and thus lose its present real powers to heal and to harm'.[2]

The Elevation of Mary: Have we made Mistakes?

Today Mary appears to be in a vacuum. Despite the annual increase in attendance at major Marian shrines, younger generations of Christians no longer know who she is. Her help is not asked for, her companionship not sought. Perhaps we have made some mistakes in our treatment of Mary over the centuries with the result that she is currently not taken seriously by many modern Christians. For too long, we have jealously guarded images of Mary that have ceased to be credible in our contemporary world. We have been afraid to let go of the woman with the veil and we have cast a slight on her character by claiming that stone statues have moved, have shed salty tears and even drops of blood. In the history of humankind, few women have been bestowed with so many faces.

Her icons and images increased and multiplied, reaching their zenith in the Middle Ages. During this long period, Mary was elevated at times to Christ-like status and even at times to God-like status. For example, Archbishop John the Geometer (c. 990) sees the part played by Mary in salvation history to be of equal value to that of Christ on the cross. He claims that she suffered even more for our sins than he did. The Benedictine abbot, Arnold of Bonneval (c. 1156), also recognises Mary as being equal to Christ since Christ bled through his flesh where Mary bled through her heart. He goes on to say that as ordinary creatures bend their knee to Jesus so he, in turn, bends his knee to Jesus' mother. Richard of St Laurent (c. 1245) prefers to sidestep God altogether when reciting the 'Lord's Prayer' and prays instead, 'Our Mother, who art in heaven …'. One final example of this arguably shocking elevation of Mary can be seen in the Franciscan preacher Bernardine of Siena (d. 1444) whose pious exaggerations led to absurdities. According to Bernardine, even when Mary was still in the womb, she had the use of her own free will. Not only this, but she also completely understood everything about Christ. That included an understanding of how he took human form at the time of his incarnation. Bernardine claims, therefore, in order to understand this great mystery, Mary had to go so far as to ensnare the Wisdom of God. Taking account of these few brief examples from former times, we can see that Christians courted a tradition where the image of Mary truly reached divine status. Christ was relegated to second place while Mary took her place beside God the Father.

Confusion between Mary and Christ

From medieval ages onwards devotion to Mary continued to grow in many diverse ways. In the minds of the devotees the contrast between Christ and his mother grew ever more confused. She came to be seen as the kind Mother who could be approached whenever a devotee was in trouble or badly needed something. Christ the Judge was far less likely to grant the request. Mary was warm and feminine whereas Christ was cold and masculine. Mary could be touched by tears and heartbreak whereas these human emotions were not as likely to evoke a positive response from Christ. It can hardly be doubted that while many millions of Christians throughout the centuries would tell of Mary's subordination to Christ, their devotion to her was far from subordinate. Many of the faithful have spent as much time and more in prayer at the altar of Our Lady than they have spent in prayer to Jesus at the Sacred Heart altar. As Christians, we know that we cannot worship Mary as worship is given only to God.

Throughout the centuries, while the Catholic Church never officially accepted such elevation of Mary, it nonetheless may have indirectly supported it through the proclamations of the 'Immaculate Conception' (1854) and the bodily Assumption into Heaven (1950). However, all that changed with the coming of the Second Vatican Council (1962–1965) and Chapter 8 of *Lumen gentium*. Debates ensued as to whether or not the Council Fathers denigrated Mary by playing down her role when they allocated her only one chapter in the Council documents rather than giving her an entire document of her own. Spretnak, for example, maintains that the Catholic Church made their mistake when the Council Fathers played down her importance, with the result that she has faded to insignificance in the minds of the faithful.[3]

Yet, if the Church did play down the role of Mary, it was not without good reason, for given her history, it may be asked where devotion to Mary ends and worship of her begins? Not surprisingly, Mackey asks, 'What, then, is the status of Mary in the public theology and doctrine of the Roman Catholic Church? Always flirting with the divinity of Mary, I should be inclined to answer, but always finally, officially and loudly denying it'.[4] This is a bold statement indeed but, on reflection, we have seen that Mackey is not far from the truth.

Perhaps Mackey's answer to his own question shocks us. A response such as this asks us to look again at Mary's extraordinarily complex history. Johnson gets it right when she says: 'While an historical woman obviously dwells at the root of this whole phenomenon, there has been a plasticity to her image that has allowed the Christian imagination to create widely different marian symbols ... '[5] If we are to value the heritage of one of the most celebrated religious figures of the Christian tradition, we must return again to the stories from where she came. If we want to understand Mary, we find her at the heart of the scriptures. This does not imply that we necessarily strip her of all the images and symbols that have accrued to her person over the centuries. However, in order to gain insights into this remarkable woman of Nazareth, in order to re-build a relationship with her, we do not begin with her elevated or fantastic titles. Rather, we ground our understanding of her in the history of her own simple life. No matter how far we go with our images and symbols of Mary, we always keep our focus on her roots and the reason for her existence. She is the mother of Jesus, not the Christ; she is Mother of God, not God.

What our troubled Church of the early twenty-first century requires is a credible understanding of Mary. We need to reclaim her but not in the form of a divinity or a semi-divinity. If we look at the scriptures, we will see that above all else Mary is a human being. She walked with us as a human being long ago in Nazareth and she continues to do so today. Mary is not standing beside Christ facing us, an image often seen in paintings in the middle of the last century. Instead, she is standing beside us facing Christ. From the scriptures, she reaches across a two-thousand-year span to be with us in our 'dark night of faith', just like the one she herself experienced long ago. As we go back in time, we keep in mind that the Second Vatican Council itself diligently returned to the scriptures for evidence of Mary's role in the history of salvation[6] and also that the scriptural accounts of Mary are, in fact, sparse. This ordinary woman struggled throughout her life to understand a wilful son from the time he was born, through his getting lost in the Temple (Lk 2:41-49) to his death on the cross (Lk 23:1-47). We stand in Mary's shoes as she takes that curious journey from the moment of her son's conception to his rising from the dead.

Mary Nestles in the Scriptures

It all began with the Annunciation. Luke's gospel portrays a frightened but strong woman. According to Luke, an angel came to Mary, wished her peace and informed her that God had greatly blessed her. She would become pregnant and give birth to a son, the son of the God most high. This girl of about fifteen years was 'deeply troubled' by the message. Added to her anxiety was her fear. In her humanity and lack of comprehension, she questioned how this could not happen to her because she was a virgin. Luke the Evangelist writes an entire section showing how difficult it was for Mary to grasp the situation in all its mystery (Lk 1:26-38). Nonetheless, such was her courage that she gave her consent, a consent that was not passive. Instead it required her free cooperation although she could not have possibly foreseen the future or the pain it would bring. Here we have our first glimpse of the human Mary.

So her story commences. In the Gospel of Matthew (Mt 1:18-21), Joseph receives the angel's message informing him of the miracle conception. When Joseph discovers that Mary is pregnant he is about to break the relationship privately and only changes his mind when he is told that the child is of the Holy Spirit. This must have been a troubling time for Mary. As the scripture scholar Meier claims:

> Joseph was already betrothed to Mary; consequently, even before he took her into his home for regular sexual relations, he counted himself as her 'husband' and had legal rights over her. If found pregnant by another man, Mary could, according to the strict letter of the Law, be put to death. Joseph is in a dilemma. He is 'just' in a double sense: he wishes to show loyalty and

kindness to Mary, yet he must satisfy the requirement of the Law not to countenance adultery. He seeks to satisfy both desires by giving Mary the prescribed document of divorce privately ... he apparently does not ask himself how this act would protect Mary from public shame when she must soon bear a son without benefit of husband. Actually the only way Joseph could save Mary from disgrace would be to marry her.[7]

Furthermore, imagine Mary's heavy heart and her weariness in the following scriptural excerpts. Soon after the announcement of her own pregnancy, Mary goes to visit her cousin Elizabeth. She does so out of concern for this elderly woman who is also pregnant. Scripture accounts tell us that Mary travels alone to a town through the hill country (Lk 1:39-45). Consider also Mary's fear at a later time when, according to Matthew, she had to flee from the marauding Herod and his killing of all male children under two years of age (Mt 2:13-15). Her worry would have been compounded by the prophecy of Simeon that a sword would pierce her heart (Lk 2:34). All Mary could do, according to the gospels, was to ponder these things (Lk 2:19). This is Mary's faith. Her pondering highlights a woman who struggles with her faith and suffers for doing so throughout her lifetime. It tells of a mother who does not understand the true nature of her son's mission.

The Test of Mary's Faith

We might even argue, looking back, that Mary did not appear to receive much gratitude from her son for her loyalty. For example, at twelve years of age, Jesus got lost in the Temple. Mary must have been desperate with worry until they found him after three days. When Mary asked why he had done this to them, they were answered, 'Why did you have to look for me? Didn't you know that I had to be in my Father's house?' (Lk 2:48-50). The scripture then tells us that they did not understand. Another moment of misunderstanding came when Jesus was preaching to his followers. Here someone told him that his mother, brothers and sisters were standing outside waiting to see him. It would have been expected that he would have gone out to them but instead he simply replied that those who heard the word of God and kept it were his mother, brothers and sisters (Mt 12:48-50). Jesus, of course, as we now know, is using this as an example to explain to his

EXPLORING THEOLOGY

followers that discipleship is of the utmost importance. His followers must be ready to leave family and friends to join the fellowship of believers, but what was going through Mary's mind at this stage? She knew the danger of the political situation and the power of the mighty Roman rulers. Yet, Jesus did not respond to her or consider her fears by offering her some kind of explanation for his actions.

If we look to the Gospel of John, we also see the same peculiar relationship Jesus appeared to have with his mother – a relationship which tested her faith if not her patience. When Mary asks Jesus to do something about the shortage of wine at the marriage feast of Cana, his reply, at face value, appears somewhat abrupt. 'You must not tell me what to do … My time is not yet come' (Jn 2:4). Mary ignored his response. She told the servants to fill the wine jars with water, knowing in her heart that he had the power to do something. He did. He performed his first miracle and turned water into wine. Yet, at the end of his life on earth, despite her loyalty, her fear, her concern and her worry, there is no record that Jesus rewarded her with anything. Consider, for example, the most important mystery of the Christian faith – Christ died and rose from the dead. He chose a woman, Mary Magdalene, for this remarkable revelation and not his mother (Mk 9:11). After the Resurrection, the Christian scriptures make no mention of Jesus visiting his mother. Again she did not receive a reward or an explanation of the kind we might imagine she ought to have had.

The Enduring Image of Mary's Faith

In this respect, of all the images that have ever been bestowed on Mary, there is one that endures. It is the image that portrays Mary as the great woman of faith. As a woman she lived the life of the poor and the marginalised at that time. She lived among a colonised people who were in subjugation to the great Roman Empire where women were of little account. Within the context of that structural oppression, Mary was not a totally independent woman who could plan her life freely. Like many Jewish women, she had to follow the directives of her parents, her husband and her religious and political leaders. She was a woman deprived of fundamental human rights. For these reasons, Mary can be best symbolised as a woman of faith, as a woman for today. She is in solidarity with those who know the meaning of suffering, humiliation, oppression and the loss of loved ones through illness and death. Mary lived through the trauma of having to bury her son. She is the living example for all Christians because, like us, she had to cope with the ordinary, perplexing, frightening and mysterious events of life. In this respect, Mary is much less a symbol of divinised perfection than a woman of faith. Instead, she is a dynamic model of earthly, human struggle, the model of a pilgrim people on a journey towards God.

Conclusion

Mary's is the kind of faith we can understand today. She is a woman who speaks to us down through the centuries, a woman we can identify with. Her story tells of someone who tries hard to come to terms with the fact that her offspring is the Son of God; her story travels the ages. We empathise with the mother often confused and hurt by the apparent aloofness and abrasiveness of her own child. Yet she never abandons him. Nowhere in the gospels does Mary appear out of the presence of her son. From the Annunciation to the cross, she is at his side despite her difficulties and her battles. Mary's faith never gives up. It is a faith close to the struggle that takes place in the human heart of every believer. In her faith, she reaches out to others, confident that her son will be at our side as she intercedes with God to free the rich and the poor, the lowly and the mighty, the male and the female of all creation. In this respect, we visit the great shrines of Lourdes, Guadalupe, Fatima and Medjugorje hoping for a cure, for food for the soul or in desperation for an answer to a prayer. Sometimes we go simply in search of peace. Pilgrims neither care about the scorn of the sceptics nor do they seek authentication of visions or rumours of visions. Long may our visits to the Marian shrines continue, so long as we do not make the mistakes of our foreparents in not recognising the place and role of the mother of Jesus. We have no doubt that Mary, the woman of faith, will hear us.

Notes

1   George Tavard, *The Thousand Faces of the Virgin Mary*, Collegeville, Minn.: The Liturgical Press, 1996.
2   Marina Warner, *Alone of All her Sex*, London: Weidenfeld and Nicholson, 1976, p. 339.
3   Charlene Spretnak, *Missing Mary: The Queen of Heaven and Her Re-Emergence in the Modern Church*, New York: Palgrave Macmillan, 2004.
4   James Mackey, 'The Use and Abuse of Mary in Roman Catholicism', *Who Needs Feminism?* London: SPCK, 1991, p. 101.
5   Elizabeth Johnson, *Truly our Sister*, London: The Continuum International Publishing Group Inc, 2003, p. 5.
6   Second Vatican Council, *Lumen gentium*, Dublin: Dominican Publications, 1975.
7   Joseph Meier, *Matthew*, Dublin: Veritas, 1980, pp. 6–7.

Further Reading

Johnson, Elizabeth, *Truly our Sister*, London: The Continuum International Publishing Group Inc, 2003.

Mackey, James, 'The Use and Abuse of Mary in Roman Catholicism', in R. Holloway (ed.) *Who Needs Feminism?*, London: SPCK, 1991, pp. 99–116.

Meier, Joseph, *Matthew*, Dublin: Veritas, 1980.

Second Vatican Council, *Lumen gentium*, Dublin: Dominican Publications, 1975.

Spretnak, Charlene, *Missing Mary: The Queen of Heaven and Her Re-Emergence in the Modern Church*, New York: Palgrave Macmillan, 2004.

Tavard, George, *The Thousand Faces of the Virgin Mary*, Collegeville, Minn.: The Liturgical Press, 1996.

Warner, Marina, *Alone of All her Sex*, London: Weidenfeld and Nicolson, 1976.

CHAPTER 12

ESCHATOLOGY:
HOPE SEEKING UNDERSTANDING

Dermot A. Lane

Introduction

For a large part of the history of Christianity the focus of eschatology has been on the study of the four last things which are usually understood to be death, judgement, heaven and hell. Eschatology literally means the study (*logos*) of the last things (*eschata*). In the past, eschatology usually came at the end of Christian doctrine and it treated, in a rather individualist manner, the person as they faced the prospect of death, a subsequent final judgement and eternal life in either heaven or hell.

One of the most significant developments in eschatology in the twentieth century has been the rediscovery of the primacy of the advent of the end (the *eschaton*) in Jesus the Christ, crucified and risen. It is only in the light of the end of time revealed 'in Christ' that a truly Christian theology of the last things can be worked out.

In the mid-1960s eschatology was given a new lease of life through the writings of Johann-Baptist Metz and Jürgen Moltmann, who drew attention to the neglect of hope within theology and the need to reintegrate eschatology into the mainstream of Christian theory and praxis. Others, like Karl Rahner and Wolfhart Pannenberg, emphasised the importance of Christology for a balanced understanding of eschatology. In the late-1990s, as a result of a renewal in Pneumatology (the study of the Holy Spirit), there has been a growing awareness of the centrality of the Spirit to eschatology.

In this overview chapter we shall summarise first of all the teaching of the Catholic Church on eschatology since the Second Vatican Council (1962–1965). This Church teaching will be easily misunderstood if it is not accompanied by some principles of interpretation and so it is necessary to outline guidelines for the interpretation of eschatology (hermeneutics or interpretation theory). Mention of interpretation demands that consideration be given to the modern and postmodern contexts in which eschatology exists at present. Since eschatology deals with the destiny of the individual, particular attention must be given to anthropology. The centrepiece of eschatology is Christology, which gives both shape and substance to Christian hope.

The Teaching of the Church on Eschatology from Vatican ll Onwards

It would be misleading to suggest that Vatican II set out to construct a systematic eschatology. In truth, there is very little formal eschatology in the Council documents. Yet, the few eschatological statements that do exist are quite significant and signal a shift in emphasis.

The *Dogmatic Constitution on the Church* (1964) contains a short chapter devoted to 'The Eschatological Nature of the Pilgrim Church and Her Union with the Heavenly Church' (Ch VII). This chapter reminds us that we are living in the end times: 'Already the final age of the world is with us (cf. I Cor 10:11) and the renewal of the world is irrevocably underway' (a. 48).

In the *Pastoral Constitution on the Church and the Modern World* (1965) a number of important developments are discernible in articles 38–43. For example, article 38 talks about those who are called 'to give clear witness to the desire for a heavenly home', whereas others are called 'to dedicate themselves to the earthly service of humanity'. Of the latter group, it points out they can 'make ready the material of the celestial realm', thus highlighting the existence of important links between historical existence and eternity. Those who are dedicated to the service of humanity in this life can 'give some kind of foreshadowing of the new age to come' (a. 39). In the same vein this document points out that 'the expectation of a new earth must not weaken but stimulate our concerns for cultivating this one' (a. 39). Indeed, the Council describes those who 'knowing that we have no abiding city but seek one which is to come' as 'mistaken' (a. 43). The document goes on to state that there must be no false opposition between social activity and religious life.

A further emphasis implicit in the eschatology of Vatican II is the way the Council puts Christ at the centre, claiming that Christ 'is the goal of human history, the focal point of the longing of history and of civilisation, the centre of the human race, the joy of every heart and the answer to all its longings' (a. 43; see also GS a. 10 and 12; AG a. 8).

These scattered eschatological references are notable for the way they talk about the advent of the end (*eschaton*) rather than the last things (*eschata*), for the value they place on the significance of earthly activities for the world to come and for the focus they give to the possibility of a social eschatology.

In 1979 the *Congregation for the Doctrine of the Faith* (CDF) issued an Instruction 'On Certain Questions Concerning Eschatology'. The context of this document was a view being put forward, initially in 1969 and more extensively in 1977, about 'Resurrection in Death' by the German theologian, Gisbert Greshake. Greshake's theology of 'Resurrection in Death' seemed to call into question the need for and the credibility of the classical notion of 'an intermediate state'. By emphasising 'Resurrection in Death' Greshake also seems to eliminate the necessity of a general judgement and resurrection of humanity at the end of time.

In response, the CDF reaffirms classical eschatology: the general resurrection of the dead at the end of time, the immortality of the soul after death and the existence of heaven, hell and purgatory. The immortality of the soul is described in terms of the 'spiritual element [that] survives and subsists after death'. The same congregation also warns against 'arbitrary imaginative representations' of the hereafter, which can be 'a major cause of difficulties that Christian faith often encounters'. Instead, it must be recognised that 'neither scripture nor theology provide sufficient light for a proper picture of life after death'. This Instruction concludes by emphasising on the one hand 'a fundamental continuity between our present life in Christ and the future life' and on the other hand 'a radical difference between the present life and the future'.

In 1994 the universal *Catechism of the Catholic Church* set forth its teaching on eschatology by offering a commentary on the last two articles of the Apostles Creed: 'I believe in the Resurrection of the Body and Life everlasting.' The Catechism outlines what it means by 'Christ's Resurrection and ours' (CCC 992–6). It notes that in death there is a 'separation from the body', with the human body decaying and the soul going to meet God (CCC 997). The Catechism then goes on to say that God will reunite the body with the soul through the power of Jesus' Resurrection at the end. As to 'how' the resurrection takes place, the Catechism says that this 'exceeds our imagination and understanding' and 'is accessible only to faith' (CCC 1000). Next the Catechism deals with death, which it says is 'the end of earthly life' and 'a consequence of sin'. Death, 'shrouded in doubt', has been transformed through the obedience of Christ onto death.

Under the final article of the Apostles' Creed, namely life everlasting, the Catechism discusses six areas: particular judgement, heaven, purgatory, hell, last judgement and the hope of the New Heaven and the New Earth. Concerning the New Creation, the Catechism 'affirms the profound common destiny of the material world and man' (CCC 1046). The visible universe 'is ... destined to be transformed' (CCC 1047). The approach of the Catechism in its treatment of eschatology is Trinitarian, Christological, ecclesiological, relational and communion-based. In many respects it could be said that the Catechism expands and elaborates on the content contained in the 1979 Instruction of the *Congregation for the Doctrine of the Faith*.

Principles of Interpretation

This teaching of the Church on eschatology will be easily misunderstood unless it is accompanied by some principles of interpretation. Eschatological statements are different from other theological statements in so far as they try to talk about a future that has not yet happened. Further, eschatology uses a highly pictorial language which is always in danger of being literalised. Consequently, it is important to have some guiding principles for the interpretation of eschatology.

The first principle of interpretation is to state that eschatology is not some idle speculation about the future, nor is it some kind of report of what goes on in the next world, nor is it a prediction about the end of the world. Instead, eschatology is about hope seeking understanding, more specifically about a particular hope-filled interpretation of human experience in the light of the Christ-event. Eschatology seeks to explore, analyse and interpret the potential within human experience for fulfilment and transformation in the future. Eschatology looks at present experience against the background of the salvation offered by Christ to see what it promises for the future. According to Rahner, eschatology entails a transposition of present experiences of salvation from a mode of beginning into a mode of consummation. The range of experiences in question is quite varied. For example, the human capacity to become, to grow and to develop are seeds of a future that bear a promise of fulfilment. The quest for justice, which lies at the origins of eschatology in the Hebrew Scriptures, implies an underlying order of right and wrong that one day will see the triumph of good over evil. Further, there are those experiences in life when we move beyond our lacklustre selves to step outside the temporal, when we rub shoulders with another dimension in life, whether in good conversation, in trusting relationships, in listening to good music, or being absorbed by the needs of others. In addition, there are those experiences of enjoyment which even Frederick Nietzsche had to admit 'seek to be eternal'. But most of all it is the experience of love, or perhaps the absence of love, that awakens hope in the future. Of course, these positive experiences must be balanced by the negative experiences of life such as evil, suffering and death. Indeed, there is an important sense in which negative experiences can be equally if not more powerfully the midwife of hope in the future.

The key to the interpretation of these experiences is the historical reality of the life, death and resurrection of Jesus as the Christ summed up in the New Testament and kept alive by the Church in the Christian tradition. The Christ-event is understood to have absolute significance for the future of humanity, history and creation. Above all it is the Christ-event that opens up new possibilities and promises for the world in the present and the future, and it is these new perspectives that constitute the heart of Christian eschatology. Indeed, one way of describing eschatology is to see it as the application of Christology to the self, humanity and creation in a mode of fulfilment. It is against this background that Karl Rahner claims that Christ is the hermeneutical principle of all eschatological statements. In particular, it is the Paschal Christ, the Crucified and Risen One, who gives us an embryonic view of the future of humanity and the world.

A third principle guiding the interpretation of eschatology concerns the question of language. Eschatology statements are symbolic, dialectical and analogical. Symbols point beyond themselves to a dimension of life that is not readily available to human experience. The symbol is not the reality symbolised and yet that reality is only available through the mediating power of symbol. The perspective of dialectic, preferred more by Protestant theologians, highlights the need for negation and usually grounds itself in the cross of Christ. The doctrine of analogy, more favoured among Catholic theologians, signals the limitations attaching to all eschatological statements while seeking to assert negatively the truth within its positive statements. Within analogy there is a dynamic movement from affirmation to negation and from negation to further refinement. Of critical importance to analogy is the awareness that we know more by way of negation than by way of affirmation. Further, the range of what we do not know surpasses the little we do know, or to put it in the words of the Fourth Lateran Council (1215), the similarity that exists between God and creatures is outweighed by a greater dissimilarity. This important theological principle must also be applied to eschatology and in particular to our limited understanding of the *eschaton*. What Aquinas says of God applies with particular force to eschatological statements: 'the ultimate of the human's cognition of God is to know that he/she does not know God.'

A fourth and final principle guiding the understanding of eschatology is the importance of the practical and ethical import of its statements. An authentically Christian eschatology is one that generates a *praxis* of liberation in the present in the name of the coming Reign of God. Eschatological statements stand out as a critique of the cynicism, fatalism and apathy in a world that has given up on the possibility of improving the quality of life in the present for the future. Eschatology, therefore, seeks to generate a dynamism directed towards the work of justice on behalf of humanity and the well-being of the earth in the passionate belief that love's labour endures unto eternal life.

The Contemporary Context of Eschatology

It is impossible to understand eschatology without reference to its particular social and cultural context. It is context that gives shape and form to contemporary expressions of eschatology. One of the most significant contextual shifts within Catholic theology in the twentieth century has been the transition from a classical, fixed understanding of culture to the emergence of a historical consciousness. The culture of historical consciousness recognises the contingent character of events within history and this clearly has implications for the way we construct a theology of history and providence as underlying suppositions of eschatology. The making of history, which is always self-involving, carries with it a burden of responsibility in the exercise of human agency. History, therefore, is not predetermined but open-ended and thus subject to the influence of the *praxis* of individual and social liberation. Historical consciousness calls forth a new sense of shared responsibility for the shape of the world in the present and the future. The possibility of making, unmaking and remaking history opens up new questions for eschatology at the beginning of the third millennium.

A second point relating to context concerns the highly ambiguous legacy of the Enlightenment, which came to expression in the project known as modernity. Much has been achieved through modernity, especially in terms of the promotion of human rights, the recognition of equality, the search for justice, the protection of human freedoms and the removal of superstition from religion. These gains of modernity have not, however, always been incorporated into modern eschatologies. The reasons for their neglect is that other aspects of modernity have been unsympathetic to the construction of eschatology, especially a social eschatology. For example, the rise of individualism and the cultivation of the shining-self-sufficient-subject of modernity has no need of eschatology. Similarly, modernity's myth of progress, the promise of endless growth and the politics of social evolution have taken over the role of eschatology in modern theology. Likewise, the modern denial of death and the covering over of so much suffering in history has paved the way for the promotion of a purely secular utopia. Lastly, the promises of science to deliver new freedoms and advance social emancipation have had the effect of sidelining eschatology within contemporary thought.

In recent times these dreams of modernity have been found to be wanting and even deceptive in some instances. So much of what went under the myth of progress has turned out to be regress and certain forms of modern development have brought about significant underdevelopment in their train. Inattention to the consequences of the actions of the modern experiment has resulted in the deterioration of the quality of existence: congested cities, deforestation and global warming. Most of all in recent decades the autonomy of the human subject within modernity has been decentred by a variety of critiques coming from feminism, ecology and the new cosmologies.

These problems and others with modernity have given birth to the vague, illusive and deliberately ill-defined movement known as postmodernity. Postmodernity is more a mood than a movement, more a protest against modernity than a worked-out philosophy, more a reaction against the universal rationalist claims of modernity than a clear alternative. Postmodernity in contrast to modernity seeks to promote the cultivation of particularity, difference and otherness; it expresses a strong 'incredulity towards meta-narratives'; it speaks out in defence of the unspeakable, the unrepresentable and the unpresentable.

For many, the logic of postmodernity seems to be one of radical deconstruction leading to fragmentation, relativism and, ultimately, nihilism. One of the most immediate casualties of postmodernity is eschatology in so far as postmodernity dissolves the human subject into an empty site designed for linguistic exchanges and also reduces history to a collection of disconnected fragments. However, before rushing in to adopt this largely negative assessment of postmodernity, it must be noted that there are some affinities as well as other radical differences between postmodernity and Christian eschatology.

The most obvious affinity between postmodernity and eschatology is the adoption of the way of negation, or the *apophatic* tradition. Both postmodernity and eschatology emphasise what is unknowable, unrepresentable and unsayable concerning the future.

A second affinity between postmodernity and eschatology is the way in which postmodernity deconstructs all affirmations in the name of something other – even though it is impossible to name this other. The nearest postmodernity comes to naming this 'something other' is to call it the 'possibility of the impossible', 'the thought that cannot be thought', the future that exists beyond the horizons of the foreseeable. Yet some postmodernists are prepared to talk about 'religion without religion' or 'the other without being' or the 'messianic without messianism' (J. Derrida). These positive 'negations' contain a faint echo with classical eschatology, which openly acknowledges that it does not know the future and that it is impossible to express it adequately.

A third affinity between postmodernity and eschatology is the deep suspicion postmodernity has towards all meta-narratives. Eschatology, of course, cannot succeed without some meta-narrative, especially the narrative of the creation, redemption and the consummation of all things in Christ. Nonetheless, eschatology shares some suspicion with postmodernity about those narratives that claim to know too much about the end of the world, the nature of the *parousia* and the character of eternal life.

In spite of these affinities there are serious differences between postmodernity and eschatology. For example, Christian eschatology affirms the centrality of God's promises revealed in the Passover of the people of

Israel, confirmed in the Paschal Mystery of Jesus Christ and manifested in the eschatological outpouring of the Spirit at Pentecost. Further, eschatology is constructed in and around the narrative of a fundamental unity between the action of the Holy Spirit in creation, redemption and the consummation of all things in Christ. In addition, eschatology and postmodernity differ radically on the issue of anthropology, as we shall see below. Lastly, eschatology affirms a continuum between the past, the present and the future within its statements about the meaning of history.

Anthropology

It is most of all in the area of anthropology, namely the question about what it means to be human, that the modern and postmodern contexts of eschatology are most problematic. The human subject, conceived as self-sufficient by modernity and as an empty site for social transactions by postmodernity, is in crisis and therefore in need of a new configuration.

The exalted and exaggerated self of modernity (going back to Descartes (1596–1650)) has given rise to a self-sufficient individualism. This strong individualism has little need of eschatology since, as Gabriel Marcel (1889–1973) was fond of pointing out, 'hope does not exist at the level of the solitary ego'; instead, hope is only possible at the level of *us*. Indeed, it is only through an awareness that 'Self knows that self is not enough' (Brendan Kennelly) that the movement of hope happens and the construction of eschatology begins to take place. The human self is aware that it cannot survive death on its own and that it is only because the self is graced and loved by God that it has a future beyond death. It is the experience of loving and being loved that assures a future for the self. However, each of these moves is unavailable to and unnecessary for the independent-shining-self-sufficient-subject-of modernity.

At the other end of the spectrum there is the deconstructed self of postmodernity, which is even less available to eschatology. According to postmodernity, the human self is something of an empty site around which a great variety of transactions take place, a little like a crossroads that facilitates the movement of traffic. For example, Michel Foucault holds that 'man is an invention of recent date' who will be 'erased like a face drawn in the sand at the edge of the sea'. According to Richard Rorty, the human self is simply a social construct resulting from cultural creations and linguistic networks that enables human exchanges to take place. Strictly speaking, the human self is purely contingent, having no underlying or enduring thread/substance/reality. For postmodernity there is no human nature or material common to human beings. As Richard Rorty sums up: 'There is nothing deep down inside us except what we have put there ourselves.' In similar fashion, Jean-Francois Lyotard holds: 'Each of us knows that our self does not amount to much.'

The reconstruction of the human required for a viable eschatology needs to take account of the variety of impulses coming from other sources. There is first of all the reaction against the individualism of modernity coming from feminism, ecology and cosmology. Feminism, in its great variety, places a strong emphasis on the self as relational. Environmentalists emphasise the 'connected self' as that which exists in dependence on the rest of nature and creation. Cosmologists talk about the individual as cosmic dust in a state of self-conscious freedom as embodied: 'We are all made of the ashes of dead stars.' These different though complementary perspectives suggest that the whole of life, in particular human life, is organically inter-connected, inter-related and inter-dependent. This perspective on human identity prompts the formulation of the following principles in the reconstruction of anthropology: to exist is always to co-exist, to be is always to be in relationship, self-discovery arises through surrender to the other.

A second impulse on the nature of the human self comes from the work of Paul Ricoeur as expressed in his book, *One's Self as Another*. According to Ricoeur, the human self is only available in narrative form and this narrative is more often than not a point of historical arrival rather than a point of departure. What is distinctive for Ricoeur about the human self is the pivotal role that action plays in the constitution of the human self. The self is not available through a process of introspection; instead, the self comes into view through a process of interpersonal action and reaction with the other as part of an ongoing narrative.

What is significant about these relational and narrative anthropologies is the existence of an active self that is open and unfinished: the self is a work of art-under-construction through the action of others and ultimately the grace of the Holy Spirit. Given these perspectives on human identity, eschatology emerges not as something additional or extrinsic to anthropology. Primarily, eschatology is, as Rahner frequently pointed out, anthropology in a mode of fulfilment or anthropology conjugated in the future. Further, this kind of anthropology, namely a relational anthropology, sees the human subject as one who is in touch with God at the beginning of life and not simply at the end of historical existence. Third, a relational anthropology opens up the way for the development of a social eschatology in both the present and the future.

Christology

These comments on the links between anthropology and eschatology lead quite naturally into Christology, which is the bridge between anthropology and eschatology. There can be little dispute about the centrality of Christology to eschatology or indeed of the suggestion that Christ is the hermeneutical principle for interpreting eschatological statements. This Christological focus within eschatology, however, has not always been to the fore in the history of Christian thought. The most obvious example of a break in the link between Christology and eschatology is the emphasis often given to the last things or *eschata* at the expense of the advent of the new end or *eschaton* 'in Christ'.

To say that Christ is the hermeneutical principle of eschatological statements means that we must be able to recognise the shape of the Christ-event within eschatological statements – something that is not always apparent in, for example, some theologies about the immortality of the soul, heaven and hell.

The Christ-event is best summed up in terms of recognising the theological significance of the life, death and resurrection of Jesus as the Christ. The Second Vatican Council affirms that 'Christ, the New Adam … fully reveals humanity to itself and brings to light its very calling' and also emphasises the Paschal Mystery of Christ as the centrepiece of salvation history (GS 22). Equally, as already noted, Vatican II describes Christ as the goal, ground and centre of human history.

The New Testament points out that God 'has made known to us the mystery of his will, according to his good pleasure that he set forth in Christ, as a plan for the fullness of time, to gather up all things in Him, things in heaven and things on earth' (Eph 1:9-10). The letter to the Colossians claims that Christ 'is the image of the invisible God, the first born of all creation … in Him all things hold together; He is the beginning, the first born from the dead' (Col 1:15). The future, therefore, is Christomorphic.

In the early Church there was a sense that an eschatological breakthrough had occurred in the historical life, death and resurrection of Jesus. The earliest interpretations of the historical life of Jesus are thoroughly eschatological. For example, Paul says that Christ has 'abolished death, brought life and immortality to light' (2 Tim 1:10). In virtue of the Christ-event, we are now living in 'the end of ages' (1 Cor 10:11) and in the 'latter times' (1 Tim 4:1) and, therefore, all are encouraged 'to put away the old man and put on the new man' (Ep 4:22; Col 3:9). Because Christ is 'the first born among many' (Rom 8:29; Col 1:18) and 'the first fruits of those who have fallen asleep' (1 Cor 15:20) Paul can say that since 'all die in Adam, so all will be made alive in Christ' (1 Cor 15:22).

Further, this experience and understanding of Jesus as the Christ is something that affects not only human existence but also the direction of material creation itself: '… for creation itself will be set free from its bondage and will obtain the freedom of the glory of the children of God' (Rom 8:21). The Christ-event, therefore, reconfigures our understanding of God in relation to the future of humanity, of history and of creation.

This sense of eschatological breakthrough is so strong in the early Church that initially Paul believes that the return of Christ (*parousia*) is imminent and so his early theology emphasises resurrection and *parousia*. With the passage of time there is a shift from resurrection and *parousia* to death and resurrection, with resurrection taking place after death (2 Cor 5:1-10; Phil 1:21-23; Phil 3:21), and later to a theology of being and becoming 'in Christ' in the present.

Within this theology of Paul there are two key points to be noted. The early Church had a strong belief that the future has already dawned 'in Christ' and has, therefore, taken a hold of the present. The future is not something that we are waiting for to take place; instead, the future is here already *in embryo* in the Paschal Mystery of Jesus Christ and the Pentecostal event. This emphasis on the future as already given 'in Christ' stands out as a critique of those particular eschatologies that give priority to the future without adverting sufficiently to what has already happened in the historical death and resurrection of Jesus. A fine balance must be maintained between the past and the future, which brings us to the second point.

In the theology of Paul there is a creative tension between what has 'already' taken place 'in Christ' and what is 'not yet' achieved, between being 'in Christ' and becoming 'in Christ', between the indicative statements such as 'you are in Christ' and the imperative statements that 'you must put on Christ'. In Paul there is a dialectic between the already and the not yet, a paradox of dying and rising 'in Christ', a mysticism of being and becoming 'in Christ'. Whichever emphasis is taken here there is always a historical process of being conformed and configured not to the death of Christ, not to the risen Christ, but to the crucified *and* risen Christ as *one* eschatological reality.

Conclusion

The challenge facing eschatology in the twenty-first century is in part the task of enabling the biblical imagination to interact and transform the secular imagination of the twenty-first century. This is not a matter of simply reproducing the biblical mindset in the twenty-first century but rather of facilitating some form of creative interaction between the past and the present. An important requirement in enabling this mutual transformation to take place will be a recovery of the place of memory within Judaism and early Christianity. Memory and imagination are inseparable and constitute the building blocks for the reconstruction of eschatology for the third millennium.

Further Reading

Grey, Mary C., *The Outrageous Pursuit of Hope: Prophetic Dreams for the Twenty-First Century*, London: Darton, Longman and Todd, 2000.

Kelly, Anthony, *Eschatology and Hope*, New York: Orbis Books, 2006.

Lane, Dermot A., *Keeping Hope Alive: Stirrings in Christian Theology*, Dublin/New York: Veritas/Paulist Press, 1996 and Oregon: Wipf and Stock, 2005.

Phan, Peter C., *Responses to 101 Questions on Death and Eternal Life*, New York: Paulist Press, 1997.

Rahner, Karl, *Foundations of the Christian Faith: An Introduction to the Idea of Christianity*, translated by William V. Dych, London: Darton, Longman and Todd, 1978.

SECTION III

CHRISTIAN MORALITY

CHAPTER 13

CATHOLIC ANTHROPOLOGY
Ethna Regan

Introduction

Who are we? What ought we become? How do we get there?

These are questions that philosophers and theologians explore in a formal way, questions that art, literature and music engage creatively with, questions that are asked implicitly and explicitly by all of us who confront the mystery of being human and the demands of that mystery as we encounter it in situations of pain and loss, joy and hope, and even in the mundane of daily struggle. This essay will examine some aspects of Catholic Christian theological anthropology and the importance of the human person in our moral theology.

Imago Dei

> God created humankind in his image: in the image of God he
> created them; male and female he created them.
>
> (Gen 1:27)[1]

Christian anthropology, like that of Judaism, is theocentric: it understands the human person in relation to God. Judaism holds that each human being is created *betzelem Elohim*, in God's image, and thus has inalienable dignity. This is the greatest principle of the Torah[2] and the fundamental text for biblical anthropology. The Genesis story of creation, while not answering all our questions regarding the creation of the world and the origins of humanity, continues to be central to ethical reflection. The following are five key insights which still provoke our moral imagination as we struggle with the meaning of human life and our place in creation:

- All of creation is good and the human person is placed in the centre of God's creative work.
- The human person – male and female – is made in the image of God.
- The notion of *Imago Dei* grounds the inalienable dignity of the human person and the sacredness of human life.
- The human person is made for communion with God and this communion is essential for human flourishing. The person, as *imago Dei*, is social and partnership between man and woman is the primordial form of communion between persons.
- The concept of *Imago Dei* is the basis for the distinction between human beings and the rest of creation: we have responsibility, before God, for the flourishing of life.[3]

Sometimes a distinction is made between the 'image' and 'likeness' of God: while 'likeness' was probably added for emphasis, early Christian reflection on *imago Dei* used the term to suggest a developmental anthropology wherein the 'image' referred to our creation and 'likeness' pointed to our eschatological perfection. Irenaeus suggested that the image of God is present in the actual moment of creation and that we move, with the grace of the Holy Spirit, on a path towards greater 'likeness' to God.[4] Thus reflection on the human person as *imago Dei* points to the moral life as a journey and from its beginnings Christian anthropology stresses the interweaving of nature and grace in any consideration of the human person. Grace is not a thing to be possessed or lost, but God's own life through the Holy Spirit who accompanies and empowers human persons in their efforts to grow in the likeness of God.

The God of the Hebrew Scriptures, who formed the human person from dust of the earth and from God's own breath, is understood as a God of history, involved in the history of the people of Israel, a history which simultaneously reveals Godself and the implications for the human person of being in the image of God. As Christians we believe that this God of history became radically historicised – enfleshed – within history. In the New Testament, the biblical story of creation is interpreted 'Christologically', i.e. in relation to the person of Jesus Christ. Christ is called 'the image of the invisible God, the firstborn of all creation' and the 'second Adam'.[5] Our

EXPLORING THEOLOGY

relationship to Christ, of the first to the second Adam, points to the fact that we are not yet truly ourselves as *imago Dei*, that we are on a journey to becoming our true selves, and that in Christ we see who God truly is and who we are intended to become. We can speak of Christ not only as *the* Image of God but also as *the* exegete of the human person. In his life, death and resurrection the questions of who we are, where we are going and how we get there find radical answers.

As a theological term, *Imago Dei* is evocative rather than strictly descriptive and the history of theological anthropology is an attempt to come to terms with its meaning. Its interpretation over the centuries has been rich and varied, focusing at different times on different dimensions of the human person that are in the image of God, dimensions such as rationality, freedom, moral capacity, creativity, relationality and power of self-determination. In the struggle to illuminate the practical and political implications of *imago Dei*, theology showed itself vulnerable to the same dangers as philosophical anthropology, e.g. universal assertions of human dignity, which incorporated careful categories of practical exclusion based on race, class or gender. The view of the human person as *imago Dei* grounds one of the principles of Catholic social teaching, the dignity of the human person. This means that no matter what level of ability or virtue, each person has intrinsic value and the person – even in error – never loses the dignity of being in the image of God. This is a primary reason for Catholic opposition to the death penalty.

Sin and Freedom

While there is a common perception of Catholicism as being obsessed with certain kinds of sin, an obsession that many people associate with inculcating a deep sense of guilt, our basic theological position is that there is a fundamental goodness in human beings as *imago Dei*, redeemed by Christ and empowered by the grace of the Holy Spirit. Distortions in the Catholic tradition used the language of sin in a controlling way, with the consequent detrimental effects on people; however, the intention of such language is to be liberative, to help us respond to the question, 'how do we get there?'

Sin is the term used to describe moral evil from the perspective of theological ethics rather than philosophical ethics. Sin, in essence, is a religious concept; it makes sense only in relation to God. Genesis continues from the creation story to offer an explanation of the spread of evil, suffering and death which, although we do not take it literally, still offers important insights that provoke our moral imagination as we reflect on how the human person as *imago Dei* is bruised and damaged by sin:

- Sin denies the goodness of creation and damages human embodiment.
- Sin undermines human dignity and de-sacralises human life.
- Sin distorts and potentially refuses communion with God.
- Sin weakens human sociality and wounds the primordial communion between persons.
- Sin abuses our responsibility for the flourishing of life, moving from a relational *imago Dei* to an inflated anthropocentrism that is marked by possession, consumption and destruction.

The biblical perspective on sin presents sin as both a state and an act (an ethic of being and doing), as personal and deliberative, coming from the depth of a person, from the heart. Sin – even our most seemingly intimate – has a social and relational impact.

While sin refers primarily to the actions of persons – what we do and fail to do – for which we are responsible, that responsibility is already shadowed by the sins of others and vulnerable to the experience of being born into historical and cultural contexts that are bruised and damaged by sin. This is what Catholic moral teaching means by the doctrine of original sin. While contemporary theology does not speak of being 'born with' original sin, nor hold with Augustine that the sin of Adam and Eve is transmitted biologically through the generations, it articulates the reality of this sinfulness that exists prior to our personal acts of freedom, in terms of its 'universality' and 'inescapability' for all human persons. Original sin thus makes possible actual sin and social sin. However, the doctrine of original sin is always subordinate to the doctrine of grace, for Paul reminds us that where sin abounds grace abounds even more.[6]

While the notion of sin only makes sense in relation to God, the sinfulness of a person, act or situation can only be properly evaluated in terms of human freedom. Richard Gula, writing on the centrality of freedom to the moral life, comments that 'without it one cannot speak of being moral persons at all'.[7] One element of freedom is freedom of choice: we choose in a variety of situations, some of greater depth than others. Indeed it sometimes seems that the human person's capacity for choice is the dominant moral characteristic appealed to in contemporary ethical conversation. In moral theology we locate freedom of choice in the larger context of the freedom of the person to shape their own personhood. The term used to refer to this capacity is 'basic freedom'. The human person is not only the subject who acts (or is acted upon) but is also the subject who becomes. The term 'fundamental option' is used to try and articulate this exercise of human freedom in its most basic sense, i.e. taking responsibility for ourselves, for the kind of person we want to become in relation to God and others. This decision arises from the deepest core of the person, akin to the biblical concept of heart; it is not a momentary choice or one particular action, but the basic direction of the many different decisions and actions that constitute a human life. The fundamental option can be expressed or changed in a particular act, but not every particular act involves the fundamental option of the person.

Karl Rahner's theology offers us a vision of a world of grace, in which freedom is always graced freedom, given and sustained by grace.[8] The human person, with the aid of God's grace, has sufficient freedom to make a fundamental option. The fundamental option is formed and actualised through the historical choices and actions of the person. Despite the vulnerability of our own responsibility and despite the bruised contexts in which our lives are embedded, we have a capacity to be receptive to God's grace – God's own self-communication – in the world. The emphasis on grace in relation to the moral life leads us to see the exercise of our basic freedom and the fundamental option not so much as a superhuman act of will – although our choices for love may often be costly and difficult – but as a responsive option that confirms us in our humanity.

Does this mean that if our most serious concern is with our fundamental option, with the disposition of our heart in relation to God and others, that we do not have to be concerned with the seriousness of our concrete choices and actions? Some theologians raise concerns about the possible separation of the inner self, where true responsibility is thought to lie, from concrete actions and choices, suggesting that it could lead to a denial of the serious implications of some of our actions. The most helpful way of answering these concerns is to view the fundamental option as corrective: it broadens a purely acts-focused morality without denying the serious consequences of such acts and it directs us to consider the person in his or her entirety.

All our freedom is situated freedom and insights from the human, physical and social sciences remind us that even our apparently freely chosen actions are choices made somewhere between freedom and determinism. Our theological anthropology, while acknowledging the situatedness of human freedom, holds that basic freedom cannot be negated. The insights of contemporary trauma therapy about the fragmentation of the self that results from trauma and abuse, fragmentation that impedes the development of an effective sense of agency, challenge us to examine the impact of such fragmentation on the exercise of basic freedom.

Unlike original sin, actual sin involves free choice and such choices involve responsible and informed freedom. One can only speak properly of sin when there is some insight into the degree of knowledge, freedom, intention and responsibility involved. The Catholic moral tradition identifies three criteria to determine whether or not a person has committed a mortal sin: grave matter, full knowledge and full consent. All three criteria are involved in the determination of a sin as mortal. Thomas Aquinas described mortal sin as an 'aversion from God', aversion from the fullness of humanity that our being *imago Dei* calls us to. Mortal sin means that an action, or series of actions, results in the death of charity in the human heart. We cannot doubt that such a possibility exists but whether mortal sin is as frequent as sometimes suggested merits serious consideration.

The basic meaning of sin is mortal and all other sins are sins by analogy. Choices which do not come from the core of the self – while not in themselves deadly – can shape our inner core and the direction of our life. These venial sins 'wound' love within us, potentially deflecting us as we journey towards what we are meant to become as human beings. Venial sins point to a lack of congruence between our actions and what we are trying to be. While the Church insists that the essential categories of actual sin are mortal and venial, there is discussion of a third category of 'grave' sin.[9] This attempts to articulate that something may not be merely 'venial' but neither might it be absolutely destructive, or that virtuous actions can be carried out by persons who also engage in seriously sinful behaviour.

Even the most integrated reflection on sin tended to focus on interior states and individual actions to the neglect of social realities. The language of social sin marks a new emphasis, a systematic articulation of an understanding of the relationship between personal and communal justice that is as old as the Hebrew Prophets. Social sin is sin in an analogous sense, for only individual persons can sin. Structures of sin are rooted in personal sin, but personal sin is impacted by institutions. Individual choices can be at the heart of injustice but individual conversion is not sufficient to root out social sin in our world, for our lives are embedded in cultures and systems that are in need of transformation. One of the modern martyrs, Archbishop Oscar Romero of El Salvador (1917–1980), offers an insightful definition of social sin: 'the crystallization of individual egoisms in permanent structures which maintain this sin and exert its power over the great majorities.'[10] Structures affect the acts of persons and are interwoven into those personal acts of sinfulness. Social sin is not a peripheral concern; the poor are the majority of humanity, thus poverty and injustice are questions for both theological anthropology and moral theology. To work for justice and peace in the midst of poverty and violence is to engage with the two possibilities of human freedom, grace and dis-grace.[11] Theology emerging from contexts of social injustice has taken the social dimension of grace seriously, reminding us that all grace *is* inherently social, that grace becomes real in history and that realisation can take public and political expressions.

Because of the complexity of human persons, actions and structures, reflection on human sinfulness necessitates its differentiation into concepts of original sin, actual sin (mortal and venial) and social sin. While such categorisation sometimes functioned in a legalistic way which did not necessarily either enable people to grow in their humanity or communities to grow in greater justice, our own experience shows us that the object of sin differs and that there are evident degrees of gravity in sinful actions. The awareness of the complexity of human sinfulness points to the connection between the ethics of being and the ethics of doing, highlighting how sin affects the fundamental dimensions of being human, distorts the image of God within us and slows that journey towards greater likeness of God, the full humanity to which we are called.

Centrality of Personhood in Moral Reflection

This essay began with a reflection on the human person as *imago Dei*. While this view of the human person was never abandoned by moral theology, there was a neglect of it as a central moral metaphor in favour of language of 'human nature'. The movement to a more adequate consideration of the human person flows from the twentieth-century 'recovery of experience as an integral element' of theology[12] and from what Bernard Lonergan describes as a shift from a 'classicist' worldview which views the human person as 'possessing' an eternal and unchanging nature – with the consequent deductive moral reasoning – to a worldview marked by historical consciousness which takes seriously the particular and contingent dimensions of the human person, without overlooking what human beings have in common, leading to a more inductive form of moral reasoning.[13]

Dignitatis humanae, one of the most important documents of Vatican II, grounded the right to religious freedom in the dignity of the human person. The significance of this appeal to human dignity may not strike us today but it exemplifies what has been described as a shift in theology from language of 'human nature' to that of 'human person'. This shift has been the most noticeable change in moral theology since the Council. The human person – adequately considered – is the basis for moral reasoning and objective moral standards are related to the totality of the human person.

What are the criteria for what Louis Janssens calls an 'integral and adequate' consideration of the human person in moral decision making? Some common dimensions emerge in the work of a number of theologians who work within this broadly 'personalist' – not individualist – approach to morality: the human person as embodied, social, historical, free, fundamentally equal but unique and open to transcendence. This personalist perspective is a contemporary exploration of the indicative and imperative that is the human person as *imago Dei*. Janssens suggests that the integration of these dimensions of the human person form a criterion for assessing the morality of human action: an action is morally right if it is beneficial to the person adequately considered in his or her totality, i.e. as embodied, historical, free and to his or her relationship with others, with God and with the world.[14]

Each dimension of the human person is incarnated in a particular gender and race and located in a particular cultural and historical context. Liberation theology, emerging first from Latin America, spoke from the specific experience of the poor human person, the victim of history. It exposed undifferentiated theological references to the human person and challenged historical consciousness to take seriously the notion of historical responsibility, described sometimes as a shift to praxis. These 'shifts' in how we understand the human person and the implications for moral reasoning are sometimes understood as shifts that substitute e.g. a concern with praxis as a substitute for a concern with the human person as subject. On the contrary, the shifts can be viewed as intensifications rather than substitutions, as attempts to articulate a more rounded anthropology, a more coherent vision of human being-acting, enabling a more creative and historically responsible form of moral reasoning.

Conclusion

Catholic theological anthropology grapples with the questions: Who are we? What ought we become? How do we get there? It reminds us of the interconnectedness of human origins (protology), human destiny (eschatology) and morality. It holds to the intimate connection between God's call and human flourishing, seeking to present an integral and multi-dimensional anthropology, a view of moral reasoning that evaluates the human person in his or her totality and a commitment to historical responsibility in the face of poverty, injustice and violence, keeping in mind that we hope both within history and for a liberation that goes beyond history. Catholic anthropology has a basic confidence in the goodness of human persons, a confidence which coexists with an acknowledgement of grace and dis-grace within history. This basic confidence, which could be termed 'hopeful realism', includes the faith that it is possible to have reasonable public discourse with men and women of good will about what it means to be human and the responsibilities flowing from that humanity.

The Church is sometimes described as an 'expert in humanity',[15] with an expertise emerging from knowledge of the depths of the human heart. In recent years, the gap between our proclaimed ethic and our operative ethic has bruised the capacity of the Church to witness to that expertise. Our challenge is to acknowledge with humility that dis-grace, that bruised moral capacity. We must examine our own structures of sin, even as we challenge the de-humanising structures and assaults on human dignity in our world. We move forward remembering that the moral life is a journey on which the Pilgrim God accompanies us and the deepening of our humanity is the graced process of becoming more like the God in whose image we are made.

Notes

1   See also Gen 5:1-2; 9:6. Note the reference to 'image' and 'likeness' in Gen 1:26.

2   C.G. Montefiore and H. Loewe, *A Rabbinic Anthropology*, NY.: Schocken, 1974, p. 172.

3   Some theologians suggest that the term 'created co-creator' might be a more dynamic and ecologically responsible term than *Imago Dei*.

4   Bishop of Lyons in the second century.

5   Col 1:15; 1 Cor 15:44-48.

6   Rom 5:20.

7   Richard M. Gula, *Reason Informed by Faith: Foundations of Catholic Morality*, New York/Mahwah, NJ: Paulist Press, 1989.

8   For a concise introduction to a range of themes in Rahner's theology, see William Dych's *Karl Rahner*, London and NY: Continuum, 2000.

9   See Pope John Paul II's *Reconciliatio et paenitentia* – Apostolic Exhortation on Reconciliation and Penance in the Mission of the Church Today (1984) paragraph 17.

10 Found in his Second Pastoral Letter, 1977.

11 This word is used by the Brazilian theologian Leonardo Boff in his book *Liberating Grace*, trans. by J. Drury, Maryknoll, NY.: Orbis Books, 1979.

12 Dermot A. Lane, *The Experience of God: An Invitation to do Theology*, Dublin: Veritas, 2003, p. 16.

13 See 'The Transition from a Classicist World-View to Historical Mindedness' in James E. Biechler (ed.) *Law for Liberty*, Baltimore: Helicon Press, 1967, pp. 133–136.

14 'Artificial Insemination: Ethical Considerations', *Louvain Studies* 8 (Spring 1980) p. 13. The influence of Louis Janssens is clear in Richard Gula's writings on the human person.

15 A phrase used by Pope John Paul II, which he attributed to Pope Paul VI.

Further Reading

Dych, William V., *Karl Rahner*, London: Geoffrey Chapman, 1992.

Gula, Richard M., *The Call to Holiness: Embracing a Fully Christian Life*, New York: Paulist Press, 2003.

Harrington, Donal, *What is Morality?*, Dublin: Columba Press, 1996.

Sachs, John R., *The Christian Vision of Humanity: Basic Christian Anthropology*, Collegeville, Minn.: The Liturgical Press, 1991.

CHAPTER 14

AN INTRODUCTION TO CATHOLIC MORAL THEOLOGY: THE CHRISTIAN CONTRIBUTION TO MORALITY

Niamh Middleton

Introduction

Morality is a human phenomenon. It is often pointed out that what distinguishes the human species from all others is the ability not only to discern the difference between right and wrong on a practical, daily basis but to seek ultimate definitions in the abstract of what constitutes the highest good. Indeed, the desire to comprehend and define absolute goodness, to understand and grapple with the mystery and problem of evil, amounts to a quest that can be traced back to the earliest civilizations. To be a morally upright person who lives in accordance with a high behavioural code is a possibility open to any human being, whether that person is religious or not. A person who has an atheistic or agnostic outlook may succeed in living a good and conscientious life, while someone who frequents church, mosque or synagogue may have a surface piety but fail to practice what they preach.

The Roman Catholic Church has, in fact, a high opinion of the essential goodness of human beings and of the human capacity for moral discernment. Many of its most well-known moral teachings – on issues such as social justice, medical practice, sexual behaviour, religious freedom – are derived from the 'natural law', an approach to moral decision making that pre-dates Christianity and has its roots in Greek and Roman antiquity.

The natural law approach to morality holds that the basis for distinguishing between right and wrong is to be found in our common human nature. In other words, how we should behave is inseparable from who and what we are as human beings. Any natural law formulation is therefore based on a particular definition of human nature, and there have been numerous such definitions. The natural law formulation used by the Church was devised in the thirteenth century by St Thomas Aquinas (c.1227–1274), who succeeded in achieving a synthesis between Greek and Roman thought on the one hand and Christianity on the other. The natural law therefore is not a creation of the Church, but an adaptation of classical philosophy to Christianity. This essay explores the specifically Christian contribution to morality. Before doing so however, we will take a brief look at how St Thomas defines human nature, and how this definition allows the *magisterium* (teaching authority) of the Church to arrive at some of its moral teachings.

Aquinas' Definition of Human Nature

Aquinas envisages the human species as an integral part of a cosmos that includes all physical and spiritual life, from plants at the lower end to God at the summit of creation.

For him, the human person is a combination of body and soul, or matter and mind. Aquinas defines our physicality in terms of two powerful instincts: the survival instinct and the reproductive instinct. In this regard, Aquinas' view of human nature has been vindicated by scientific discoveries from the eighteenth century onwards that have shown survival and sexual instincts to be fundamental to the evolution of species, including our own species. Aquinas defines human intelligence/spirit in terms of our rational powers. It is our rationality that distinguishes us from other animals; we are rational creatures because God has infused each one of us with a rational soul.

We will now consider some of the moral norms that Aquinas derives from his account of human nature. These norms, as well as many others that have their basis in the natural law, are central to the Church's traditional moral teachings. On the most basic level of human nature, we share with all other life on earth – plants and animals – the need to survive. Each and every one of us has a powerful survival instinct, though we may not become consciously aware of it unless we find ourselves in a life-threatening situation. We are therefore obliged to take care of our health in every way possible. The requirement to nurture and protect our lives and the lives of others gives rise to some of the Church's strictest moral prohibitions: murder, abortion and euthanasia are considered to be among the gravest sins. The second powerful instinct is one that we share with other animals: the instinct to procreate and rear offspring. From this aspect of human nature the Church derives one of its most important moral principles, known as the unitive–procreative principle. This principle states that since sexual intercourse throughout nature involves physical union between male and female and the consequent production of young, the natural law commands that every sexual act should involve the union of two bodies and openness to procreation. These two dimensions of the sexual act must not be separated, as God has created us this way to accomplish his purposes and for our own good. Thus the use of contraceptives, which separate union from procreation, is forbidden. By the same token, techniques such as IVF, which involve the creation of new life in a laboratory setting, are also forbidden. The Church uses this principle in the formulation of many of its sexual norms, of which I have mentioned just two.

Although the human species is integrally related to all other life on earth through survival and procreative instincts, we are also distinguished from the rest of creation by our unique rational powers. These powers enable us to develop sophisticated cultures, societies and institutions. Most importantly, our rationality allows us to enter into relationship with God and to cooperate in the task of caring for creation. This third and most important dimension of our human nature obliges us to live in civility with one another, to be good citizens and make a contribution to society, to nurture an aesthetic sense, to search for the truth of existence and to seek to know God. In summary, Aquinas defines a human being as a unique combination of body and spirit, who has been created by God to enjoy the pleasures of both the senses and the spirit. If we abide by the laws of our nature, we will achieve harmony between body and soul. Crucially, Aquinas maintains that human nature does not fundamentally change, and that, therefore, morality does not change.

The natural law approach to moral decision making is not without its critics, both inside and outside the Church. Much of the criticism centres on Aquinas' second level of human nature and the unitive–procreative principle. The moral norms forbidding contraception and IVF, for example, are often criticised as harsh and legalistic. In the first instance they do not take into account individual circumstances which can be difficult and even harrowing; in the second they impose a blanket ban on couples who suffer the pain of infertility from availing of techniques that could allow conception to occur. Many moral theologians within the Catholic tradition also argue that this natural law theory, based as it is on a somewhat static account of human nature, does not allow for the possibility that human nature may evolve and change through time. Those who subscribe to the latter view believe that if human nature changes, then moral norms must also change. Whatever one's point of view regarding human nature, it cannot be denied that those who criticise the legalism of traditional natural law morality are making a valid point when they express doubts about the application of general moral principles to all individual moral dilemmas, especially those which involve difficult, dangerous and sometimes tragic circumstances. In our discussion so far, we seem to have travelled far away from the Palestine of two thousand years ago and the itinerant preacher and teacher, Jesus. The question is, if the natural law can be discerned by all reasonable human beings who reflect on our common human nature, does our Christian identity make any difference to how we make moral decisions? Or as one student put it: 'What does all this legalism have to do with Jesus?'

The Law of Love

Although the Church draws on the natural law for much of its moral teaching, the most important source of moral guidance for all Christian denominations is the Bible, and especially the New Testament, where the story of the life, death and resurrection of Jesus is recounted. However, those who study the gospel texts in the hope of finding neatly formulated lists of moral dos and don'ts will be disappointed. Jesus does not pass judgement on others or tell them what they should not do. In fact, he made a point of standing up for those who were generally thought of as 'bad' people, 'sinners' in the language of the time.

Strictly speaking, Jesus was not a moralist. He was a deeply religious Jew who prayed constantly and experienced a very close relationship with God, whom he referred to by using the intimate term 'Abba'. As anyone who reads the gospels attentively must admit, Jesus lived in a way that was *the* model of perfect love for others, to the extent of laying down his life in the service of sinful humanity. In the manner of his living and dying, he revealed a new way to understand morality and to live a good life. This new concept of morality is as fresh, as challenging and as startling to today's readers of the gospels as it must have been to those who witnessed the words and acts of Jesus at first hand. Love is the main theme of Jesus' life and his teachings. Whereas codified lists of laws such as the ten commandments or the natural

EXPLORING THEOLOGY

law generally consist of statements that begin with 'thou shalt not' or 'you should not' or 'don't do' this or that, Jesus said things like:

> But I say ... Love your enemies, do good to those who hate you, bless those who curse you, pray for those who abuse you. If anyone strikes you on the cheek, offer the other also; and from anyone who takes away your coat do not withhold even your shirt. Give to everyone who begs from you; and if anyone takes away your goods, do not ask for them again. Do to others as you would have them do to you. (Lk 6:27-31)

We often associate morality with prohibitions, but the command of Jesus was as positive and dynamic as it could possibly be. Jesus was born, however, into a society and culture that had grown legalistic in its interpretation of Jewish religious law, known as the Torah. It had also reached the stage where, to be considered one of the righteous as opposed to a 'sinner', it was necessary to be able to afford an education. To be educated in that era was to know the scriptures: the Law and the Prophets. The many that were too poor to afford an education were inevitably classed as feckless and immoral, incapable of virtue and piety since they could not know enough about the law to fulfil complicated religious duties. Jesus, a rabbi who is portrayed in the gospels as a teacher, preacher and healer of great eloquence and popularity, not only defended such 'sinners' and aligned himself with them, but pointedly ignored some of the minor details of the law himself. He was frequently rebuked by the religious authorities for the fact that his disciples did not fast (Mt 9:14 par). He himself was rebuked by the Scribes and the Pharisees for healing a man with a withered hand on the Sabbath, which provoked him to anger. We are told that 'he was grieved at their hardness of heart' (Mk 3:1-6). Jesus replies to their criticism by quoting the prophet Isaiah: 'This people honours me with their lips, but their hearts are far from me; in vain do they worship me, teaching human precepts as doctrines' (Mk 7:6-7). Referring to the rules regarding ritual cleanliness he says:

> Do you not see that whatever goes into a person from outside cannot defile, since it enters, not the heart but the stomach, and goes out into the sewer? ... It is what comes out of a person

that defiles. For it is from within, from the human heart, that evil intentions come: fornication, theft, murder, adultery, avarice, wickedness, deceit, licentiousness, envy, slander, pride, folly. All these evil things come from within and they defile a person. (Mk 7:18-23)

Jesus came up against increasing opposition from the religious authorities for consorting with 'sinners' and failing to observe every aspect of the law. Indeed, this behaviour was partly responsible for the conspiracies that arose against him and that eventually led to his crucifixion. Clearly, Jesus could never be described as 'legalistic' or judgmental in moral matters. Does this mean that he was against formal moral systems such as the Torah? What would he think of the norms of the natural law were he alive today?

The Law of Love and the Law of Nature

Jesus, as we have seen, was a devoutly religious Jew. A comprehensive study of the gospels leaves the reader in no doubt that Jesus had an intimate knowledge of the Jewish scriptures; he was the interpreter *par excellence* of the law and the prophets. He states unequivocally: 'Do not think that I have come to abolish the law or the prophets; I have come not to abolish but to fulfil' (Mt 5:17). Laws, prescriptions and norms are necessary in the formation of character and in the formation of a people, and the Jewish people were the product of a relationship between themselves and God (Yahweh), that was based on covenant law going back to Moses' reception of the ten commandments on Mount Sinai over a thousand years before the birth of Jesus. Israelite society was one that valued justice, mercy and honesty above all else. It was a society marked by concern for the vulnerable in society, particularly widows and orphans. In his criticisms of the legalistic approach that had developed in the Judaism of his time, Jesus was reminding his peers of the 'spirit' rather than the 'letter' of their law. On being questioned by a scribe as to which commandment was the greatest of all, Jesus replies:

The first is, 'Hear O Israel: the Lord our God, the Lord is one; you shall love the Lord your God with all your heart, and with all your soul, and with all your mind, and with all your strength'. The second is this: 'You shall love your neighbour as yourself'. There is no other commandment greater than these. (Mk 12: 29-32)

Jesus' commandment to love was, in fact, directly derived from his religion. He believed that these commandments should take precedence over all others and that to keep them was to keep all. He shows, however, that laws and norms must not be understood as a restrictive limit on certain behaviours, but as the basis for a moral and spiritual journey towards perfection 'at the heart of which is love'. As fulfillment of the law, Jesus is himself a product of that law.

So, to answer the question of whether Jesus supported the formal moral system, we can say that Jesus was not against the law, merely abuses of the law. The key to his understanding of the law is to be found in his frequent references to the hard-heartedness that comes with a legalistic attitude; he always stresses that outward observances of the Jewish law, such as those that involve ritual cleanliness, can in no way give any indication of what is in a person's heart. It is from a person's heart that moral goodness flows. In studying the life and teachings of Jesus, the role of religion in moral behaviour also becomes clear. In coupling the commands to love God and love one's neighbour, Jesus seems to imply that in order to be able to love others there must be a prior and deep relationship with God.

We are now ready to answer the second question posed earlier of whether or not Jesus would have approved of the natural law. In making an argument in favour of the natural law approach to morality, the first thing to be noted is that the Israelites of two thousand years ago did not face the moral dilemmas that have been brought about by modern inventions in science and technology. The power over life and death that we now have through weapons of mass destruction, through the ability to prevent and control human reproduction, to create and even design life in a laboratory setting, is very recent in the context of human history. On a very basic, day-to-day level, the Christian love ethic cannot directly answer the moral questions raised by new technological, medical and scientific procedures. Nor can it always answer questions raised anew in succeeding generations relating to such issues as religious freedom, political systems, the justice or injustice of civil laws. The natural law can provide solutions to contemporary moral dilemmas.

The second thing to be noted is that there is no opposition between the natural law approach to morality and the Christian love ethic: each is informed by the other. The natural law gives rise to a codified system of norms that makes heavy ethical demands of us. However, the demands of the love ethic are even more testing. To be able to respond to the latter, one must first have been prepared through obedience to the former. There is, however, a significant difference between the natural law and the law of love; in highlighting this difference, we can begin to discern the uniquely Christian contribution to morality. The difference lies in the distinction between two words: *natural* and *supernatural*. The natural law is specific and gives clear guidance and instruction. Most of all, its norms relate to everyday aspects of life: to social, political, health, medical and sexual matters; hence the use of the word 'natural' to describe it. These norms relate to our human nature and to our natural lives. Jesus' commandment to love, on the other hand, is the demand of the new Covenant inaugurated by him, a covenant that both fulfils and transcends the old Covenant established by Yahweh with the Jewish people. The new Covenant surpasses the natural law by calling upon Christians to live out not just a natural but also a supernatural mode of moral existence. What exactly does this new Covenant of love require of Christians?

The Christian Contribution to Morality

Jesus lived a perfected mode of human existence because he was himself fully divine as well as fully human. His interactions and relationships were a manifestation in human terms of his Trinitarian existence with the Father and the Holy Spirit. Jesus had an exemplary knowledge of the relationship between love, truth and morality. Through his life, death and resurrection, he has made this moral wisdom available to each and every individual who is prepared to travel in his footsteps. Most importantly, the risen Jesus gifts us with the supernatural virtues of faith, hope and charity. These *theological* virtues are not only inspired by the example of Jesus: they transcend the natural and are of divine origin. According to the Catechism:

> The theological virtues are the foundation of Christian moral
> activity; they animate it and give it its special character. They
> inform and give life to all the moral virtues. They are infused by

God into the souls of the faithful to make them capable of acting as his children and of meriting eternal life. They are the pledge of the presence and action of the Holy Spirit in the faculties of the human being. (CCC 1813)

Through faith, we believe in God, in his goodness and power, in all that he has revealed to us even during periods when we may become aware of great evil in the world, or suffer disaster or misfortune ourselves. We must bear witness to our faith even through persecution and even if our faith turns us into objects of derision. The theological virtue of hope enables us to desire the happiness of the Kingdom of heaven and trust in the promises of Christ at all times, including times of discouragement, abandonment and difficulty. The apostle Paul depicts the virtue of charity thus:

> Charity is patient and kind, charity is not jealous or boastful; it is not irritable or resentful; it does not rejoice at wrong, but rejoices in the right. Charity bears all things, believes all things, hopes all things, endures all things ... So faith, hope and charity abide, these three. But the greatest of these is charity. (1 Cor 13:4-7, 13)

As human beings, we all have the ability to love and to accept love from others. St Paul's wonderful description of the virtue of charity refers to a perfection and purification of our natural ability to love that is effected by the power of grace and inspired by the example of Jesus. We have noted his criticism of those who ignore the big issues of justice, mercy and compassion while indulging in condemnation of those who fail to comply with minor details of the law. Jesus makes it clear that in order to be his disciple it is necessary to follow the example he has set rather than a system of laws, norms and rules.

Clearly, the virtues of faith, hope and love make great spiritual demands of us and are dependent on divine revelation and grace. Those who practice the theological virtues have surpassed the natural or the 'human' virtues: this divinely inspired morality enhances and perfects *natural* morality. Although the demands of the natural law can sometimes be difficult to discern, they are always easier to discern than to perform; all of us from time to time may need supernatural assistance both to understand and to obey the norms of the natural law. As the words and example of Jesus himself show, in order to consistently know and do the good, we must first 'love the Lord our God'.

The crux of Jesus' teaching is encapsulated in the statement, 'If you continue in my word, you are truly my disciples; and you will know the truth and the truth will make you free' (Jn 8:31). This statement reverses common presuppositions about moral progress. Normally, we are taught behavioural rules and regulations by parents, teachers and others with moral or legal authority over us and then we put their instructions into practice: we learn and then we act. To be a disciple of Jesus, we must first act by following practically in our lives the model of love lived out by him in word and deed; only *then* will we learn the full implications of what it means to be a Christian. If we fail in love, punishment will come internally from a tender conscience as opposed to authority figures. Further, what we learn will amount to far more than how to behave. We are assured that we will come to know *the* truth – that elusive truth sought by all of the greatest writers, philosophers and poets.

To understand the full significance of this promise that Jesus made, it helps to distinguish between two different kinds of knowledge: knowledge that is *epistemological* and knowledge that is *ontological*. Epistemology refers to the kind of knowledge most associated with teachers; it is directly taught through oral instruction or books. Ontology on the other hand refers to a knowledge that would be better termed wisdom; a knowledge of how to *be* in the world. It cannot be reduced to morality alone, yet moral goodness is its foundation. Needless to say, one's level of intelligence is irrelevant to the attainment of true wisdom. Unlike the kind of knowledge that is found in books, this is a type of knowledge that is equally available to all. Through this wisdom, the true disciple of Jesus will be freed from an attachment to the material goods of this earth that can lead to spiritual enslavement and from the general fears and anxieties that are the human lot. Each person who travels in the way of Christ will find his or her own unique version of 'the truth' and make his or her own unique, indispensable contribution to the 'Kingdom of God' that Jesus came to inaugurate.

Conclusion

It is no surprise, therefore, that Jesus did not leave behind him a set of moral norms or absolutes as other religious teachers have done; instead he left a perfect example of love in word and deed for those who wished to be his disciples. This does not imply that codified systems of morality are to be dispensed with; to be ready for the Christian call a moral 'apprenticeship' is necessary. However, those who achieve the wisdom of which Jesus speaks will, like him, know how to live according to the spirit and not the letter of the law. They will not rush to judgement or condemnation. They will have the courage to stand up and be counted in the face of injustice wherever they find it. Their moral influence will be accomplished through example; their deeds will spring from a loving heart that is the fruit of a transformed character and not from a set of rules imposed from without. St Augustine described this state of affairs best when he said, 'Love, and what you will, do'. Those who live as Jesus did no longer need to be taught from without; they are led interiorly by the Holy Spirit and because they love, whatever they 'will' must of necessity be oriented toward the good. The Christian call to morality goes far beyond the duty to live up to one's responsibilities; it is a call to sainthood.

Further Reading

Gula, Richard M., *Reason Informed by Faith*, New York: Paulist Press, 1989.

O'Connell, Timothy E., *Making Disciples*, New York: Crossroad, 1998.

Connors Jr, Russell B. and McCormick, Patrick T., *Character, Choices & Community: The Three faces of Christian Ethics*, New York: Paulist Press, 1998.

Fernández, Aurelio and Socías, James, *Our Moral Life in Christ*, New Jersey: Scepter Publishers; Chicago: Midwest Theological Forum, 1997.

Harrington, Donal, *What is Morality?*, Dublin: Columba, 1996.

Kennedy, Terence, *Doers of the Word: Moral Theology for the Third Millennium*, Liguori, Missouri: Triumph Books, 1996.

CHAPTER 15

MORAL DECISION MAKING, CONSCIENCE AND CHURCH AUTHORITY

Patrick Connolly

Introduction

Making an ethical decision is a process which involves many factors. This article explores how a thoughtful Catholic can relate to conscience and to the teaching authority of the Church when discerning appropriate moral behaviour in his or her daily life.

Broadly speaking, in many areas of life in the West it is clear that Catholicism's strong communal and corporate core is in tension with the current stress on individual choice and self-fulfilment. This is especially obvious in how Catholics arrive at moral decisions. Many Catholics believe that one is entitled to make up one's own mind about moral questions without much reference, if any, to external religious authority, and that one can do what one decides in moral matters, provided the rights of others are not affected. In western societies, where individual freedom is valued above all else, there is little difficulty in accepting the role of 'conscience', though how that term is understood varies in popular discourse. However, in this climate it is often difficult for Catholics to perceive the relevance of teachings and arguments which are rooted in Christian tradition and which are put forward by Church authority. Indeed, to acknowledge the insights of Church teachings in making individual moral decisions may sometimes be seen as reducing personal autonomy and individual dignity. This is partly illustrated in the way that many moral issues are now spoken of colloquially as an individual's 'private business', though one wonders if people really believe that any area of morality is an exclusively private concern.[1]

Social Context

Catholic Christians in the western world do not live in an ecclesial bubble but rather in a culture sceptical of authority. This is not an entirely regrettable development, as in the past argument from authority was often used arbitrarily to end moral discussion among Catholics. In contemporary western societies people can sometimes be dismissive of the Catholic tradition and teaching on morality, as if it has little or nothing to offer the twenty-first century. The reaction comes not only from those unsympathetic to Catholic moral reasoning but sometimes also from sincere practising Catholics. Aside from its wider origins in a general scepticism about all types of authority in society, this reaction also often arises because ecclesial authority has been discredited in recent times by the handling of clerical child abuse scandals, so that Catholics can be sceptical about moral guidance from the Church's leadership even if it simply expresses the accumulated insights of the Catholic moral tradition. Our western society places much emphasis on forms of public authenticity and accountability, and so the Church's teaching authority itself is seen to have lost popular credibility because of mistakes by individual Church leaders. While it is true that the Catholic understanding of teaching authority does not ultimately depend on the personal merits or otherwise of individual popes and bishops, leaders and teachers who are authentic and effective Christian witnesses are heard much more willingly.

Another factor behind the current situation is the experience in the past of authoritarianism in the Church, in that governing power in the Church has often been used (and misused) to bolster its teaching authority. Governing power and teaching authority are of course distinct, but in practice can be intermingled, in a fashion which does not always help teaching authority.[2] Taking for a moment the example of Ireland, there has probably been an overreaction to the memory of Catholic moral authoritarianism. Although many younger people have never personally experienced such authoritarianism, the memory of it has taken hold of the modern Irish consciousness in such a dramatic way that there has been a conflation of the experience of different generations, leading now to an almost instinctive scepticism or even occasional knee-jerk rejection of moral statements from Church leaders. This, of course, is partly the institutional Church's own fault, as the severe and rigid way in which moral teaching was often presented in the past laid the cultural seeds for today's unsympathetic harvest, though nowadays it tends to be forgotten that such moral authoritarianism was shared by many people besides bishops.

Moral Decision Making and the Concept of Conscience

While offering guidance, the Church or its individual ministers cannot dispense people from personal moral decision making nor relieve people from dealing in conscience with a moral issue. This, of course, is not to deny that seeking pastoral advice in the context of a person's concrete circumstances should or may be helpful in coming to an ethical decision. Ultimately, however, moral responsibility must be allowed to rest where it belongs – with the individual.

Central to how the individual Catholic struggles with moral responsibility and decision making is the concept of conscience. Conscience is the consequence of accepting the responsibility of human freedom. As opposed to a life of uncritical conformity to an external imposed moral code, conscience arises from 'the appropriation of one's existence, the ready acceptance that life has been chosen and that what has to be chosen above all is responsibility for one's self ...'.[3] Fundamentally, conscience is the name given to that in us which responds to the moral – it is an aspect of our consciousness, the one which is aware of the distinction between good and evil and which urges us to do good and avoid evil. A person's conscience is formed by education, beginning as a child at home and then in formal schooling, by the inheritance of values and principles which comprise the moral 'code' of the community of which he or she is a part, and by various influences (media, religion, etc.).

As a theological term, conscience is sometimes distinguished at three different levels:

- a generalised awareness of the difference between right and wrong;
- a grasp in general terms of various individual moral values (e.g. justice);
- where the moral value is translated into particulars, in other words, what we ought to do in a particular situation.[4]

At this third level, conscience is a personal act of judgement about a particular action that has been done or, more usually, an action that one is thinking about doing. A person may be conscious of not having acted in the past in a particular way that he or she should have, or may be uncertain of the moral probity of the action. Often, however, conscience is used to refer to present or future decisions relating to moral issues that confront the person.

In this context, conscience is a reasoned judgement about what one should or should not do in a particular set of circumstances. It is the diligent application of what one knows to the moral appraisal of a particular act, in the light of one's personal values and religious beliefs, the convictions one has about what is right and wrong, and the experience one has gained in life about what is usually the outcome in similar situations. The judgement of conscience, therefore, is certainly not the simple freedom to do just what I like or want. Of course, the word 'conscience' can be misused as an alibi for a defiant, obstinate inability to correct myself and an unwillingness to listen to anyone else. However, in fact, conscience engages the person in an authentic search to find the right answer, to ensure that the judgement one arrives at is, as far as possible, in accord with the objective truth. Vatican II summed this up when it said: 'The more a correct conscience holds sway, the more persons and groups turn aside from blind choices and strive to be guided by objective norms of morality.'[5]

Hence, conscience is not just 'doing what I feel is right'. Conscience is not mere subjective instinct and the consequent absence of doubts, yet neither is it simply an intellectual endeavour. It does draw on the emotional and intuitive aspects of the personality in judging what is right in a given situation. Therefore, conscience is rightly connected with the emotions, especially with the feeling of guilt when our conscience accuses us of something, but also sometimes with peacefulness, which is associated with the freedom of a clear conscience. While conscience is not to be simply equated or confused with feelings, the emotions are indeed important in the moral life. Our conscientious judgements are never purely intellectual. For instance, guilt is good and proper, provided there is real fault and the guilt is proportionate to the gravity of the fault. On the other hand, disproportionate guilt is unhealthy, because it involves feelings of guilt which do not correlate with the seriousness of the fault, if indeed there was any moral fault at all. Our upbringing and moral education has significant influence on how our emotions and conscience relate, and we should be aware that this varies among people.[6] While acknowledging that there are always emotional elements involved, simply feeling guilty or content about some personal act is not the same thing as the judgement of a mature conscience. It is important to remember this in what appears to be an increasingly emotive culture.

Experience also teaches us that conscience can be frail and fallible. All sorts of factors can lead to a mistaken conscience: a deficient moral sense, false ideas, prejudices, social pressures, negligence, etc. Using traditional language, conscience is said to be correct when it accords with the objective truth; otherwise, it is called erroneous.

So far, one might be forgiven for thinking that God does not seem to figure much in the topic of conscience. However, the Catholic understanding of conscience also sees it as humanity's most secret core and sanctuary, where the person is alone with God. The Second Vatican Council observed that in the depths of his or her conscience a person detects a law which the individual does not impose on himself or herself, but which nonetheless holds the person to obedience, and this voice of conscience summons the person to love good and to avoid evil – this is all because in the heart of humanity there is a law written by God.[7] This thinking reflects the teaching of St Paul's Letter to the Romans:

> When Gentiles who have not the law do by nature what the law requires, they are a law unto themselves, even though they do not have the law. They show that what the law requires is written on their hearts, while their conscience also bears witness and their conflicting thoughts accuse or perhaps excuse them. (Rom 2:14-15)

Our conscientious choices are not simply judgements to do or not to do certain things; through our actions we are also deciding what kind of people we wish to be – just or unjust, faithful or unfaithful, truthful or untruthful, committed or uncommitted, etc. We are deciding to accept or reject God's love and God's claims on us. In short, we are responding, positively or negatively, to God.

The Primacy of Conscience

Once the final judgement of conscience has been made, it then becomes a command, addressing its dictate to the whole person and obliging the person to act according to it. The principle of the primacy of conscience arises from the premise that one must be true to one's deepest thought-out convictions. This principle means that one must follow the sure judgement of conscience, even when, through no fault of one's own, it is objectively in error. The primacy of conscience as the subjective norm of morality is an age old principle in the Church, as illustrated in the thought of St Thomas Aquinas (c. 1227–1274) who taught that even an erroneous conscience must be followed, provided it is certain of itself. Not following a *bona fide* (L. 'good faith') informed conscience would involve not being true to oneself. Historically, the primacy of conscience has been obscured in practice by authoritarianism in the Church, but the principle as such has never been denied.[8]

The primacy of conscience, while respecting the individual's personal integrity and freedom, does not amount to subjectivism, or mean liberation from the demands of truth. While conscience is the ultimate *subjective* measure of the goodness or evil of what we do, it does not decide on the *objective* correctness of what we do. Conscience does not decide moral principles or norms: '... one's conscience is relevant for deciding *what to do*; *it governs acts*, not principles'.[9] In other words, if I follow my conscience I am not immune from doing wrong.

As has been mentioned above, one is bound to follow even an erroneous conscience. It is wrong to act against one's beliefs and convictions, but it can be wrong to have arrived at these beliefs and convictions in the first place by not taking the time or trouble to find out what is good and true, or by having neglected or blanked out the memory of innate truths placed deep in our being by God our Creator. In this case the person is not without fault. The fault lies not in the present act, not in the present judgement of conscience, but in closing oneself, probably over a period of time, against the promptings of truth deep within one's heart:

> We must do what we sincerely believe to be right but how we came to that sincere belief may be questionable. Sincerity is a serious, ongoing task.[10]

For this reason, Vatican II speaks of the possibility of a person's conscience gradually becoming blind from being accustomed to sin.[11] On the other hand, a person may not be blameworthy because error of conscience can also be the result of what is traditionally called invincible ignorance, an ignorance of which the individual person is unaware, and which the person is unable to overcome by himself or herself.

In short, as the present Pope (previously as Cardinal Ratzinger) has stated: '… the vulnerability of conscience, the possibility of its being abused, cannot destroy its greatness.'[12]

The Church and Moral Decision Making

In Catholic doctrine the Word of God is given to the entire Christian community by the power of the Holy Spirit. This basic conviction is prior to the doctrine of an apostolic ministry which has the responsibility of safeguarding the authentic proclamation of God's Word, and for formulating teaching. The Church's teaching office (the Pope and the bishops, the Magisterium) has its authority by virtue of inheriting the apostolic mandate to teach in the name of Jesus Christ. The Magisterium does not and cannot make behaviour as such moral or immoral, but rather can only teach what it believes to be already moral or immoral. This is not simply a question of reflecting the consensus of the views of Catholics today, but also of being faithful to Scripture and Tradition, to God's message and a Church that extends across the centuries. The teaching role of the Pope and bishops is not to impose highhandedly from without but to be the advocate of the Christian memory, to illuminate, elucidate and defend it.[13]

There is a popular assumption that the Church's moral teachings can or should only be accepted to the extent that one agrees with the reasons advanced to uphold these teachings – in other words, the teaching is only binding insofar as its supporting reasoning convinces the listener. This means that the Church's view is regarded as one opinion among others, perhaps highly regarded, but only to be accepted if its accompanying argumentation convinces the individual. To complicate matters, the arguments are sometimes not seriously studied, or half-understood, or reduced to simplistic legalistic rules. Christian morality is not fundamentally about norms, though it cannot function without them. The popular assumption conflicts with the Catholic understanding that Magisterial teaching carries more authority than just its supporting arguments, because of the Catholic conviction that the Holy Spirit guides the Church. The

Catholic trust is that the Spirit will not lead the Church into error, and that the bishops appointed to lead the Church can discern the Spirit, and, when faithfully following the Spirit, will not lead believers seriously astray.[14] In other words, according to Catholic thinking, in moral decision making and forming one's conscience, one ought to give Magisterial teaching a strong preference over alternative view points, and the Catholic presumption is always in favour of the teaching's correctness. Such a strong presumption is of course in tension or in even direct conflict with our society's growing disillusionment with established authority structures, civil and ecclesial, which is accompanied by a corresponding fallback on an over-stated moral autonomy reluctant to accept that Catholic teaching may have some compelling insights, especially if these are at odds with the biases and blind-spots of our western culture.

Hence, for the Catholic, consideration of an issue is not supposed to be confined to the arguments proposed in favour of a particular teaching, but rather also to take account of the belief that the Church is more than just another opinion-former in the marketplace of ideas. Church teaching is not, of course, totally independent of its supporting arguments, because these help make it possible for a Catholic to understand and make the teaching his or her own. Receiving a Church moral teaching with openness and sincerity, giving it serious attention and trying to appropriate it personally through study and prayer are what is expected of a committed Catholic, in informing his or her conscience. In making moral decisions in conscience, the Church's teachings are a caution against the rationalisation of one's own prejudices and feelings, especially in a 'convenience' culture which exalts self-affirmation and self-fulfilment, and which often regards commitment as an unattainable ideal. On the other hand, it must be acknowledged that after much serious effort, a sincere committed person may nonetheless still find it difficult or impossible to accept a particular teaching, and that must be profoundly respected. The interplay between conscience and authority, sometimes leading to tension, will always be present in the Catholic Christian community. In the final analysis, the Church's moral authority consists of an appeal to the consciences of people to accept that what it says is true, so conscience always remains the definitive focus of moral decision making and the sure judgements of conscience must be followed.

Conclusion

In moral decision making, conscience is the final arbiter, in the sense that the ultimate responsibility for choosing what to do rests with the individual person and the person must do what he or she thinks is right and good. The Catholic view of conscience holds in tension the dignity and freedom of the human person, the teaching authority of the Church and the search for moral truth.

Notes

1   See the interesting commentary on this question by L. Hogan, *Confronting the Truth: Conscience in the Catholic Tradition*, London: Darton, Longman and Todd, 2001, pp. 18–20.

2   See B. Hoose, 'Notes on Moral Theology: Authority in the Church' in *Theological Studies*, 63 (2002), pp. 107–109.

3   V. McNamara, *The Truth in Love: Reflections on Christian Morality*, Dublin: Gill and Macmillan, 1988, p. 157.

4   See R.M. Gula, *Reason Informed by Faith: Foundations of Catholic Morality*, New York: Paulist Press, 1989, pp. 130–135.

5   Vatican II, Pastoral Constitution on the Church in the Modern World, GS 16. In a similar vein, Pope John Paul II stated more strongly: '... the maturity and responsibility of these judgements ... of the individual ... are not measured by the liberation of conscience from objective truth, in favour of an alleged autonomy in personal decisions, but, on the contrary, by an insistent search for truth and by allowing oneself to be guided by that truth in one's actions.' John Paul II, *VS*, Encyclical Letter on Certain Fundamental Questions of the Church's Moral Teaching, Dublin: Veritas, 1993, no. 61.

6   We cannot deal here with the difference between conscience and the psychological phenomenon of the super-ego, the term given, after Freud, to the mechanism for regulating behaviour acquired by the child under direction of the parent; there is some vestige of this in everyone. See J.W. Glaser, 'Conscience and Superego: A Key Distinction' in C. Ellis Nelson (ed.) *Conscience: Theological and Psychological Perspectives*, New York: Newman Press, 1978, pp. 167–188.

7   See Vatican II, GS, Pastoral Constitution on the Church in the Modern World, no. 16.

8   See G.V. Lobo, *Christian Living according to Vatican II*, Bangalore: Theological Publications, 1980, p. 336.

9   Irish Catholic Bishops' Conference, *Notification on Recent Developments in Moral Theology and their Implications for the Church and Society*, no. 10(e), July 2004, available

at www.catholiccommunications.ie/PastLet/moraltheologyjuly2004.pdf. Accessed 5 February 2007.

10   Irish Catholic Bishops' Conference, Pastoral Letter, *Conscience*, Dublin: Veritas, 1998, p. 11.

11   See Vatican II, GS, Pastoral Constitution on the Church in the Modern World, no. 16.

12   J. Ratzinger, 'Conscience in its Age' in J. Ratzinger, *Church, Ecumenism and Politics: New Essays in Ecclesiology*, Slough: St Paul Publications, 1988, p. 169.

13   See J. Ratzinger, Address to the American Catholic Bishops, 'Conscience and Truth', no. 3A, Dallas, February 1991, accessible at www.ewtn.com/library/curia/ratzcons.htm. Accessed 5 February 2007.

14   The precise extent and limits of the Magisterium's authority in moral teaching is much debated among the theologians and cannot detain us here. See, for instance, Hoose, op. cit., pp. 109–115.

Further Reading

Bretzke, J.T., *A Morally Complex World: Engaging Contemporary Moral Theology*, Collegeville, Minn.: The Liturgical Press, 2004.

Harrington, Donal, *What is Morality?*, Dublin: Columba, 1996.

McNamara, Vincent, *The Truth in Love: Reflections on Christian Morality*, Dublin: Gill and Macmillan, 1998.

CHAPTER 16

AN INTRODUCTION TO CATHOLIC SOCIAL TEACHING

Donal Dorr

Introduction

God did not create us to exist as isolated individuals. Each of us is born into a family and we grow up in local communities, which in turn are located within nations and these nations form part of the global society. Furthermore, we humans are an integral part of the animal world; like the other animals we depend utterly on the plants, which in turn are in dynamic interaction with the minerals in the soil, the sunshine and the rain. In fact, we are made up of the same atoms and molecules as the animals, the plants and the inanimate world – and our whole world is such an integrated interdependent system that it has been called 'Spaceship Earth'.

In the broadest sense the term 'Catholic Social Teaching' would refer to all aspects of our relationships with others – with family, friends, communities, the wider human society, the animal and plant world and with the inanimate world. Traditionally, however, the phrase has usually been understood in a more restricted sense, namely, as referring to the relationships between people in the *public* sphere. In this sense it covers issues about how society is organised at economic, social and political levels. Within the past generation we have come to realise that we need also to include – and to emphasise – the ecological level, because global warming and other environmental problems are now threatening the balance of life on earth.

In this chapter I shall be looking at Catholic teaching on political, economic and environmental questions; this will also include taking account of gender and cultural issues. But it is important to note that all this needs to be balanced by looking at the Christian understanding of interpersonal relationships – for instance, family relationships, sexuality, friendship and small-group relationships, as well as issues about *in vitro*

EXPLORING THEOLOGY

fertilisation, genetic modification and when it is lawful to allow a person to die. These are topics which I am not treating here because they do not come under the heading 'Catholic Social Teaching' in its usual sense.

Principles and Developing Guidelines

As Christians we believe that church authorities are assisted by the Holy Spirit in formulating official Catholic social teaching. This teaching is based largely on reflection by discerning Christians and theologians, together with formal and informal ecumenical and inter-faith dialogue and taking account of developments in the wider human community. The more obvious sources of social teaching are Scripture and the past tradition of the Church. It must, however, be added that the inspiration of the Spirit may come also through more secular sources. For instance, much of the Church's recent thinking and teaching on democracy, human rights, ecology and the role of women was first worked out by people who were not Catholics, and perhaps not even Christians.

Catholic social teaching is not a set of detailed and unchanging rules which have come down from on high. It is rather a set of principles and guidelines which have emerged over the centuries as Christians tried to work out in practice how best to put into practice the virtues of love, justice and solidarity. Catholic social teaching is not a monolithic system. It allows for some degree of variation to take account of cultural diversity; this aspect will have to become more evident in future as the Church's centre of gravity moves southwards, away from the western world.

The Church's guidelines on social justice have changed and developed over the years. This is partly because of changing circumstances, for instance, advances in technology and communications. It is also partly because we have learned by experience that some approaches work better than others; the history of eastern Europe in much of the last century has shown the problems which arise when the state tries to exercise centralised control over all aspects of economic activity.

The Church's social teaching will continue to develop in the future as new issues come to the fore; for instance, there is room for further development as regards how best to deal with globalisation and with ecological issues. However, the more fundamental elements will remain the same – especially the central virtues of solidarity and respect. Other key words and phrases which are prominent in Catholic social teaching are: fundamental human rights, structural justice, subsidiarity, participation, partnership, sustainability, option for the poor, reconciliation and peace. The sense in which these are understood should become clearer as we go through a series of different items which cover the main areas of Catholic social teaching. Some of these items are fundamental principles while others are more in the nature of practical guidelines where there is room for some change or development.

A basic source for Church teaching on all these issues is the *Compendium of the Social Doctrine of the Church*. In what follows I shall give some references from this book under each heading. (Note that all the references are to paragraph numbers.) Many further references can be found in the very comprehensive index of the *Compendium*.

1.   Solidarity (n. 192–6)

At the heart of Catholic social thought and action lies the notion of *solidarity*. Its meaning was well spelled out by Pope John Paul II in the 1987 encyclical, 'On Social Concern'. The pope sees solidarity as a virtue which calls us to react responsibly and morally to the fact that we are interdependent. It involves overcoming our distrust of others and committing ourselves to cooperating with them and to working for the common good of all. The virtue of solidarity goes further than justice or fairness; it causes those who are powerful or wealthy to feel responsible for those who are weak or poor and makes them ready to share what they have with them. This virtue of solidarity applies not only to individuals in their interpersonal relationships but also to whole classes of people and to countries in their relationships with other countries, since they too are linked in an interdependent system. In his account of solidarity the pope insists that the powerful must not try to dominate those who are weaker; there must be deep respect for the value systems of the different cultures.

2.   Dignity and Rights (n. 81; 152–7)

The dignity of each human person must be respected. This is shown in practice by respecting his or her fundamental human rights. The Catholic approach to human rights does not start from just listing a whole series of rights which are somehow to be seen as self-justifying. Instead we see fundamental rights as deriving from human dignity. The test for whether a person's dignity is being respected is whether his or her rights are respected. We do not claim to have worked out an exhaustive list of human rights, but many of them are well known. These include the right to life, to security, to work, to a family income, to the ownership of property, to an education; the right to freedom of conscience; the right to have one's culture respected; the right not to be discriminated against on the basis of gender, race, wealth, or social status; prejudices such as racism, homophobia and sexism must be challenged.

One of the most important of all human rights is the right of people to *participate* in the making of all decisions which affect one's life and the life of the community (n. 189 – 91). If people have the right to share in making the decisions that affect their lives, then they are in a position to ensure that their other basic rights will be respected and that true justice and peace will prevail.

3. Ownership of Property (n. 171–81)

Humans are the stewards of the goods of the earth and have a duty to respect them and use them for the benefit of all. In some tribal societies the ownership of land and other immovable goods is held in common. But in the western and westernised world the right to own private property, including land, is a practical necessity; experience has shown that in our cultures it is the only effective way in which the dignity of the person can be safeguarded. However, the right to private property is not an absolute value; it takes second place to the right of all people to benefit from the goods of the earth. This means that civil authorities have the right and duty to put restrictions and conditions on the ownership and use of private property in order to protect and promote the common good.

4. Development and Respect for the Environment (n. 446; 451–86)

All people and all peoples have a fundamental right to integral human development. The style of development fostered by governments and international agencies must be one that is sustainable and ecologically sensitive and viable – one that enables humans to live in partnership with nature. For instance, it should be one that minimises pollution, uses renewable energy sources and limits fishing catches to ensure that stocks are not exhausted. All this is summed up nowadays by saying that we must respect the integrity of creation. As of now there is no firm Catholic teaching on the controversial issue of genetic modification and the use of what is called a 'terminator gene'. However, there is a weight of evidence to show that, in actual practice, these are being used more to serve the interests of four major transnational corporations than to benefit the poor.

5. *The Common Good (n. 61; 385)*

Society is not just a collection of isolated individuals; it is rather a community composed of diverse elements where all are called to be in solidarity with each other and to cooperate together for the common good. The primary community is the whole human race rather than individual nations.

The idea of 'the common good' plays a central role in Catholic social teaching. It is by no means the same as 'the greatest benefits for the greatest number of people', since that might suggest that one would be entitled to deprive a small minority of fundamental rights in order to benefit a large majority. Working for 'the common good' involves respecting the dignity and rights of each person while fostering the welfare of the community as a whole. The common good of all people cannot be attained when the government of any individual country single-mindedly pursues the national interest of that country without taking due account of the welfare of the people of other countries. So the common welfare is to be promoted by cooperation under the auspices of international agencies such as those of the United Nations family.

Within countries, society should be organised in a way that allows for dialogue between its different sectors and does not foster polarisation between different social classes or other groupings. Furthermore, the model of development chosen must be one which lessens rather than widens the gap between those who are privileged and those who are under-privileged in the economic, social, sexual, political and cultural spheres. The Church recognises that this can take place under any one of a variety of socio-political and economic systems, no one of which is proposed by the Church as 'the right way'. The Church does, however, hold that the values and principles of Catholic social teaching provide useful criteria for evaluating the various possible systems.

6. *Subsidiarity (n. 185–8)*

The authorities in society have a sacred duty to promote the common good. The common good of society requires that all agencies – political, social and economic – respect the principle of subsidiarity. This principle of subsidiarity is one of the most important elements in Catholic social teaching and it is one that has been accepted in principle by the European Union. It means that responsibility is to be exercised as far as possible at a lower level rather than a higher level. This indicates that the state should not try to control matters which are more appropriately left to regional authorities or local councils, or to professional bodies. Similarly, the EU Commission should not try to control matters which are more appropriately left to national governments.

The principle of subsidiarity involves putting significant limits to the power of state authorities. It means that some of the authority exercised in the past by the state must now be passed *downward* to regional or local authorities; but it also means that there are situations where it is more appropriate that some of that authority should be passed *upward* to international agencies. One might think here of EU fisheries policies. There is no general rule or guideline that can automatically tell us what the appropriate level is for decision making about a particular item. That has to be decided on the basis of the particular circumstances and of previous experience. The common good normally requires that the decision-making bodies at every level be monitored at a higher level to eliminate or minimise abuses. If the principle of subsidiarity is applied also in economic matters it leads to the 'small is beautiful' approach, which involves using local food and materials as far as possible.

There is a particular issue in regard to the extent to which the state should be involved in *economic* affairs. Up to the time of Pope John XXIII's ground-breaking social encyclical *Mater et Magistra* in 1961, church authorities were inclined to assume that, in general, the less the state intervened in economic affairs the better; although they did insist that the state has to intervene in some situations in order to protect the poor. Pope John's encyclical took a more favourable view of a 'welfare state' approach. Nevertheless, the Church still favours a 'free enterprise' economy; however, it is also very aware of the abuses that arise in a system of unbridled global capitalism (n. 335).

7.   Work (n. 101; 255–322)

It is mainly through our work that we humans exercise our role as stewards of creation, protecting and ennobling nature and ensuring that the goods of the earth are fairly distributed. The dignity of the human person is very closely related to the character of the person as a worker. Work should be of a kind that enables people to find personal fulfilment in it. Though it may at times involve toil, work is basically good and necessary for humans.

In his 1981 encyclical 'On Human Work' (*Laborem exercens*), Pope John Paul II insisted that the fundamental basis for determining the value of work is not the usefulness of the object produced but the fact that the one doing the work is a human person. This implies that work must not be treated as just a commodity, to be sold and bought in accordance with 'the law of supply and demand'. The human person has a fundamental right to work – work which is not to be mere drudgery but creative, fulfilling work. Furthermore, workers are entitled to share in any decision making that will affect them; it is also appropriate that workers should share in the profits that are the result of their labour.

Workers have a right to form trade unions to help them defend their rights, such as just wages or safe and humane working conditions, and also to negotiate about the general economic policies and structures of society. The strike weapon may be used as a last resort in struggling for justice and for the rights of workers, but it should not be used as an instrument of 'party politics'.

8. The Family (n. 209–214; 248–254)

Each family is entitled to an income sufficient to meet its basic needs and to provide a degree of security for its future. It may be necessary for the state or local authorities to provide 'family support' where the family income is otherwise insufficient. Family income should be adequate to ensure that it is not necessary for *both* parents of young families to leave the home each day to go out to work. There should be practical financial recognition that caring lovingly for children in the home is real and valuable work. Those who take on this task – usually women – should not be penalised economically for doing so.

9. Women (n. 111; 295)

There is a fundamental equality of dignity between women and men. It is immoral to discriminate against women on the basis of gender. However, the different qualities of women and men means that some roles in society are generally more appropriate for women and others for men.

Women should not be forced to fit into an economic system which was developed in a way that catered mainly for the needs of men. Therefore, various professions should be re-organised in a way that does not put women at a disadvantage, especially those women who choose to devote time to child bearing and caring for young families.

10. *Structural Justice and Preference for the Poor* (n. 201; 333)

Structural injustice arises when one nation, race, class, gender, group or individual has undue and unchecked power and is therefore in a position to take advantage over others. Examples of structural injustice are international trading agreements which are biased against primary-producing countries (e.g. countries dependent on the export of tea, cocoa or sugarcane). Governments and international agencies have a grave duty to promote structural justice, correcting such imbalances. Note that even those who act justly in their inter-personal relationships may well be operating political or economic mechanisms that are structurally unjust – or benefiting from them.

Civil authorities and all who hold power in society must show particular concern for the poor, for racial or cultural minorities, for migrants, for asylum-seekers and political or economic refugees, for those who are physically or mentally disabled, for people who are old or infirm, for those of a minority sexual orientation and for any other groups or individuals who find themselves on the margins of society or vulnerable to exploitation. It is vital that ordinary citizens watch out for injustices and put pressure on the civil authorities to respond firmly to abuses – particularly new or expanding areas of exploitation, such as the drugs trade and the trafficking of women and children for commercial sex.

Within the past generation we Christians have come to recognise the call of the Church at every level to make a 'preferential but not exclusive option for the poor' (n. 182; 449). We are called, through our work and our lifestyle, to model for civil society ways of promoting structural justice by giving a privileged place to those who have been disadvantaged or oppressed. Needless to say, the Church itself in all its institutions and procedures must give witness to its commitment to justice.

11. *Civil Authorities* (n. 393–416)

The Church favours a genuinely democratic system of government in society. Church teaching understands human authority to be derived ultimately from

God. However, it also recognises that the secular political world has a certain autonomy. This means that governments derive their power directly from the citizens and that it is lawful to seek to change the government.

Citizens have a duty to obey the civil authorities except where the demands are clearly unjust or immoral. Legitimate authorities are entitled to impose penalties for breaches of just laws. However, imprisonment or other punishment must respect the dignity of the person; harsh and degrading penalties are not acceptable and torture can never be justified. In recent years the highest Church authorities have taken a firm stand against capital punishment.

Nowadays, even governments have a duty to respect higher authorities – they are obliged to cooperate with international agencies and to make them more effective and more just.

12. Resistance (n. 400–1)

Oppressed groups and all citizens have a right and a duty to work by lawful means for the replacement of any government which notably and consistently fails to respect fundamental human rights. Violent resistance to an existing government is almost invariably unjustified. The Church does not exclude in principle the possibility of a justified war of liberation. However, it teaches that in practice such violence would almost certainly do more harm than good; normally, therefore, other forms of resistance must be used instead.

13. Peace and War (n. 488–515)

Peace is not the mere absence of war; it requires the establishment of an order based on justice and love. According to Catholic social teaching, the development of international institutions and the nature of modern warfare make it highly unlikely that a war between states could be justified. However, one cannot in principle exclude the possibility, as a last resort, of a justified recourse to armed resistance against unjust aggression or against sustained oppressive tyranny.

The use of weapons of indiscriminate mass destruction cannot be justified; and to rely indefinitely on such weapons as a deterrent is also unjustified. There is a lack of full agreement among theologians and church authorities as to the morality of holding such weapons as a deterrent on a purely interim basis. At present, the balance is tipping against the holding of such a deterrent. The Church teaches that state authorities should respect the consciences of individuals who conscientiously renounce the use of violence and refuse to bear arms.

14. *Peacemaking and Reconciliation (n. 516–20)*

Catholic social teaching gives a high priority to peacemaking and it emphasises the importance of working for reconciliation and for the healing of long-standing grievances. It strongly favours the development of international institutions, including those which are directly related to peacemaking, mediation and peacekeeping, as well as those concerned with the protection of human rights and those which foster peace in the long-term by promoting closer economic and political cooperation between nations.

Conclusion

The overall purpose of the Church's social teaching is not to provide a book of rules. It is rather to offer Christians and members of the wider human community some guidelines on how to live out, in our daily lives, our love for God, for our neighbours near and far and for the beautiful and fruitful world in which we live.

Further Reading

Pontifical Council for Justice and Peace, *Compendium of the Social Doctrine of the Church*, London and New York: Burns & Oates, 2005.

Dorr, Donal, *Spirituality and Justice*, Dublin/Maryknoll: Gill and Macmillan/Orbis Books, 1984.

Galilea, Segundo, *The Beatitudes: To Evangelize as Jesus Did*, Maryknoll: Orbis Books, 1984.

McDonagh, Sean, *Passion for the Earth: The Christian Vocation to Promote Justice, Peace and the Integrity of Creation*, Maryknoll: Orbis Books, 1995.

O'Brien, David J. and Shannon, Thomas, *Catholic Social Thought: The Documentary Heritage*, Maryknoll: Orbis Books, 1992.

CHAPTER 17

CATHOLIC THEOLOGY OF CREATION
Sean McDonagh

Introduction

> In the beginning when God created the heavens and the
> earth …

The first line of the Bible tells us that the world was created by a loving, personal God. The world is good in itself; God contemplates what he has done and found that 'it was good' (Gen 1:10, 13, 18, 21, 26). This statement is very important. Israel grew up cheek by jowl with cultures which maintained that the spirit world was created by a god or a good spirit and that matter came from an evil spirit. The Genesis story rejects this radical dualism.

The creation account in Genesis 1:1-2:4a comes from a liturgical source. The text has a ritual cadence and structure, finely tuned by decades of use in the temple worship. Even in translation one can sense the majesty and rhythm, 'God said, "let there be light" … God said, "Let there be a dome in the midst of the waters"', building up to a climax in Gen 2:3, 'God blessed the seventh day and hallowed it, because on it God rested from all the work that he had done in creation'.

In reading the text or, better still, listening to it being read aloud, it is obvious that the author did not set out to give a scientific account of creation in either an ancient or modern sense. While it builds on the cosmology of the day, it was written to answer the more basic questions – who created the world and why? The answers were clear and emphatic. God created the world and sustains it by his power. There is nothing hidden from God's domain. God's creative outpouring reaches its zenith in the creation of man and woman.

Let us make humankind in our own image, according to our likeness; and let them have dominion over the fish of the sea, and over the birds of the air, and over the cattle, and over all the wild animals of the earth, and over every creeping thing that creeps upon the earth ... God blessed them, and God said to them, 'Be fruitful and multiply, and fill the earth and subdue it.' (Gen 1:26-28)

The repercussions of this command, 'to fill the earth and subdue it', have had a profound impact on the way Jews and Christians have related to the natural world. The New Revised Standard Version of the bible uses the phrase 'subdue it', while other translations use the phrase 'have dominion over it'. Given that this initially appears to be a controlling stance towards nature, some people, such as the American historian Lynn White, maintain that our modern ecological problems stem from 'the orthodox Christian arrogance towards nature'. However, we must ask ourselves, does the Genesis text support such human arrogance towards nature? In response we can say that the injunction makes sense in the light of the urge within many Middle Eastern cultures to control the chaos and subdue the wilderness. Nevertheless, many modern biblical scholars insist that the Divine command cannot be interpreted as a licence for humans to change and transform the natural world according to any human whim or fancy. The order is, in fact, a challenge to human beings to imitate God's loving kindness and faithfulness and act as his viceroy in relationship with the non-human component of the earth.

This would appear to be the original meaning of the Hebrew word *radah* (subjugate) used in the Genesis text. Like viceroys of the king, men and women were expected to be just, honest and render real service. They were forbidden from exploiting the people or the earth.

Furthermore, exegetes today remind us that the first account of creation does not end at Gen 1:31 with the creation of humans. It ends rather in Gen 2:3 with the Sabbath rest of God. The Sabbath was a very important institution for the people of Israel both for the well-being of humans and other creatures.

The second account of creation (Gen 2:4-3:24) is a much older account than the first account. In this story, the author sets out to situate the history of God's saving activity on behalf of Israel within the broader parameters of human and cosmic history. For the author, the same God who brought Israel out of Egypt and bestowed on her the land of Israel was the One who had created the world and all human cultures. In this creation story the author deals with themes which were common among cultures of the Near East. These included the creation of the world, an initial state of paradise, the origins of tribes, institutions such as marriage and universal questions like the origin and meaning of suffering, evil and death. Given Israel's unique experience of Yahweh, the reality of evil demanded a special answer. Israel knew from experience that Yahweh is full of loving kindness and compassion and that he had rescued them from oppression in Egypt. Yet evil was an ever-present reality in the world around them and even in their personal and collective lives. The question arose: how can one explain the emergence of evil if God is good? It could not originate from a rival spirit co-equal with God; therefore, it had to have come from some primordial disobedience by humans themselves.

In comparing the two accounts of creation, the first thing that strikes one is that the second account is more rooted in the earth. Humans are created from actual earth; God formed man from dust from the ground and breathed into his nostrils the breath of life, and man became a living being. Humans come alive because Yahweh breathes a living spirit into them. Yahweh's involvement with humans does not end with creating and setting them loose to do as they please. Immediately, 'the Lord God planted a garden in Eden, in the east and there he put the man whom he had formed' (Gen 2:8). The text tells us that God 'took the man and put him in the garden of Eden to till it and keep it' (Gen 2:15). And the Lord God commanded the man, saying, 'you may freely eat of every tree of the garden; but of the tree of the knowledge of good and evil you shall not eat, for in the day that you eat of it you shall die.' Human activity was circumscribed by God's command to 'till and keep'. The Hebrew words used here are *abad* and *shamar*. *Abad* means 'work' or 'till', but it also has overtones of service, while *shamar* means 'keep', with overtones of preserving and defending from harm. This account cautions about the limits of the earth, with the command not to eat the fruit of the tree of knowledge of good and evil.

The third chapter of Genesis goes on to recount how Adam and Eve transgressed God's command and ate of the fruit of the tree. In their pride and arrogance they wished to take complete control of their own destiny and be 'like God, knowing good and evil' (Gen 3:5). These fantasies were quickly dashed. Their act of disobedience severed their intimate friendship with God (Gen 3:8) and transformed their human situation. Pain, suffering and death entered into the human condition (Gen 3:16, 19b). Moreover, the Fall also ruptured their relationship with nature. It was no longer the bountiful and fruitful garden (Gen 2:9), but it became antagonistic and inhospitable: 'cursed is the ground because of you; in toil you shall eat of it all the days of your life; thorns and thistles it shall bring forth for you' (Gen 3:17b-19).

Noah

The Noah story (Gen 6:11–9:17) has a profound message for the modern world where so many creatures are facing extinction because of human activity.[1] God commanded Noah to conserve nature. In the wake of the flood Yahweh renews the command of Gen 1:28. This time the covenant is entered into not merely with humans but with all creation (Gen 9:8-17). God spoke to Noah and to his sons: 'As for me, I am establishing my covenant with you and your descendants after you, and with every living creature that is with you, the birds, the domestic animals, and every animal of the earth with you, as many as came out of the ark …' God said, 'This is the sign of the covenant that I make between me and you and every living creature that is with you, for all future generations: I have set my bow in the clouds, and it shall be a sign of the covenant between me and the earth' (Gen 9:8-14).

Yahweh, the creator, is also the saviour of Israel. Therefore, he is not a remote God uninvolved in the world. Yahweh is a caring God who practices good husbandry and looks after all his creatures by 'giving them their food in due season' (Ps 104:27). It recalls that, 'You visit the earth and water it, you greatly enrich it; the river of God is full of water; you provide the people with grain' (Ps 65:9). He is also a God who is faithful both to the human community as well as all creation (Gen 8:22; 9:9-13).

The Covenant Tradition

The community of Israel was not born out of the fact that they shared a common language or a common cultural experience. Rather, Yahweh chose as his people a group of oppressed slaves; he liberated them and invited them into a covenant relationship (Ex 19:3-9; 24:3-8). For this reason, the covenant and its renewal played a dominant role in the history of Israel down through the ages. At crucial moments in its history, such as when it entered the land of Israel, the community renewed the covenant (Jos 24:1-28). Prophets like Amos, Hosea, Isaiah, Jeremiah and Ezekiel reminded the people when they had been unfaithful to the covenant and challenged them to return to its spirit (Jer 31:31; Ezek 36:26-32).

The Covenant Law or Torah covered not just religious observances and moral behaviour but every aspect of life (Ex 20:1-17). Much of the Torah deals with Israel's relationship with God, with fellow Israelites and with outsiders. Nonetheless the demand for stewardship and respect for animals is not omitted. In the Book of Exodus, respect for Yahweh's sovereignty, care for the earth, concern for the poor, sensitivity to the needs of both wild and farm animals, all come together.

> For six years you shall sow your land and gather in its yield; but the seventh year you shall let it rest and lie fallow, so that the poor of your people may eat; and what they leave the wild animals may eat. (Ex 23:10-12)

Respect for birds and domestic as well as wild animals was also enjoined in the Law. 'You shall not muzzle an ox while it is treading out the grain' (Deut 25:4). This thoughtful and respectful attitude is extended further to include all wildlife:

> If you come on a bird's nest, in any tree or on the ground, with fledglings or eggs, with the mother sitting on the fledglings or on the eggs, you shall not take the mother with the young. Let the mother go, taking only the young for yourself in order that it may go well with you and you may live long. (Deut 22:6-7)

Despite what I have written above, some commentators stress that the Jewish tradition gives more prominence to human-divine and inter-human relationships. There is no denying that these insights emerged at a time when the impact of human activity on the natural world was nowhere as noticeable or destructive as it is today. Nonetheless, it is worth remembering that the Jewish tradition was flexible and adaptable. Covenants in Israel and elsewhere in the ancient Middle East were sealed by ritual activity. In Exodus the covenant between Yahweh and his people was sealed through the sacrifice of oxen, the sprinkling of blood and finally a meal (Ex 24:3-8, 9-11).

The same urge to seal the covenant with a meal carries over into the New Testament. Before his sacrifice Jesus breaks bread and shares the cup (Mk 14:17-25; Mt 26:20-29; Lk 22:14-23; 1 Cor 11:23-33). The early Church continued to recall the death and resurrection of Jesus 'by breaking bread' (Acts 2:46). Down through the ages, members of the Christian community have brought to the Eucharist the fruits of the earth transformed by human labour. As with the ancient covenants in Israel, the Eucharist calls to mind the graciousness of God in creating and redeeming his people. In the Eucharist, the Christian community is recreated by recalling the mighty deeds of God. Like the father who in answer to his son's query, 'what does this ritual mean?' (Ex 12:26), recounts the *Haggadah* or story of liberation, the Christian community, in celebrating the Eucharist, recalls the story of God's faithfulness and loving kindness by creating our world and redeeming his people.

Unfortunately, in the present Roman Missal the focus on creation is often hurried and perfunctory. Eucharistic Prayer II is a good example. We glide over the stupendous reality of creation in a single line – 'He is the Word through whom you made the universe'. The Preface of Sundays in Ordinary Time V is more sensitive:

> All things are of your making, all times and seasons obey your laws, but you chose to create men and women in your own image, setting them over the whole world in all its wonder. You made them the stewards of creation, to praise you day by day for the marvels of your wisdom and power through Christ our Lord.

It is obvious that the creation theme offers extraordinary opportunities for Christian communities in different parts of the world to praise God from the depths of their own experience of nature. Each region, or more accurately each bioregion could celebrate a different dimension of creation in their Eucharistic celebrations. People living in mountain regions could incorporate their experience together with all the creatures and plants which live with them into their hymn of praise. Those living near the seashore in tropical regions can incorporate the world of wonder, beauty, symmetry and abundance that is revealed in the coral reefs and the mangrove forests.

In recalling God's graciousness in the context of the life, death and resurrection of the Lord, our gifts are transformed into his body and blood. Christians believe that as members of a community we share the gifts of Christ's body and blood. But this breaking of the bread and pouring out of the cup reminds us of Christ's sacrifice – that his life was poured out for others to bring salvation, wholeness and peace to humanity and the earth.

Prophets

The prophets in Israel were not seers who gazed into a crystal ball to foretell the future. They were people who were called by Yahweh to remind Israel to be faithful to the covenant. The aim of the prophet was to help the people to see the designs and hear the call of God in the present moment. They challenged, cajoled and inspired Israel with hope, when the sky was full of dark clouds and no bright dawn seemed to be spreading from the horizon. The prophets were very much aware that the earth would also punish those who by their extravagant consumption oppress the poor and destroy the earth (Joel 1:4).

> Is not the food cut off before our eyes, joy and gladness from the house of our God? The seed shrivels under the clods, the storehouses are desolate; the granaries are ruined because the grain has failed. How the animals groan! The herds of cattle wander about because there is no pasture for them; even the flocks of sheep are dazed. (Joel 1:16-18)

Prophets challenged the political and religious leadership of their time. For this reason they were often made unwelcome by people who were associated with the institutions of state or religion such as kings or priests. The prophet Amos was seen as a troublemaker (Amos 7:10-14).

Unfortunately, the various institutional watchmen, including religious leaders, have failed to understand the magnitude of the ecological crisis that has been unfolding during the past fifty years. Prophets like Rachel Carson,

E.F. Schumacher, who have warned us, have been ignored. Only in the late 1980s did politicians and religious leaders begin to wake up to what is happening to the planet. Yet, even at this late stage they have little positive guidance to offer beyond vague generalities. How different contemporary leadership is from the concrete options laid out before the people by the prophets in the Bible.

Psalms

During worship Israel celebrated in song its faith in Yahweh and how he related to Israel as a people and to the natural world which he created.

> For the Lord is a great God, and a great King above all gods. In his hand are the depths of the earth; the heights of the mountains are his also. The sea is his, for he made it, and the dry land, which his hands have formed. (Ps 95:3-5)

The praise of God was not confined to humans alone. In Psalm 148 the psalmist invites all of creation, animate and inanimate, human and non-human, to praise God, conscious of the fact that without this vast symphony, fitting praise of God would be incomplete (Ps 148:1, 2-4, 7-12). When creatures are forced over the precipice of extinction, the praise which that particular creature renders to God is silenced for ever and thus the chorus of creation is impoverished.

> Praise the Lord from the heavens … Praise him, Sun and Moon, praise him, all you shining stars! Praise him, you highest heavens, and you waters above the heavens! … Praise the Lord from the earth, you sea-monsters and all deeps, fire and hail, snow and frost, stormy wind fulfilling his command! Mountains and all hills, fruit trees and all cedars, wild animals and all cattle, creeping things and flying birds! (Ps 148:2-4, 7-10)

There is no other place where Yahweh's concern for his creation and knowledge of its intimate working is better expressed than in Psalm 104. The psalmist begins with an image of Yahweh working meticulously, like a careful tent maker, to create the heavens the clouds and the winds:

Bless the Lord, O my soul. O Lord my God, you are very great. You are clothed with honour and majesty, wrapped in light as with a garment. You stretch out the heavens like a tent, you set the beams of your chambers on the waters, you make the clouds your chariot, you ride on the wings of the wind, you make the winds your messengers, fire and flame your ministers. (Ps 104:1)

Jesus' Respect for the Natural World

A Christian theology of creation has much to learn from the attitude of respect which Jesus displayed towards the natural world. The disciples of Jesus were called upon to live lightly on the earth – 'take nothing for your journey, no staff, nor bag, nor bread, nor money – not even an extra tunic' (Lk 9:1-6). Jesus constantly warned about the dangers of attachment to wealth, possessions or power. These are in many ways what is consuming the poor and the planet itself. 'How hard it will be for those who have wealth to enter the kingdom of God!' (Mk 10:23; Lk 16:19-31; cf. Mt 19:23-24; Lk 18:18-23). 'You fool! This very night your life is being demanded of you. And the things you have prepared, whose will they be?' (Lk 12:16-21). There is no support in the New Testament for a wasteful, throwaway consumer society which destroys the natural world. The modern world produces mountains of non-biodegradable rubbish or, worse still, produces toxic waste when, for example, plastics or styrofoam cups which are used once are eventually destroyed.

Thoughout his ministry Jesus shows an intimacy and familiarity with many of God's creatures as well as the processes of nature. He is not driven by an urge to dominate and control the world of nature. Rather, he displays an appreciative and contemplative attitude towards creation which is rooted in the Father's love for all creation: 'Consider the ravens. They neither sow nor reap; they have neither storehouses nor barn, and yet God feeds them' (Lk 12:24). We need not be constantly fretting about acquiring more goods. God will provide for our legitimate needs: 'Of how much more value are you than the birds!' (Lk 12:24).

The gospels tell us that nature played an important role in Jesus' life. At his birth, Luke tells us that he was laid 'in a manger, because there was no place for them in the inn' (Lk 2:7). He was first greeted by people who were 'keeping watch over their flock by night' (Lk 2:8). Mark tells us that the spirit drove him into the wilderness. 'He was in the wilderness forty days, tempted by Satan; and he was with the wild beasts; and the angels waited on him' (Mk 1:13).

The time which Jesus spent in the desert was the most formative for the messianic ministry which he was about to embrace. In order to be fully open and receptive to his call, Jesus forsook the company of people and regularly returned to the hills to pray and commune with the Father (Mt 17:1; Mk 6:46; Mt 14:23). We know that he prayed on the hills before making important decisions like choosing his disciples (Lk 6:12). His ministry was not carried out just in synagogues or in the temple. In Matthew's gospel, the beatitudes and subsequent teaching were delivered on a mountain (Mt 5:1-7:29). Much of his teaching and miracles took place on the shores of the Sea of Galilee (Mt 13:1-52; Mk 4:35-41; Jn 21:1-14). The miracle of the loaves occurred in a 'lonely place' (Mt 14:15-21; Lk 9:10-17; Jn 6:1-13).

Many of his parables centred on sowing seed (Mt 13:4-9, 18-23; Mk 4:3-9, 13-20; Lk 8:5-8, 11-15), vines (Jn 15:1-17; Mk 12:1-12; Mt 21:33-44; Lk 20:9-19), lost sheep (Lk 15:4-7; Mt 18:12-14) or shepherds (Jn 10:1-18). His teaching is regularly interspersed with references to the lilies of the field (Lk 12:27), the birds of the air (Mt 6:26) and the lair of foxes (Lk 9:58). He was Lord of creation and could calm the waves (Mk 4:35-41; Mt 8:23-27; Lk 8:22-25), walk on the water (Mk 6:48-49) or when food was needed multiply the loaves (Mt 14:13-21; Mk 8:1-10; Lk 9:10-17; Jn 6:1-13).

Like most great religious personalities he was a great healer. He cured the sick and restored them to health (Mt 12:9-14; Mk 3:1-6; Lk 6:6-11). He cured the paralytic (Mk 2:1-12), the man with a withered hand (Mk 3:1-6), the woman who had been stooped for many years (Lk 13:10-17), the man who had been paralysed for thirty-eight years (Jn 5:1-15) and restored sight to the man born blind (Jn 9:1-41). While individuals are restored to health by each act of healing, the healing ministry of Jesus was not confined to individuals. Each healing was a sign that challenged the social or religious prejudices of the time. They also sowed the seeds of healing within the community itself, as it was opened to the transforming power of God's compassion and graciousness.

In his preaching Jesus identified himself with the natural elements of water (Jn 4:13-14), bread (Jn 6:48) and light (Jn 8:12). He presented himself as the good shepherd (Jn 10:11; Mk 6:30-44) who came that 'they may have life, and have it abundantly' (Jn 10:10b). He rode into Jerusalem on a donkey (Mt 21:1b-5) and in Mark's gospel (16:15) the disciples were called to take the Gospel to all creation. Finally, in and through his death, Jesus participated in the most radical way in one of the key processes of nature.

Christian Faith in Jesus as Centre of Creation

The ministry of Jesus was not confined to teaching, healing and reconciling humans and all creation with God. Paul tells us that Jesus himself is the centre of all creation:

> He is the image of the invisible God, the first-born of all creation; for in him all things in heaven and on earth were created, things visible and invisible, whether thrones or dominions or rulers or powers – all things have been created through him and for him. He himself is before all things, and in him all things hold together. (Col 1:15-18)

Jesus is the word and wisdom of God who existed with God from the beginning. In the prologue of John's gospel, the birth and life of Jesus is framed within the widest context of cosmic history. He is active in bringing forth creation; through him the universe, the earth and all life was created (Jn 1:3-5). All the rich unfolding of the universe, from the first moment of the fireball, through the formation of the stars, the moulding of planet Earth, the birth and flowering of life on earth and the emergence of human beings, is centred on Christ. Hence all of these crucial moments in the emergence of the universe have a Christological dimension.

In the man Jesus, God who was active from the beginning in bringing forth the universe 'became flesh' (Jn 1:14). The redemption which he accomplishes does not come by way of discarding, denigrating or abandoning the material world, but by transforming it from within. In John's gospel Jesus' incarnation is seen as an outpouring of God's love for the world – 'for God so loved the world that he gave his only Son, so that everyone who believes in him may not perish but may have eternal life' (Jn 3:16).

The leadership which Jesus gives in the New Testament is always a leadership of service. This leadership involved accepting death joyfully. Paul in Philippians goes on to say: 'And being found in human form, he humbled himself and became obedient to the point of death – even death on a cross' (Phil 2:6-8). In the contemporary situation, Christian service must mean working for a more peaceful, just and sustainable world. Only in this way can people of this and future generations experience the abundant life which Jesus promised (Jn 10:10).

The resurrection of Christ is the beginning of the new creation (2 Cor 5:17-19). The writers of the New Testament are at pains to affirm the visible, bodily nature of Christ's resurrection. Through the reality of Christ's resurrection all visible created reality is touched, given a new significance, transformed and taken up into the life of the Trinity. Paul states: 'God was in Christ reconciling the world to himself' (2 Cor 5:19, cf. Col 1:20). In this text Paul is affirming that all reality is interconnected, sequentially linked over time and ultimately grounded in God. The Preface of Easter IV in the Roman Missal echoes this belief: 'In him a new age has dawned, the long reign of sin is ended, a broken world has been renewed and man is once again made whole. The joy of the resurrection fills the whole world.'

The resurrection is the cosmic sign of hope. All creation is united in Christ and therefore everything has a future in God, through Christ. This hope for wholeness or redemption is anchored in the presence in the world of the spirit, who despite past human failures and sins can bring forth new things (Is 43:19; Ezek 37). This grace allows the believer to look forward confidently to the future and not be mired in the past either of our own individual or our collective failures. This is a profoundly liberating experience for the believer and can release new energies to bring about a healing of creation.

In the classic text of Romans Paul likens the yearnings of creation for redemption with similar human desires. Within the plan of God realised in the resurrection of Christ, humans can help bring about this cosmic redemption.

> We know that the whole creation has been groaning in labour pains until now; and not only the creation, but we ourselves, who have the first fruits of the Spirit, groan inwardly while we wait for adoption, the redemption of our bodies. (Rom 8:22-24)

The Fathers of the Church

The Fathers of the Church, beginning with the early 'Apologists' like Justin Martyr, Theophilus of Antioch and Tatian, developed a theology of creation. Very often, this was elaborated in opposition to the prevailing Gnostic dualism, which depicted the created world as radically deficient and often insisted that the body was evil. The Fathers affirmed the goodness of creation since it was created by the one God. To distinguish the Christian understanding of creation from that which was current at the time in some of the philosophical schools, the Apologists stress that God did not create the world through the mediation of spirits or from pre-existent matter, but that the world was created out of nothing (*creatio ex nihilo*).

The Fathers did not seal off a discussion of natural theology from the doctrines about Christ (or Christology). In much of the patristic literature Christ is portrayed as the ruler of the universe. The theology of Irenaeus of Lyons is one of the best examples of the Fathers' setting Christ at the centre point and culmination of creation.

One of the most important features of the patristic period was the rise of monasticism. One could easily interpret the flight from the world as a radical rejection of every aspect of the created order and therefore argue that the patristic period had little to add to a theology or spirituality of creation. There is no doubt that the 'athletes of God' were fleeing what they saw as the decadence, especially of urban life. Yet the early monks or hermits sought out the wilderness precisely because it had an inherent capacity to reveal the presence of God. When St Anthony, the father of monasticism, was asked, 'How dost thou content thyself, Father, who art denied the comfort of books?', Anthony answered, 'My book, philosopher, is the nature of created things, and as often as I have a mind to read the words of God, it is at my hands.'

Many legends tell how the monks also developed friendships with the animals, even predators like wolves and lions. The feeling of dread, which a human might normally be expected to have towards a lion, is often replaced by an attitude of mutual help and friendship. There is a profound moral and religious message in the fact that holy people were considered to have friendly relationships with wild animals, even lions. The authors of these stories may wish to call the attention of Christians to the fact that holiness of life can even be appreciated by the 'wildest' of creatures and that, in living out the life of the new Adam, the monks were recapturing the original friendly relationship which existed between all the animals in Paradise prior to the fall. The Isaiah text obviously helped spread this belief in the Judaeo-Christian tradition (Is 1:6-7).

The sensitivity of the Greek Church to the created world can be seen in a prayer attributed to St Basil the Great (c. 330–379):

> O God, enlarge within us the sense of fellowship with all living things, our brothers, the animals, to whom thou gavest the earth as their home in common with us.
> We remember with shame that in the past we have exercised the high dominion of man with ruthless cruelty, so that the voice of the earth, which should have gone up to thee in song, has been a groan of travail.
> May we realise that they live not for us alone but for themselves and for thee and that they love the sweetness of life.

Celtic Spirituality

Local churches in Ireland, England, Scotland and Wales have much to learn from early Celtic spirituality, which was very much attuned to the presence of the Divine in the world of nature. This spirituality grew out a marriage between the pre-Christian and the Christian traditions.

As in the Eastern monastic tradition, friendship with animals marked the lives of holy people. St Columban (c. 559–615) was well known for the austerity of his monastic rule, yet was also known to be friendly to animals. Legends which grew up around him at Luxeuil in France picture squirrels and doves playing in the folds of his cowl. Birds also approached him and nestled in the palms of his hands and even wild animals obeyed his commands. In his sermon 'Concerning the Faith' he tells the reader that, 'If you wish to understand God, learn about creation'.

Benedictine and Franciscan Threads in the Christian Tradition

It is important to look briefly at some approaches to the natural world which are inspired by the biblical perspective and which, in varying degrees, have helped shape Christian consciousness through the centuries. The first two approaches emerge from the Benedictine monastic tradition and the experience of St Francis of Assisi (c. 1182–1226). Many people are familiar with these visions of the natural world, because they have left an indelible stamp on western European agricultural and aesthetic traditions. The third strand arises from the writings of Hildegard of Bingen (1098–1178). Her writings have only become well known in recent years; hence her impact, to date, is still very limited.

Benedictine Care for the Earth

From the seventh century onwards, a network of Benedictine monasteries was established in western Europe. St Benedict of Nursia (c. 480–c. 547), the father of western monasticism, decided that his monks should live together in a stable community. The rhythm of the monastic life written into his famous Rule included liturgical and other forms of prayer, manual work and study. This inclusion of manual work was, in a sense, a revolutionary departure from the old way. Greek and Roman scholars in general showed disdain for manual work. They felt that it was degrading for the scholar to engage in such a lowly task. By combining work and prayer, Benedict ennobled all kinds of manual work. He also insisted that each monastery should be self-sufficient, so the range of manual work included domestic chores, crafts, garden work, tilling the soil and caring for domestic animals. The stability of the monastery meant that the monks had to learn to cultivate the soil in a renewable way.

The Benedictine model of relating to the natural world was marked by gratitude for the good things of the earth and respect for the earth in order to ensure its continued fruitfulness for human beings. Humans were called to be faithful stewards of the world and not to abuse the earth. But the point of departure was always the human perspective. The drive to domesticate nature and to bring it under human control was very much at the centre of the Benedictine tradition.

Franciscan Fellowship with all Creation

Unlike St Benedict, St Francis of Assisi was a nomad at heart. He and his friars, who were street preachers, were constantly on the move. They had no possessions and were expected to live lightly on the earth, being a burden neither to the earth nor to those who met their subsistence needs. In opting for the nomadic life, Francis abandoned any *homo faber* (humans as artisans) role for the brothers. There was no urge to remake the world, not even in the garden tradition of the Benedictines. The natural world was not seen from a utilitarian perspective, as providing food, clothing and shelter for human beings. Rather, there was a sense of joy, wonder, praise and gratitude for the gift of all life. For Francis, every creature in the world was a mirror of God's presence and, if approached correctly, a step leading one to God. What emerges here might be called a fellowship approach to creatures. In his 'Canticle of the Creatures' Francis showed a kinship with and deep insight into the heart of all creation – animate and inanimate – which was probably unrivalled in the whole European experience.

Hildegard of Bingen: The Greening of the Earth

The approach of Hildegard of Bingen adds a unique dimension to those of both Benedict and Francis. Unfortunately, her writings are not widely known. Selections from her writings have only been published in English in the past few decades. This remarkable woman – poet, musician, painter, visionary, tanist, herbalist, counsellor to Popes, princes and Councils of the Church – has a unique contribution to make to the western Christian's appreciation of the natural world. Her approach to the earth delights in its 'greening'. The Divine is present in the 'greening' of the earth in a way reminiscent of the fertility poetry of the pre-Christian Celtic religion of much of Europe. In her writings, Hildegard captures and celebrates the uniquely feminine experience of the most intimate processes of the natural world. The taming, organising skills of Benedict and even the fraternal solicitude for all creatures of Francis are valuable elements of a masculine approach to reality. But Hildegard celebrates the feminine, fertility dimension. Her poetry pulsates with a rapturous, sensuous love for the earth. It is full of ardour and passion. In the following poem she delights in the love of the Creator for his creation and does not feel constrained to shy away from explicitly sexual language:

> I compare the great love of Creator and creation to the same love
> and fidelity with which God binds man and woman together.
> This is so that together they might be creatively fruitful.[2]

The Church and the Natural World

It is a fact of recent history that the Catholic Church has been slow to recognise the gravity of the ecological problems facing the earth. She has not been alone. Most of the institutions of society – schools, governments, the media, financial and industrial corporations – have also refused to see what is happening to the delicate fabric of the earth. They have been lulled into a false sense of security by some of the successes of modern technology and have failed to understand the urgent need to face the despoilment of creation. Unless they become aware very quickly of the ecological crisis, human beings and the rest of the planet's community will be condemned to live amid the ruins of the natural world. At last the Church is beginning to wake up to what is at stake. In 1987 John Paul II's encyclical *Sollicitudo rei socialis* (SRS) addressed the issue.[3]

Ecology and Recent Church Documents

It is not easy to find any reference to the environment among the mountains of documents that have come from Rome in recent decades. In fact, recent Church teaching on the role of people vis-à-vis the rest of creation has failed to take into account an important strand within biblical literature, found, for example, in the Book of Job, especially Chapters 38 and 39. These chapters reject an exclusively human-centred view of creation. Despite its great achievement in helping to bring the Catholic Church into modern times, Vatican II did not engage in any detailed exploration of ecological issues. It subscribes to what is called a 'domination' theology, which sees that the natural world is there for humankind's exclusive use. 'For man, created to God's image, received a mandate to subject to himself the earth and all that it contains, and to govern the world with justice and holiness' (GS 34). It did not challenge humans to respect other life forms, obey ecological laws and work to establish more just human societies within the limits of the natural world. Only in 1988 do we find any serious caution about the 'consequences of haphazard industrialisation' (SRS). Yet even there, the momentum to pollute the earth, which is built into our modern industrial consumer society, is not examined or critiqued in any detail.

On 1 January 1990, Pope John Paul II published his World Day of Peace Message, 'Peace with God the Creator, Peace with All Creation'. This is the first papal document devoted exclusively to environmental concerns. It is written in a lively style; its coverage is comprehensive; the analysis is incisive and the text reverberates with a note of urgency. Throughout the document the Pope insists that environmental degradation must be a concern of every individual and every institution: ultimately, it has an essential moral and religious dimension.

In this document ecological problems are named in a much more detailed manner than in previous documents. Not content with enumerating ecological problems, the Pope looks below the surface at the root causes of the devastation. 'First among these is the indiscriminate application of advances in science and technology.' This critique of technology constitutes a major shift in emphasis in recent papal teaching that I am sure will not be welcomed by the captains of industry.

Equally unpalatable for many environmental consultants is the reminder that the standard of living which many people in the First World enjoy is obtained at the expense of Third World people and the earth itself. The Pope warns that:

> modern society will find no solution to the ecological problem unless it takes a serious look at its lifestyle ... Simplicity, moderation and discipline, as well as a spirit of sacrifice, must become part of everyday life, lest all suffer the negative consequences of the careless habits of a few.

The document 'Peace with God the Creator, Peace with All Creation' is a landmark in the greening of the Church. One hopes and prays that the Pope's voice will be heard and acted upon in parishes, church schools and dioceses around the world.

In 2004 the Pontifical Council for Justice and Peace published the *Compendium of the Social Doctrine of the Church*. Chapter 10 is devoted to protecting the environment. It is one of the shortest and least competent chapters in the book as it fails to capture the magnitude of the ecological crisis and the urgency with which it must be faced. The extinction of species only merits a half a paragraph and global warming a single paragraph.

Conclusion

The biosphere recognises no divisions into blocs, or alliances of systems. In ecclesiastical terms this means that there are no Catholic lakes, Protestant rivers or Muslim forests. We all share a common earth and, in the face of a threat to the survival of a large segment of the creatures of our planet, we should unite our efforts to protect God's creation. We need to have ecological theology at the heart of our Catholic faith. It should spill over into our prayer life, our celebration of all of the sacraments, our ethical reflections and actions and our spirituality. In the face of the magnitude of ecological destruction every faith must begin to confront the ecological crisis if it wishes to have its message taken seriously in the contemporary world. In this chapter I have only touched the surface in terms of developing a truly vibrant ecological theology which must now be at the heart of our Christian/Catholic faith. Every community must attempt to do this and the shape of that theology will be different because human communities live in different ecosystems. However, such an opening up to the world under the guidance of the Holy Spirit, the Spirit of Life, could bring forth a new spring for the Catholic faith.

Notes

1   I outline the threat of extinction in my book, *The Death of Life: The Horror of Extinction*, Dublin: Columba, 2005.

2   Hildegard of Bingen, *Liber vitae meritorum*, 5.31.39, p. 197.

3   John Paul II, *Sollicitudo rei socialis*, 1987, no. 34.

Further Reading

Edwards, Denis, *Ecology at the Heart of Christian Faith*, New York: Orbis Books, 2006.

McDonagh, Sean, *To Care for the Earth*, London: Geoffrey Chapman, 1985.

_____ *The Greening of the Church*, London: Geoffrey Chapman, 1990.

_____ *Passion for the Earth*, London: Geoffrey Chapman, 1990.

_____ *Greening the Christian Millennium*, Dublin: Dominican Publications, 1999.

_____ *Patenting Life? Stop! Is Genetic Food Forcing us to Eat Genetically Engineered Food?*, Dublin: Dominican Publications, 2003.

_____ *Dying for Water*, Dublin: Veritas, 2003.

_____ *The Death of Life: The Horror of Extinction*, Dublin: Columba, 2006.

_____ *Climate Change: The Challenge to Us All*, Dublin: Columba, 2006.

SECTION IV

Christian Prayer

CHAPTER 18

MAKING SAINTS THROUGH THE LITURGICAL YEAR

Raymond Topley

Introduction

It is said that our diaries and calendars are our 'literary fingerprints'. They reveal who we are and what it is we are most interested in. Likewise, the Christian calendar or liturgical year, as it is sometimes called, reveals the pre-occupations and concerns of the community of Jesus. By means of it the Christian community shapes the annual cycle of time in accordance with its own particular agenda of making Christian disciples and, in the process, making saints. At the time of the dying of Jesus the Christian liturgical year did not exist. The calendar was devoid of any Christian content. Today it is a highly sophisticated liturgical and catechetical instrument designed to proclaim Christ and promote holiness among his followers. Accordingly, the liturgical year has a legitimate and important place in the curriculum of Christian religious education given that the latter, also, is concerned with bringing people to maturity of faith and holiness of life. To understand the significance of this assertion one needs to appreciate the Christian year's overall structure.

The Plan of the Liturgical Year

The 'shape' or structure of the liturgical year may best be understood through the concept of 'cycle.' This kind of language sits easily in any discourse on time, given the never-ending cyclical nature of each emerging year with its regular sequencing of seasons. A variety of religious cycles exists within the Christian year, namely, Sunday, Easter, Christmas, the Sanctoral and the Marian. Each of these possesses its own particular characteristics. Additionally, there exists a certain inter-relatedness between the various cycles. To appreciate such connectedness and purposefulness it is necessary to survey each cycle separately.

The Sunday Cycle

The genesis of the liturgical year is to be located in one particular event, the Resurrection of Jesus, occurring on 'the first day of the week'. On the evening of that initial Christian Sunday, Jesus appeared among his disciples and the first commemoration of this auspicious event was exactly one week later when the assembled disciples were once again visited by the Risen Lord. Thus, the Sunday Cycle was set in train by Jesus himself along with his community of disciples. Arising from such beginnings one can appreciate the observation of the Second Vatican Council that 'Sunday takes its origin from the very day of Christ's resurrection'. What this implies is that the meaning and significance of Sunday is to be quarried out of the resurrection stories found in the final chapters of the Gospels. A simple glance at these narratives reveals a staggering range of activity on the part of the Risen Lord over the course of these first two Sundays of the Christian era. Along with being raised from the dead, he appears to his followers, breaks bread (Eucharist) with the Emmaus-bound travellers, grants power to forgive sins, bestows the Spirit and missions his followers to go and proclaim the Gospel to all. Little wonder then that this day of relentless activity on the part of the Risen Lord, which suggests the content and spirit of all future Sundays, should become known by the faith-filled appellation, 'The Lord's Day'.

Even this cursory analysis is sufficient to disclose the underlying thrust of the day as one of utmost significance in the liturgical calendar. It is a day for remembering the Lord. Simply stated, it is the Lord's Day, understood in the fullest possible sense of divine 'ownership'. It is not for the faithful Christian to decide unilaterally how it ought or ought not to be spent. Divine 'lordship' of Sunday may be understood as an expression of the Risen Lord's reign in the hearts and minds of his followers. As such then, Sunday can act as a symbol for the Christian life itself. What devout Jews say about the Sabbath may be applied also to the Sunday: 'Keep holy the Sabbath, and the Sabbath will keep you holy.'

The Easter Cycle

Every Sunday, it is said, is a little Easter and every Easter is a great Sunday. This arises from the fact, essentially, that there is a common bond between the two. That common ingredient is the Resurrection. Sunday celebrates it weekly; Easter celebrates it annually. The interplay of preparation (forty days of Lent) and celebration (fifty days of Easter), of restraint and exuberance, is a characteristic of the whole of the Christian calendar. At the heart of the Easter Cycle is the Sacred Triduum of Good Friday, Holy Saturday and Easter Sunday. Over the span of these three days can be found the essence of the Christian life. In an absolute act of *kenosis* (self-emptying, self-surrender, self-offering) on Calvary, Jesus gives himself to God on behalf of the whole of humanity. The response of God to this act emerges with the dawn of Easter Sunday as *anastasis* (resurrection). Jesus' offering is accepted. The Resurrection has occurred and death, in the process, has been conquered. No longer is human death a cul-de-sac but is, rather, a highway to God. Through this new reality the meaning of death is relativised and so too is the concept of time. Jesus of Nazareth, in his human condition, had been confined, like the rest of us, to being in just one place at any one time. Now, as Risen Lord, he can be in many places at the same time. This has enormous implications in respect of Christian liturgy. What it implies is that the Risen Lord, therefore, can be truly present in liturgies today just as he was at the original events. Through religious commemoration, the past is given a new existence in the present, a fact which challenges the faith of each believer.

Such faith is exercised with particular fervour during the seasons of Lent and Easter. Lent, essentially, is about tending to one's heart, where encounter with God occurs. Christianity has ever viewed the human heart as a place where both wheat and weeds flourish and where, in the case of each person, there is to be found, as in the case of King David, both the sinner and the saint. Lent provides a renewal space for the saint in each one. It is preparation time for the celebration of the Paschal or Easter event. The true observer of Lent, accordingly, does not arrive at the Easter Vigil unprepared. One is ready to feast because one has first fasted and has very likely participated in the traditional and revered tripartite expression of Lenten observance: prayer, fasting and almsgiving.

While the period of fifty days from Easter to Pentecost is indeed celebratory, in another and very real sense, it is also preparatory. The ultimate goal of the Easter Cycle is the outpouring of the Holy Spirit at Pentecost. The gift of the Holy Spirit, the *Donum Dei*, is therefore rightly seen as the fulfilment of this cycle whose appropriate prayer is, 'Come, Holy Spirit!' Like Jesus himself, every saint is one who is filled with the Spirit, led by the Spirit and empowered by the Spirit (see Luke, Chapters 3 and 4).

The Christmas Cycle

'Come, Lord, Jesus!' encapsulates the spiritual purpose of the Christmas Cycle. The mood of the Christmas preparatory season, Advent, is one of quiet confidence and joyful expectation. The Christmas celebratory period has two expressions, one in the Christian West, the other in the Christian East. Western Christians see Christmas Day as the liturgical apex of this cycle whereas Eastern or Orthodox Christians, such as the Greeks and the Slavs, look upon the Feast of the Epiphany on the sixth of January as the religious climax of the season. While Christmas celebrates the coming of Christ into the world, Epiphany rejoices in the manifestation and significance of Christ for all peoples and not just for a chosen few. For every Christian today however, Catholic, Orthodox and Reform, the main challenge arises from the pernicious de-Christianising of this ancient feast as crass commercialism competes with Christian consciousness in the hearts and minds of all believers.

Paradoxically, at the heart of the theology of Christmas is, actually, a commerce of sorts. The 'admirabile commercium!' which is referred to in ancient Christian writings constitutes an exchange, but one understood as being transacted between the Creator and creatures in and through the instrumentality of the Virgin Mary. In exchange for a share in humanity for his Son, God offers a share in divinity. This essentially is what the mystery of the Incarnation means, namely God taking up residence within the human family. As the story of salvation progresses, the Holy Spirit comes to inhabit humanity explicitly, divinising the world and thus completing the exchange.

Christmas, therefore, along with the cycles of Sunday and Easter, can be seen to proclaim, promote and present Jesus Christ to Christian believers of every era so as to enlighten and inform in the first instance. However, an additional goal is to mould and form believers into the image of Christ. 'In your minds you must be the same as Christ Jesus', is how St Paul expresses this process (Phil 2:5). Jesus Christ is the *Sanctus* (the Holy One) *par excellence*. Taking on the mind of Christ, therefore, and being graced by Christ in and through the liturgical year is what contributes to the making of the *sancti* (the holy ones) and so it is to this agenda we now turn in considering the Sanctoral and Marian Cycles.

The Sanctoral Cycle

St Stephen, the first Christian martyr, is honoured in the Christian calendar with a feast day immediately following Christmas day. The stoning of Stephen ushered in an era of persecution for the early Church which was to last intermittently for close on three hundred years. During that time many believers were martyred for Christ. The local Christian communities, particularly in Rome where so many believers gave up their lives for Christ, recorded three details about the passing of such a witness (*martus*). First of all they would ensure that the martyr's name (*nomen*) was remembered. Second, the place (*locus*) where they were martyred was marked so that the sacrifice of Christ's death could be celebrated with a mass on the same spot each year where the martyr's own sacrifice had occurred. Finally, the *dies natale* or birthday into the new life of heaven was recorded so that the commemoration of such 'witnesses' would occur annually on the day in question. This is how the Sanctoral Cycle began.

Back then all that was needed for a person's name to be added to the canon (list) of martyrs was their dying for Christ. Nothing further was necessary by way of official sanction. It was the local Christian community which discerned who should or should not be so listed. This localised approach continued beyond the era of the martyrs (red martyrdom) to the age of the saints (white martyrdom). The former died for Christ. The latter lived for Christ. Such a one was St Patrick. To those who knew him he was a person of deep prayer, who exhibited a love for Christ and a remarkable service of others. The appellation 'saint' or 'holy one' was accordingly bestowed upon him and others like him whose lives were fully and wholly dedicated to God.

In time, however, it became clear that some form of regulating who merited or did not merit acknowledgement as a saint was necessary in order to avoid abuse of the practice. This led to the development of a process known as 'canonisation'. The overall purpose was to ensure that those who made it into the canon of saints genuinely deserved to be so listed. The initiative to have someone canonised began, as before, with the local community but the last word was reserved to the Pope after advice from theologians, bishops and cardinals. Today, candidates for canonisation need to exhibit in their lives orthodoxy (right teaching) and orthopraxis (right living). However, in addition, two miracles are required, one for beatification ('Blessed'), the first stage, and one for canonisation ('Saint'), the final stage. This requirement is understood as a 'signal' from God or a kind of 'divine signature' of approval.

Saints show clearly that holiness of life is a distinct possibility even in the most unlikely circumstances and the most unsympathetic societies. They demonstrate that discipleship of Christ, though a high ideal, is not an impossible one. Each saint, at some stage or other, has to face up to the ambivalence of the human heart and the necessity of making a radical decision for Christ and the reign of God. The crown of martyrdom, be it red or white, is never easily or cheaply won by anyone. When Lutheran pastor, Dietrich Bonhoeffer, who was imprisoned under the Nazi regime, exclaimed, 'There is no such a thing as cheap grace', these words could have been most fittingly applied to any and everyone travelling the road to sainthood. It is this struggle which, more than anything else, exhibits the glory of the saints, namely the triumph of the grace of God over all obstacles which may arise. This highlights the fact that sanctity is a work of partnership. It is a combination of God's grace, on the one hand, and human response and endeavour, on the other.

The life of a saint, however, ought not to be imagined in terms of a lone struggle or a solitary existence. The vast majority lived out their lives in the midst of their communities where they strove, despite innumerable obstacles, to work for the reign of God. Through their efforts and commitment they ensured that the will of God was given a foothold in at least one centre of consciousness, namely themselves. Their relationship with God fuelled their relationship with their fellow human beings, whom they both loved and served. Nowhere was this more evident than in the case of Mary, the Mother of Jesus.

The Marian Cycle

After her son, Jesus, Mary is the holy one, the Saint of Saints. Indeed, in some Christian communities she is referred to as Saint Mary, which is but another term for 'Holy Mary'. Little wonder then that she merits a liturgical cycle all to herself. The cycle which honours Mary may be understood as a kind of liturgical garland with various Marian feast days dispersed throughout the year. As in the case of saints, the triumph of the Paschal Mystery is evident in her life also. She is equally both Mother of God and Disciple of Christ. Indeed, she is disciple before she is mother as she had to proffer her Christlike obedience at the time of the Annunciation before she became mother. Like the saints, she is model, mentor and mediator. Her advice to the servants at the wedding feast of Cana to 'do whatever he tells you' (Jn 2:5) is of the essence of an apostle as one who is sent to proclaim Christ and the good news. The most ancient of the Marian feast days is the Assumption of Mary into heaven which is referred to among the Eastern Orthodox as her *Dormition* or 'falling asleep'. In the iconography of this mystery are three depictions of Mary. At the foot of the icon the earthly Mary is laid out on a bed in her final sleep surrounded by apostles and disciples of her son. At the top of the picture she is represented in the heavenly realm, surrounded by the heavenly host of angels and saints and the Blessed Trinity. However, the most arresting element in the icon focuses on the person of Jesus. He holds in his arms an infant-sized image of his mother whom he is bearing from earth to heaven. In this striking reversal of roles, the divine Son is parent of the human mother and is carrying her into her new life in heaven on her *Dies Natale*.

As such then the person of Mary is a figure or icon of hope for all followers of Jesus. Throughout the course of the liturgical year her story as both disciple and divine mother is told and retold. The Marian Cycle, along with the Sanctoral, the Sunday and the Seasonal cycles, plays its part in the birthing, nurturing and sustaining of ever more saints and holy ones. These follow in the steps of those who have gone before until there is fulfilled the following promise and prophecy traditionally imagined as addressed to the faithful on earth by Mary in heaven: 'What you are, I once was. What I am now, you one day will be.'

Conclusion: Pedagogy of the Liturgical Year

The liturgical year has always had an honoured place in catechetical programmes and practice, particularly during seasons such as Advent and Lent. Regarding teaching about the saints, what is necessary, however, is to endeavour to base whatever one proposes and practices as a teacher on a solid theoretical framework. Such a framework is to be found in the research and writings of Albert Bandura of Stanford University in California. Bandura, a social psychologist, developed a 'social learning theory,' which proposes that people learn values and behaviours more from each other than from pure and detached cognitive activity. For such learning to occur four conditions need to be fulfilled. Learners need first of all to be attentive and to observe the behaviour of the one held up as a model. Second, the behaviour in question needs to be retained in the learner's memory. Following this comes imitation of the particular behaviour. The final element is that of motivation whereby the behaviour is perceived as attractive and desirable. If an approach to teaching saints to people were to follow such a pattern, which Bandura also refers to as 'modelling' and 'observational learning,' one might hope to see some positive outcomes in time. By so combining developmental theory with the content and recurrence of religious feasts a catechist or religion teacher might well progress one of the principal functions of the liturgical year, namely the making of saints and the formation of disciples of Christ.

Further Reading

Bandura, Albert, *Social Foundations of Thought and Action: A Social Cognitive Theory*, Englewood Cliffs, N.J.: Prentice Hall, 1986.

Kisinski Carola, Dorothy, *The Liturgical Seasons: Catechesis for Children and their Families*, San Jose, CA: Resource Publications, 1999.

Crichton, J.D., *Our Lady in the Liturgy*, Dublin: Columba, 1997.

Johnson, Lawrence J. (ed.) *The Church Gives Thanks and Remembers: Essays on the Liturgical Year*, Collegeville, Minn.: The Liturgical Press, 1984.

Mathson, Patricia, *Seasons of Celebration: Prayers, Plays and Projects for the Church Year*, Notre Dame, IN: Ave Maria Press, 1995.

Schneider, Valerie, *Teaching Sacraments and Seasons: Reflections, Prayers and Activities for Teachers*, Mystic, Conn.: 23rd Publications, 1999.

Sweeney, Jon M., *The Lure of the Saints: A Protestant Experience of Catholic Tradition*, Brewster, MA: Paraclete Press, 2005.

Thompson, Katie, *The Complete Children's Liturgy Book: A Comprehensive Programme for every Sunday of the Lectionary*, Buxhall, Suffolk: Kevin Mahew, 1995.

Vos Wezeman, Phyllis and Liechty, Anna L., *Many Saints, Many Ways: Multiple Intelligence Activities for Grades 1-6*, Notre Dame, IN: Ave Maria Press, 2003.

Woodward, Kenneth L., *Making Saints: How the Catholic Church Decides who Becomes a Saint, who Doesn't, and Why*, New York: Touchstone, 1990.

CHAPTER 19

SACRAMENTS: KEY SYMBOLS FOR THE CHRISTIAN WAY OF LIFE

Bruce T. Morrill

Introduction

Sacraments are among the most visible, distinguishing features of Roman Catholicism. Whether the image be of a pope celebrating Mass with a crowd of thousands, or a bride and groom emerging from a village church with well-wishers spilling out behind, or a priest and mourners bearing a coffin from chapel to graveside, or a cluster of family and friends on the steps of a city parish church accompanying parents and their baby for baptism, the sacramental rituals (officially called 'liturgy') of the Church are often what first come to mind at the mention of Catholicism. In the narrowest definition of the term, sacrament refers to one of seven official rituals symbolising the meaning of Catholic faith and empowering its practice: baptism, confirmation, Eucharist, penance, anointing of the sick, marriage and holy orders. These ritual symbols, nonetheless, point to a deeper dimension of Catholic tradition that theologians call sacramentality: the belief that God is encountered in our lives on earth, that the good world created by God – however fallen and troubled – is the arena for our discovering the happiness God intends for all humanity. This happiness most often is rendered in English translations of biblical texts and prayers as blessing or blessedness. The word 'blessed,' however, should not imply some other-worldly bliss but, quite to the contrary, a profound sense of joy, of well being, of peace in life (even amidst its trials) in the presence of the God revealed in Christ Jesus.

The source of such confidence in the venture of human life, the conviction that this God can be trusted, Christians find in the life, death and resurrection of Jesus. Therein lies the heart of the Christian faith: the mystery (wonder) of God's having taken on and served, in the Jewish prophet Jesus, the human condition in all its joys and sorrows, suffering and goodness, to the point of death. In raising from the dead this Jesus, who died unjustly at the world's hands, God revealed the mystery of all our lives, namely, our passage through this world as a venture in meeting and knowing God – the loving Creator and life-giving Spirit – through our loving service of one another and all God's creation. Such knowledge is not a matter of theoretical ideas or abstract principles but, rather, a committed response of one's entire self – body, soul and spirit – to the invitation of God's life as revealed in the story of Jesus. What nurtures such a commitment, precisely as a way of life, are not abstract arguments but, rather, symbols and stories shared in traditional rituals that deeply shape and sustain the rhythms and patterns of our living. The most crucial of these ritual symbols for the life of faith and shared mission of the Church are called the sacraments.

The 'What' and 'Why' of Sacramental Liturgy

To ask the question, as many students do today, 'Why should I have to go to Mass on Sunday?' points to fundamental issues about the meaning and purpose of the Church's *liturgical* worship as a crucial, indispensable part – but *only a part* – of the entire Christian life as the worship of God. What this means – and this is quite a religious paradox – is that the practice of the Christian faith, in its origins and genuine purpose, is not about stepping out of the ordinary world (what scholars of religion call the *profane* world) into a separate, *sacred* sphere of reality. The New Testament reveals that through his life, death, resurrection and glorification Jesus has brought an end to locating God exclusively in certain fixed places or personages. If the Letter to the Hebrews and other such biblical and early Church texts speak of priest, temple, or the sacred, all of these terms only work metaphorically in the brilliant light of Christ's resurrection and ascension and the sending of his Holy Spirit into the Church for the salvation of the world. Jesus, a Jewish layman who attained the reputation of a teacher (rabbi) and prophet, was never a priest; he did not belong to the priestly caste in the temple of Jerusalem. Nor is he now *literally* – that is to say, by any sociological definition of religion – a priest. Christ does not serve in one temple somewhere on our planet but, rather, with the Father and the Spirit he is the source of salvation for all of humanity. Christians, who have all been baptised by the Spirit into Christ, now comprise the members of his body, the Church, in the world. For this reason the New Testament (1 Pet 2:5) speaks metaphorically of the entire Church as a priestly people or as a temple made of living stones. All Christians (the 'living stones') are called – and empowered by Christ's Spirit – to give glory to God by letting God shape their lives in the world according to the pattern of Christ's loving service unto death. Just as Jesus' entire life was an act of worship, so too is the *entire* Christian life.

The performance of sacramental worship or liturgy, therefore, far from being an end in itself, is for the purpose of revealing our entire lives as an ongoing act of worship, of glorifying God by sharing in God's creative and redemptive action in our world. This notion of liturgy comes from the earliest (patristic) tradition of the Church. Repeatedly over the early Christian centuries the pastors (bishops) of the Church, in their homilies and letters, taught that the glory of God and the salvation of people are utterly bound together – like two sides of the same coin. What brings honor to God, that is, what acclaims and gives thanks to the God of Jesus, is the actual, historical deliverance of people from suffering, meaninglessness and sin. The official introductions to the sacramental rites of the Roman Catholic Church today repeatedly refer to this traditional understanding of Christian worship as the *celebration of the paschal mystery*.

The word 'paschal' relates to Passover, the annual springtime feast in Judaism that commemorates God's delivering the ancient Hebrews out of slavery in Egypt into the land of Israel. It was precisely during one such Passover festival that Jesus went to Jerusalem for a confrontation with religious authorities over the mission and destiny of God's people (as a suffering servant, a light to the nations) that led to his execution by the occupying Roman forces. Christians believe, therefore, that as a prophet Jesus took on the burdens of his oppressed people at a highly symbolic moment, their annual celebration of God's redeeming them from slavery. Passover was, of course, no mere history lesson. It was an annual ritual commemoration that included a special meal with freshly slaughtered lamb, bitter herbs and unleavened bread symbolising the Jews' suffering and hasty fight from Egypt. Through the recounting of the stories and sharing of the symbolic food and drink, Passover revitalised the Jews' identity as a people and their hope that God would finally deliver them once and for all. Christians believe that in going to his death during that annual celebration

Jesus became the new Passover, the paschal lamb who 'takes away the sins of world'.

The liturgical notion of *paschal mystery* therefore bespeaks Catholics belief that in celebrating baptism, Eucharist and the other sacraments they are given a share in the saving reality of Christ's death and resurrection. Called by the risen Christ to carry on his mission of mercy and forgiveness, reconciliation and justice in the world, the succeeding generations of the early Church adopted symbols from their Jewish and pagan cultures – water, bread, wine, the imposition of hands, salt and oil – to develop rituals they believed transformed the very reality of their lives into visible signs (sacraments) of their now ascended (invisible) Lord. It was not enough just to hear or talk about what it means to be saved by Jesus; rather, the ancient Christians knew their need for ritual symbols that would suffuse their very bodies with the healing and empowering presence of Christ through the power of his Spirit. These ritual practices professed in action the Christian belief that we humans find our ultimate value and purpose precisely in and through the social, traditional and physical dimensions of our bodily existence on this earth. That was and is a claim that is far from obvious! For all the delights in the natural world our bodily senses might give us, for all the challenges and accomplishments our participation in family and social life might provide us, for all the comfort and security our cultural traditions might bestow on us, there is just as much – and tragically, often more – sickness, abandonment, pain, prejudice, conflict, failure, guilt and death. Celebrations of sacramental liturgies were and are powerful experiences revealing through tangible symbols the strong and loving presence of the Christ so often hidden and intangible in the ambiguities of our lives and world. Communally shared ritual actions, the sacraments bond the members of the Church with one another, as together they interpret the weekly and annual rhythms of life, as well as certain special, climactic moments in individuals' lives, in terms of the Christ-meaning revealed in Scripture and tradition.

Symbolising: Essential to Human Living

Catholic tradition recognises and trusts that human beings are not merely driven by animal instincts but rather find themselves continuously constructing the meaning of what they experience in their lives, often without reflection or realising it. Human individuals and societies thrive through shared traditions and the freedom of each member personally to discover one's part therein. This we do completely through our use of symbols, the words we physically produce and the array of signs and objects we use to communicate and share with one another the full range of our ideas, feelings, beliefs and commitments. Indeed, essential to human well-being is each person's sense of connection to others, of loving and being loved in friendships and family relationships, of purpose in contributing to and receiving from such wider social institutions as towns, nations, churches, ethnic groups, schools or universities, commercial companies, etc. All of this we do through shared symbols. Languages are among the most powerful conveyers of identity and worth, since they function so constantly in people's lives as to seem 'natural'. As soon as one moves to a different country (or as soon as a nation or ethnic group find themselves forced to adopt a different language), we quickly discover how much we take for granted the words and grammatical structures we use, how much our imaginations and interpretations of life are tacitly shaped by our common languages. The sharing and passing on of stories – whether they be tales of national heroes, inside jokes or memories among a group of pals, or intimate details between two lovers – is crucial to the way people acquire and maintain a sense of who they are, what they want, what or whom they are willing to suffer for, what they can look forward to.

Stories exist only in their telling and people tend to share them over food and drink. Indeed, another key symbolic activity common to all peoples is their not merely ingesting calories and hydration but their making of eating and drinking occasions for bonding with other people and even higher beings (gods, goddesses, spirits, ancestors, heavenly powers). Annual holidays or festivals are largely perpetuated by special foods and meals (ritualised eating at tables), combined with songs, stories and other objects (flowers, flags, statues, colours) symbolising the meaning of the day *and therefore* of the people and their world as they know it. Likewise, key transitional events in people's lives (what anthropologists call passage rites or life crises) including birth, coming-of-age (entering adulthood), marriage, assuming public office and death, always entail the sharing of meals. One need only consider the contemporary wedding industry to realise how important the meal is to a wedding – not to mention the singular food item of an elaborate cake. Heads of state often mark the reaching of agreements by toasting each other with valuable drinks and receive each other with elaborate banquets for which the guest lists are carefully prepared.

The scale of food rituals, however, is not normally so grand. Friends quietly revel in meeting over coffee or a pint. Only talking on the phone or briefly on the street is not sufficient for the flourishing of a friendship. Walking past pubs in Dublin any early Friday evening offers evidence for how young people ritualise the end of the work week (the daily and weekly rhythms of life) while making and maintaining friendships and intimate relationships. If one were to make the same tour of the city just one or two years later, one would discover changes in clothing and hair fashions and perhaps trends in what drinks are popular, even as the young women and men continue to share their names, interests, stories, favorite music or media stars – and thereby something of themselves. All of this is symbolism, and all of it is done by ritual patterns (how to dress, how to stand, what to say, how to order, when to arrive or leave) that those engaged in it generally follow without question, wanting to be in the middle of the scene, a part of the action.

The Sacramental Rites of the Church

People, then, largely interpret and construct the meaning of their lives through symbols and rituals that so pervade their daily and weekly life as to feel 'natural', while transitional events in the lives of individuals and social institutions occasion less frequent but more elaborate rituals explicitly symbolising the values and story of a given societal group. The Church, as a social institution with two thousand years of tradition, has its own patterns for symbolising time and ritualising key events. The central sacramental rite of the Church is the Eucharist, especially as it is celebrated on the Lord's Day, Sunday. The New Testament and other early Christian documents describe how the first generations of Christians in each city gathered every Sunday in the largest homes available to proclaim readings from the Bible (which at that time was only the Jewish scriptures), share stories of Jesus' words and deeds, read circulating letters from their key leaders (the apostles), pray for the good of the Church and world and share the bread and wine they believed became the body and blood of Christ through their giving thanks over it (Gk *eucharistein*) to God the Father. In so doing they kept the Lord's command from the Last Supper, the meal on the eve of his execution wherein he identified the typical Jewish ritual meal blessing of bread and wine with his body and blood (that is, his very life for them) as a lasting memorial.

The weekly Sunday celebration was not, however, only a recollection of what Jesus had done in the past. It was also an experience of his still being with them under the form of those symbols in the present, as well as the foretaste of the heavenly banquet they would share together with him in the future. Sunday was the day for this celebration not only because it recalled the day of the week on which Jesus was raised from the dead but also because, as the first day of the week, it symbolised the *new creation* begun in Jesus' resurrected body. The Church experienced themselves as carrying on Christ's mission under the conditions of this passing world, while finding their strength for the journey in the weekly Sunday celebration that anticipated (that is, symbolically gave them a real share in) the fullness of Christ's final victory over sin and death. Assembling on Sunday to share the Word of God and the body and blood of Christ was, and remains to this day, the fundamental symbolic ritual whereby Christians interpret the meaning, values and purpose of their lives according to the memory and active presence of the crucified and risen Jesus.

If the weekly Sunday celebration set the basic symbolic rhythm in early Christianity (annual feasts like Easter and, even later, Christmas would only slowly develop between the second and sixth centuries), baptism was the ritual for initiating individuals into the life of the Church. The climactic symbolic gesture of baptism was (and remains) the immersion or submersion in water with an invocation of the name of the Father, Son and Holy Spirit. The term 'baptism', however, referred to a broader ritual process wherein people heard the Good News (Gospel), responded with an act of faith in Jesus as Lord, were symbolically recreated in the water and received the power of the Holy Spirit. The order and details of those several elements of the baptismal process varied and the time and place for baptism was subject to each occasion. Nonetheless, the symbolism of baptism – death and rebirth by water and the Holy Spirit – in every instance not only expressed the change in life status for each convert but also *caused* that change. The water rite literally washed the power of sin and death from the new believer, while the laying on of hands and/or anointing with oil brought the power of the

Spirit upon the totality of the person – body, mind and soul. Today Catholicism continues these beliefs and ritual actions in the sacraments of baptism and confirmation.

The fundamental rites that created and sustained Christians proclaimed that sin and death no longer had power over them, that they now had the divine help they needed to pattern their lives on the self-giving love of Jesus, that they need not fear the diminishment of the body or decay of death. The fact remained, however, that people did struggle through illness, aging and death, as well as fail in their baptismal promises by sinning, sometimes even seriously. The Church developed rituals to place people undergoing these life crises in the merciful and healing hands of God through the symbolic actions and care of the local Christian community.

Illness was (and remains) an upsetting experience that can place one's personal life (as well as that of loved ones) in chaos. From both Jewish and pagan cultures the Church adopted practices of applying olive oil to the bodies of the sick and laying hands upon them. Bishops would consecrate the oil at solemn Eucharists in their communities. The invocation of the Holy Spirit on the oil changed it into a sacrament of healing for the sick. The oil was distributed and people applied it to the sick in their homes or even on themselves (sometimes drinking it). The purpose of the rituals was to draw the sick persons from their isolation and fear into the embrace of Christ, sharing one's suffering with him. As for those who were dying, the key sacrament was (and remains) the Eucharist, which in this human situation functioned as the food for the final journey from this life to the heavenly banquet, of which the bread and wine are already a foretaste. The Eucharistic ritual for the dying is called *viaticum*, which means 'going with you'. Funerals were a matter of praying confidently to God for the departed, trusting in the mercy and compassion that has been revealed in Christ. The Eucharist came to be celebrated not only for funerals but also annually on the day the person died. This was the origin of the celebration of the Eucharist on days other than Sunday.

As for Christians' failures through sin, the Church believed that such rituals as praying the Lord's Prayer (Our Father) three times a day, doing acts of charity and participating in the Sunday Eucharist healed people of most faults and failings. For the major sins of apostasy (publicly renouncing the faith), murder and adultery, however, a lengthy period of public penance and readmission to the Eucharist by the bishop was the norm for centuries. This practice, however, gave way in the west to individual confessions of sin – both grave (mortal sins) and less serious (venial sins) – with absolution by bishops or priests. The history of rites for ordaining bishops and, eventually, priests to assist them (as Christianity spread) is complex but fundamentally based on the Church's need for stable and wise leadership in continuity with the apostles, the first missionaries of Jesus.

Conclusion

The growth of Christianity as the religion of entire empires spanning Europe, Asia Minor and Africa led to the movement of the Church's sacramental rites from homes to large public buildings. The participation of large crowds anthropologically necessitated the development of more elaborate ritual gestures and heightened symbols, as well as the elaboration of language in the prayer texts and proliferation of musical chants. Up until the Middle Ages the word *sacramentum* was used in reference to any sign or symbol used in the practice of the faith. By the thirteenth century, however, theologians and councils had identified the seven ritual symbols listed in the introduction of this essay as *the* sacraments. The Council of Trent in the sixteenth century affirmed this tradition and brought much theological precision to the meaning of each sacrament, as well as mandating the revision of all ritual texts. More recently, the Second Vatican Council (1962–1965) inaugurated another period of reform and renewal for the Church's liturgy and sacraments. The hallmark of the revised rites has been their celebration in the local language of the people, their simplification and return to early Christian roots and the proclamation of scripture with preaching as integral to the practice of every sacrament. The purpose of these reforms has been to help people to participate in the rituals more actively and to hear the message of the Gospel in them more clearly. The sacramental symbols are thereby able to transform the key events, decisions and relationships of our lives into encounters with the crucified and risen Christ whose Spirit is present and active in our world.

Further Reading

Cooke, Bernard and Macy, Gary, *Christian Symbol and Ritual: An Introduction*, Oxford: Oxford University Press, 2005.

Martos, Joseph, *Doors to the Sacred: A Historical Introduction to the Sacraments in the Catholic Church*, New England: Liguori Press/Triumph Books, 2001.

Pecklers, Keith, *Worship: A Primer in Christian Ritual*, Collegeville, Minn.: The Liturgical Press, 2004.

CHAPTER 20

SACRAMENTS OF INITIATION AND RECONCILIATION

Owen F. Cummings

Introduction

The sacraments are vital stepping stones in a Catholic's journey through life. Catholics become members of the Body of Christ, the Church, through the sacraments of baptism, confirmation and the Eucharist. They are kept healthy in this body through the sacrament of penance and reconciliation. The Eucharist, as the sacrament of God's own self-donation in Christ to and for us, is the centre of the Church from which all else finds meaning.

Baptism

The most important Christian festival of the year is the Easter Vigil, usually celebrated after sunset on Holy Saturday evening. St Augustine once said that the Easter Vigil is the 'mother of all Christian feasts'. He said this because it is at this Easter Vigil that we can see all the Christian sacraments of initiation in the right sequence. The ceremony begins with baptism, followed by confirmation and ends with the Eucharist. After the Liturgy of the Word comes baptism where the celebrant says 'X, I baptise you in the name of the Father, and of the Son, and of the Holy Spirit'. After baptism comes confirmation and then, as Mass proceeds, the newly baptised receive the Eucharist since baptism finds its fulfillment in the Eucharist.

Now there are two basic theologies of baptism in the New Testament: the first, a tomb theology, is found largely in St Paul while the second, a womb theology, is principally found in St John. The tomb theology is about dying and rising with Christ. We do not grow effortlessly like plants or trees, but only through a series of dyings and risings, in the maturing rhythm of life, the rhythm of baptism.

> Are you unaware that we who were baptised into Christ Jesus
> were baptised into his death. We were indeed buried with him
> through baptism into death, so that, just as Christ was raised
> from the dead by the glory of the Father, we too might live in
> newness of life. (Rom 6:3-4)

Plunged into Christ's death in baptism, we emerge from the baptismal font
raised into his resurrected life. The living out of this baptism demands a
series of daily dyings and risings as we live out our identity in Jesus. What we
most value is established only through this lifelong personal dying and rising.
If the Eucharist is the memorial of Christ's death and resurrection, baptism
is ordered towards Eucharist.

The second theology of baptism is a womb theology, which focuses on
baptism as a spiritual 'womb' from which the baptised are born into new life
in the Church. 'Very truly, I tell you, no one can see the kingdom of God
without being born from above … without being born of water and Spirit'
(Jn 3:5-6). Baptism is imaged as a birth from above. When a child is born,
the mother puts the newborn to her breast to be fed. The sustenance and
nurture of the newborn Christian is the Eucharist, given from the breast of
Mother Church. The poet-theologian, St Ephrem of Nisibis, a fourth-
century deacon writing in Syriac, comments:

> The priesthood ministers to this womb as it gives birth;
> anointing precedes it, the Holy Spirit hovers over its streams, a
> crown of Levites surrounds it, the chief priest is its minister, the
> angels rejoice at the lost who in it are found. Once this womb
> has given birth, the altar suckles and nurtures them: her
> children eat straight away, not milk, but perfect Bread.[1]

Each of us is conceived and born into a flawed set of circumstances from the
first moment. Baptism enables us to die to our fundamental flaw by making
us the Body of Christ, by enabling our re-birth as the Body of Christ. 'Our'
is an important word here. One Christian is no Christian. We are all
together Body of Christ, Church.

Confirmation

The *Catechism of the Catholic Church* (1992) opens with a resounding acclamation of the unity and sequence of baptism, confirmation and Eucharist. As with baptism, we look to the Easter Vigil for our understanding of confirmation. The meaning of confirmation is to be understood in its location between baptism and the Eucharist. It is the event that takes place *after* baptism, and *before* God's final self-gift in the Eucharist, 'This is my body, this is my blood'.

Confirmation brings an increase and deepening of baptismal grace. The word 'grace' is an important word for Christians, but sometimes can be mistakenly thought of as a quantity. 'Grace' is simply our code word for the entire process of God's drawing us into the reality of God's own life. This process, which began in baptism, is taken further in confirmation. Confirmation increases and intensifies the relationship with God that makes us sons or daughters in the Son, uniting us more firmly to Christ. Confirmation increases the gifts of the Holy Spirit in us, the gifts already given by God in baptism, and strengthens our connection with the Church, helping to make us witnesses of Christ in everything that we say and do. What begins in baptism is intensified in confirmation and is completed in the Eucharist.

Eucharist

The Eucharist is the final sacrament of Christian initiation. The Eucharist is the central mechanism, as it were, of God's divinising us, drawing us into the life of the Trinity. The 'fundamental structure' of the Eucharist is organised around two liturgies. The first liturgy is the Liturgy of the Word and the second is the Liturgy of the Eucharist. Historically, each of these ritual actions had its origin in Jewish custom. The Liturgy of the Word came out of the synagogue service on the Sabbath day, while the Liturgy of the Eucharist came out of the table rituals of Judaism. These two rituals of Word and Eucharist came together into what we now call the Mass. It may be helpful to think of being fed by Jesus Christ at two tables, the table of the Word of God and the table of the Body of the Lord.

The Liturgy of the Word consists of the following moments: the readings from scripture, the homily, the Creed (which is patterned on belief in the Father, the Son and the Holy Spirit), and the general intercessions. In these moments, we hear God speaking to us, we profess our faith in God and we make our needs known to God. This is followed by the Liturgy of the Eucharist, which includes the presentation of the offerings, the Eucharistic Prayer and receiving of Holy Communion. The 'Preface' comes at the beginning of the Eucharistic Prayer. It does not mean preface in the ordinary English sense of the word as an introduction. Rather, it means a prayer that is said aloud and in front of the congregation. Like the Creed, the Eucharistic Prayer is also Trinitarian in structure: it is prayed to the Father, in the Son and through the Holy Spirit.

As we move into the Eucharistic prayer the language of the prayer changes. The priest moves from praying in the name of the entire assembly to speaking in the first person, in the name of Christ. The 'we' of the community that is the body of Christ becomes the 'I' of Christ, the head of his body, the Church. Christ becomes not only the one offered, but also the one who offers the Eucharist. Catholics understand the Eucharist to be the memorial of Christ's unique gift of himself on the cross. This is his sacrifice. The Eucharist is the re-presentation of this unique sacrifice here and now.

Since there is no Christ without the Church, and as Christ is the head of his body, the Church, the Church participates in the offering of Christ so that the Eucharist is also the sacrifice of the Church. In practical terms this means that the entire lives of the faithful, everything about them – their joys, works, suffering and tears – are united to and associated with this sacrifice of Christ-the-Church. Christ is present in many ways to his Church. In fact, in Catholic understanding there is nowhere that Christ is absent. Now Christ is present in a most special way in his word, in the Church's prayer, in the poor, the sick and the imprisoned, in the sacraments, in the sacrifice of the Mass, in the person of his minister and especially in the transformed bread and wine. Catholics believe that the bread and wine, by God's power and through the action of the priest, become the very body and blood of Jesus Christ, crucified and risen. When they receive these gifts in Holy Communion, they are receiving Christ and they are being received by Christ. The presence of Christ in the transformed or consecrated bread and wine is the most intense, the most full way in which Christ is present. Catholics refer to this transformation as transubstantiation. It is a complex term which means that the realities (or 'substances') of bread and wine become the reality (or 'substance') of Jesus Christ .

As we live and celebrate the Eucharist, we anticipate in hope the Parousia of the Lord. The Parousia is the final goal of creation, the second coming of Christ, the day of the Great Resurrection, the new creation. At the Parousia, our human invitation into the life of the Blessed Trinity will be creaturely complete, but that invitation to communion is already in place here and now in the Eucharist. The Eucharist is the pledge of the Parousia, the down payment on what is still fully to come.

The words of the Lord at the Last Supper point clearly to the Eucharist, the sacramental representation of his sacrificial death on the cross, as *the* sacrament of reconciliation. The priest prays the words: 'Take and eat, this is my body … Drink from it all of you, for this is the blood of the covenant, which will be shed on behalf of many for the forgiveness of sins' (Mt 26:26-27). The forgiveness of sins, reconciliation with God, is achieved by Christ's death, re-presented in the Eucharist. This makes the Eucharist in a very strict sense *the* sacrament of reconciliation, bringing about our reconciliation with God, through the forgiveness of sin. That is why the earliest Christians considered that there was no opportunity after baptism-confirmation-Eucharist to be forgiven. Sin had come to an end through this integral rite of initiation into Christ's body. Over time, however, the Church wisely saw that the forgiving and reconciling dimension of Christ's ministry among us required a discrete, though never separate, ritual action entitled penance and reconciliation, to enable us to grow morally and to become further configured to the reconciling Christ.

Penance and Reconciliation

There are three rites or forms of the sacrament in the Catholic Sacrament of Penance and Reconciliation. Rite I is the traditional one-to-one celebration of the sacrament that Catholics have been accustomed to in the course of the second millennium of Christianity. This is where the person is face to face with Christ in the person of the priest. Rite II provides for a general communal preparation for the sacrament, with individual confession of sin. This is often how children are prepared for their first experience of penance and reconciliation. They assemble together, listen to some passages from Scripture, think of their faults and failings and then make their act of sorrow or contrition to Christ through the priest. Rite III makes allowance for particularly difficult situations in which individual confession of sin is impossible, and so there is a general confession of sin followed by general absolution. What each rite has in common is the confession of sin. The acknowledgment that we are sinners and in need of healing is the base for all three rites.

'Though I fail, I weep; though I halt in pace, yet I creep to the throne of grace.' These are the words of the Anglican priest-poet, George Herbert, in his poem 'Discipline'. Configured to Jesus Christ through baptism-confirmation-Eucharist, and sustained and strengthened in him through ongoing reception of the Eucharist, our moral lives seldom match our Eucharistic identity. Made body of Christ, we do not live consistently as body of Christ. When Herbert thinks of his failings he weeps. When he considers his slow pace of maturing and growing in Christ, he keeps moving on 'to the throne of grace'. This is where the Sacrament of Penance and Reconciliation comes in. Patterned as all the sacraments are around the Eucharist, this particular sacrament heals our diseased Eucharistic lives. Made better with the medicinal grace of the sacrament in the hospital of the Church, we may continue on our pilgrimage to sanctification.

Too often penance and reconciliation is interpreted only in egocentric terms, that is to say, where the human subject/ego is almost the exclusive focus of the sacrament, and not the forgiving and healing Love that God is. In this sacrament we acknowledge that God is sheer, unbounded Love and in the presence of such a God there is the recognition that we are anything but that. In the presence of Love, moral seriousness demands our acceptance, but also our resolve, to go beyond the un-love that so often constitutes our moral lives.

Confession of sin fulfills a deep human need, a need as basic and important to life as the biological need for oxygen and light or the need for love. If we are to grow morally, we need confession of sin. Sometimes you hear the question: 'Why do we need to tell our sins to someone else, to the priest, when the God who is Love already knows what we have done, and is only too ready to forgive us?' It is much too glib to answer this question by responding, 'The priest alone is empowered to forgive sin'. While it is true that the priest is empowered to forgive our sins in the name of Jesus, we can say more about the confession of sin than that. A more satisfying answer is that if we are content to live on the surface of life, if we are content with the disfigurement and the dismemberment of humankind, if we are complacent, then we will have no *felt* need to confess our sins to another. If, however, there is authentic acknowledgment that human beings can and will do anything to each other, then we must accept the implication that our failures and sins contribute to the network of sin that threatens and destroys human life and the earth. It helps us to recognise what might be called the sociality of our sin, the infection of others by our actions. This was something well understood in the early Church in its practice of public penance. That ritual grasped that we are not atomised individuals, existing on our own in some kind of frozen individuality. In Christ we exist in and for one another. Thus, the third century Latin author, Tertullian, wrote of public penance:

> The Body of Christ does not take pleasure in the trouble of any one of its members, but grieves for each and all. With one or two individuals, there is the Church and the Church is Christ. When you cast yourself asking for prayer at the knees of the brethren, you are dealing with Christ, you are entreating Christ.[2]

The Church is communion in Christ and when one of the members of that communion is sinfully ailing, it is an occasion for all to be concerned. All share in the Christ-life together. Equally, each infects that communion of the Church with his/her own sinfulness, and so in that sense the public penance demonstrates not only the sinner's need for healing and forgiveness, but also the mutual obligations of concern for all who are Church.

If the question is then pressed, 'Why cannot a general confession of sin, as in the introductory rites of the Mass, be made without going to individual confession?' then the response must be that what is unconfessed remains unhealed. Honesty demands from us the admission that we are obscure to ourselves, to the point that we can very easily fool ourselves. We need confession of sin to another because of our innate and too obvious tendency to fool ourselves. We may not be egregious sinners, but we are sinners, and if we would be made well and whole we require the face-to-face encounter with another, with Christ. The newspapers show daily that we human beings are capable of doing anything to one another. We need to take a good and honest look at ourselves to see how we affect others negatively and to speak about ourselves to another, the priest, without any mask or excuse. Our propensity for self-evasion is so strong that we can too easily not see

EXPLORING THEOLOGY

ourselves as we really are, and justify that refusal to see in a myriad of ways. Persons-as-Church are healed of self-evasion and delusion through personal sacramental confession.

Conclusion

Sometimes it is objected that the sacrament is really necessary only in the case of grave sin. There is an element of truth in this, but it tends not to see the systemic inter-connection of all sin within the person, and so within the Church. What is forgotten is that the sacrament is called the sacrament of penance *and* reconciliation. While not all Christians may require reconciliation, all certainly require penance. By *reconciliation* is meant the formal restoration of baptised believers to the communion of the Church after serious sin. By *penance* is meant the comprehensive ongoing process, involving every feature and practice of Christian life, by which believers are more fully converted and configured to Christ. The one rite of the Church thus serves two purposes. Indeed, one could argue if the movement of penance were regularly in practice, the moment of reconciliation would be relatively unnecessary.

Notes

1   Cited in Thomas M. Finn, *Early Christian Baptism and the Catechumenate: West and East Syria*, Collegeville: The Liturgical Press, 1992, p. 155.

2   'On Repentance', 10:5-6, cited in W. A. Jurgens, *The Faith of the Early Fathers*, Vol. 1, Collegeville: The Liturgical Press, 1970, p. 131.

Further Reading

Cooke, Bernard, *Sacraments and Sacramentality*, Mystic, Conn.: 23rd Publications, 1994.

Cummings, Owen F., *Eucharistic Doctors*, New York; Mahwah, NJ: Paulist Press, 2005.

Moloney, Raymond, *Our Splendid Eucharist*, Dublin: Veritas, 2003.

Noll, Ray N., *Sacraments: A New Understanding for a New Generation*, Mystic, Conn.: 23rd Publications, 1999.

CHAPTER 21

CHRISTIAN SPIRITUALITY
Una Agnew

Introduction: Spirituality is a Way of Life

Spirituality is a hunger in the heart for love and meaning. It is a longing for
fulfilment implanted in us from birth. This desire makes us restless for
something beyond us which we may or may not recognise as God. Jesus'
words, 'I have come that you may have life and have it to the full', promise
us the fulfilment we long for (Jn 10:10). Restlessness may be the spur that
urges us to search for love and greater understanding of our destiny. Suffering
and the loss of someone dear to us plunges us into mystery and impels us to
search for deeper meaning. We search for integrity amid the multiplicity of
questions that assail us, eager to reach for what is honest and embrace what
is spiritual. The world around us may seem to thwart our best intentions and
despise our search for spiritual values. The over-arching mystery of love that
enfolds all of creation can direct our search and be a beacon of truth for
contemporary culture. Spirituality then is a search at the core of human
existence present in all the great religions of the world. Christian spirituality
can help us find meaning and support us when despair threatens.

Spirituality is Three-Pronged

Spirituality branches out in three directions at once. First, it centres on the
sacredness of the human *person* and the fire in the heart for God; second, it
directs itself towards the nearness and distance of a *God* of love and mystery;
third, it discerns how the *culture* in which we live influences and continually
affects our spirituality. When a person asks: 'What is the meaning of my life
here and now? What was I born to do? Where do I turn for help?', these are
profoundly spiritual questions. The spiritual person knows that the material
world is not the only reality; that a person is not just a statistic, a DNA code,

a genome, a chemical formula or a mere functionary. At the kernel of the self, one is oriented towards the divine somewhat as a sunflower instinctively turns towards the sun. Despite the obstacles life places in our paths, the soul possesses a homing instinct for its divine source and origin. In the well-known words of William Shakespeare, 'there's a divinity that shapes our ends roughhew them how we will.'[1]

When questions relating to God arise, a person may ask, 'Who is God for me?' I delve into mystery in search of a God who speaks to my life and answers the deepest longings of my heart. Organised religion may help me recognise God as Father, as Lover, as Companion on the journey, but each one's personal quest for God awakens in them new images born of new experiences surfacing from the depths of faith in a personal God. When the Irish poet Parick Kavanagh (no saint himself) says that 'beautiful, beautiful, beautiful God / is breathing His love by a cut-away bog', he is highlighting his personal discovery of a God in floral splendour and lavish colour, breathing love for humankind in bogland so often despised.[2] Recovery from cancer has sharpened his awareness and gratitude to a God who brings colour and beauty to his life.

The pilgrim soul today can wander, lost and astray amid the lure of commercialism. Sometimes, a restless pursuit of fame, money and pleasure causes the person to lose touch with his/her divine source and so feelings of frustration and emptiness follow. A sense of the larger mystery in life is missing. A hollow emptiness often haunts the lost or drifting contemporary spirit. In spite of desolation, an inborn capacity and hunger for the divine remains. A cry from the soul calls out to be recognised, and can survive hardship, suffering, death of friends, even cruelty and torture. The spirit of Etty Hillesum triumphed over the awfulness of Westerbork and Auschwich as Christ's spirit triumphed over the horror of his crucifixion.[3]

What is Christian Spirituality?

The person of Christ is at the centre of Christian spirituality. Christ's forgiving, healing ministry is a template for all Christian lives. He never flinched from bringing comfort to all who even touched the hem of his garment. A life lived in accordance with the example of the historical Jesus as portrayed in the gospels is the model of Christian living. Reading the gospel story is both inspiring and transforming. It forms an essential

Christian spiritual practice and is a constant source of nourishment and challenge to each culture and generation. A gospel of selfless love has inspired generations of Christians so that accumulated Christian holiness has built shrines of worship, enterprises of solidarity and networks of Christian service throughout the length and breadth of the universe. Christian love has operated especially where the cry of the poor and outcast is heard. People are called to a life of personal discipleship and loving service in imitation of Christ. Accounts of the life, death and resurrection of Jesus still have power to ignite the spirit of Christian enterprise and nourish a sense of solidarity and mission.

Christian Spirituality is Primarily Incarnational

When a person is *Christ-ened* into the Christian family the sacredness of person is fully acknowledged by the sacrament of Baptism. Water, a life-giving substance, symbolises purity and growth. The vitality and beauty of water provides a strong natural symbol for the rite of initiation into the Christian family. Just as water nourishes and cleanses so does the pouring of water at baptism signal access to the new source of life: grace. Entrance into the life of grace is a new-found immersion in love, a promise of a graced existence to counter the evil that may seek to lure us from grace. Christian spirituality calls us to realise the original blessedness of being human by responding to what is best in us. Graced living engages us in the fullest possibility of human flowering. Where before we may have struggled alone to grapple with the pull of our destiny, now, despite our imperfections, we bathe in a divine energy that fosters our graced unfolding.

Christian spirituality does not eradicate our own genetic make-up but rather accentuates the Christ-form imprinted in us as a potentiality. And so Christ becomes incarnated in us according to the blueprint of our originality. The poet Gerard Manley Hopkins has insight into Christian spirituality when he writes that, 'Christ plays in ten thousand places, lovely in limbs, and lovely in eyes not his / To the Father through the features of men's faces'.[4] Hopkins brings to mind the fact that each person bears in his or her body the traces of God and is holy simply by being the self one is born to be. Being oneself in a graced manner is our greatest personal achievement.

The Four Pillars of Authentic Christian Spirituality

Since spirituality can be nebulous and over-reliant on metaphor, some definable yardstick can be helpful in discerning the essential characteristics of a concrete, lived spirituality. Ronald Rolheiser, a favourite Catholic writer over the years, has created a convenient checklist whereby the four essential, 'non-negotiable' aspects of Catholic spirituality are outlined. His book, appropiately entitled *Holy Longing* (1999), describes his four essential pillars.[5] The first is *personal commitment to a moral life*, supported by a life of prayer. Prayer is the natural overflow of an awareness of God at the core of one's being and develops in different ways in different temperaments. A life of integity and right relationship is the natural outcome of a life of prayer. Prayer promotes reverence for self, for others and for the universe that sustains us. While Rolheiser does not make reverence for the earth explicit in his list of non-negotiables, it flows logically from his programme for moral living.

Prayerfulness and right relationship rarely comes as pure gift 'out of the blue'. It is more often the fruit of honest and sustained effort over years. Julian of Norwich achieved a life of love and contemplation only after struggling with the horrors of sin, disease and despondency in the society of her time. She countered fear of the fourteenth-century Black Death with absolute trust in God's superabundant love. Despite the climate of anxiety and fear that prevailed, her serene belief that 'All will be well' is derived from a life of faith, hope and love. Love of God and right relationship with others requires a lifelong programme of personal commitment which can rarely be achieved without the support of a prayerful and reflective community. This leads to the second pillar of Christian spirituality.

Rolheiser's second prerequisite for Catholic spirituality is a *commitment to Christian belonging*. Belonging to a faith community provides both support and challenge on the Christian pilgrimage. A praying community can challenge presuppositions, yet also provide direction and a safe port-of-call for fellow travellers. Genuine belonging in a Christian community is a prize worth fighting for and can be realised when Christians, priests and people join in solidarity for worship and good deeds. For the Irish writer John McGahern, the church spire, the smell of incense, the sound of sacred music, provided him with a source of spiritual beauty and comfort in the dismal scenario of his early family life. A Christian landscape like ours, dotted with church spires, is a constant reminder of transcendent symbols: signs reaching heavenwards reminding us that we are destined for something above and beyond us. Our churches are our heritage; they remind us that our ancestors fought hard to keep our faith alive.

The great moments of life, birth, marriage and death, are given sacramental solemnity and dignity in our Christian belonging. This belonging is developed also in less dramatic ways when small groups unite in prayer, friendship and table fellowship; reminding us that where 'two or three are gathered in my name', God is present (Mt 18:20). Belonging also provides expertise in a network of supports. Our Christian theologians guide our reflections on God and keep us free of error while different spiritualities provide for different spiritual needs and spiritual mentors and wisdom figures help us discern how God is at work among us today.

When a community-based Christian life of belonging is established, a sense of social solidarity and protection of the weakest in society tends to prevail. This *dedication to justice* is the third hallmark of a truly Christian spirituality. To live a Christian life demands the development of a social conscience along with an understanding of how unjust structures oppress the poorest and weakest in society. Christ gave us examples of his perennial concern for the outcast and marginalised. Gospel parables such as the Prodigal Son and the Lost Sheep remind us how Christ is gentle with the outcast. He often castigated those in authority who placed heavy burdens on others while they themselves lived privileged lives. Hypocrisy and injustice in society are exposed and treated more harshly by Jesus than human weakness and fallibility.

Yet authentic Christian spirituality refrains from taking the high moral ground of self-righteous indignation in the face of weakness. Christian living instead favours *mellowness of heart*, the fourth mark of authentic Christian spirituality. The secret of true mellowness is a blend of gratitude for the grace of living and joy in the lives of others. In this attitude of hospitality, the 'bruised reed' is not crushed nor the prodigal son excluded. A sense of justice and care for the less fortunate saves Catholic spirituality from any self-satisfied 'I'm-alright-Jack' attitudes. A mellow heart suggests a healthy antidote to self-preoccupation and blatant individualism. This fourth and perhaps most challenging of Rolheiser's non-negotiables requires the asceticism of loving acceptance of self and others that leads to Christian joy.

It is a far cry from the self-righteous, holier-than-thou attitudes that have often characterised Christian spirituality in the past. These four non-negotiables suggest a personal quest for integrity lived out in the presence of divine mystery in a climate of solidarity and healthy interdependence.

Balancing Essentials with Special Gifts

When we look carefully at these four non-negotiables of Christian spirituality, we can see that together they provide an essential foundation for authentic Christian living. They blend kindness with caution, simplicity with celebration and a good self-care with self-sacrifice for others. Jealous acquisition of all four does not guarantee God's grace, but rather ensures the proper conditions for authentic spiritual living. Neither will these essential components be present to the same degree in each person. Certain people live different aspects more intensely according to their calling. Some are called to lives of prayer and contemplation, others to social justice and still others to foster the ecclesial dimension of Christian living. Some have a discernible charism for communal living and liturgical prayer while others are variously gifted with care for the earth, mystical prayer or solidarity with God's poor. Mellowness and hospitality of heart becomes the specialty of those who welcome saints and sinners alike, and refuse to stand in condemnation of any. As each person struggles to preserve a balance of all four, the freedom of God's spirit is evident in individuals. In this way, Christian spirituality accumulates a rich medley of spiritualities derived from many gifts. It is in a spirit of mellowness of heart that we learn to respect and celebrate the manifold nature of God's gifts expressed in the lives of others.

The Language of Spirituality

The search for God expresses itself in metaphor as 'journey' 'seeking', 'pilgrimage' etc. More and more people are eager to discover their pathway to God and find spiritual guidance for the journey. Gurus of all kinds present themselves, eager to satisfy the spiritual needs of our time. Whole sections of bookstores are given over to Tarot, Zen and New Age invitations to spiritual knowledge and fulfilment. People become confused and even fascinated by the lure of spiritual benefits derived from Feng Sui, Tao meditation, colour therapy and art. In a contemporary post-modern ambience, the search for God may appear to be random and map-less, though the orientation of the human for the transcendent remains largely the same. The language of spirituality often reflects the driveness of the seeker. Dag Hammarskjöld (1905–1961), once Secretary to the United Nations, sensed the fear and fascination in his search for ultimate truth. He says:

> I am being driven forward
> Into an unknown land.
> The pass grows steeper,
> The air colder and sharper.
> A wind from my unknown goal
> Stirs the strings
> Of expectation.
> Still the question:
> Shall I ever get there?
> There where life resounds,
> A clear pure note
> In the silence.[6]

Spiritual journeying is both compelling and terrifying since it faces us with mystery.

For those who have surrendered to the mystery of love in their lives, a language of love and desire has flowered throughout the centuries. Mystics are ordinary people keenly aware of a fire and an energy that burns within them. It was such a fire that St John of the Cross (1542–1591) experienced as a hidden flame of love for God. St Francis of Assisi (1182–1226), fired by joy, surrendered his possessions for a life as 'God's troubadour', bearing the wounds of Christ and witnessing to Christian joy. St Paul single-handedly organised the early Catholic Church, spurred on by energy and verve for which the only explanation was 'Christ in me'. St Teresa (1515–1582), the Spanish mystic, was conscious of walking in God's company as she reformed a great religious order in the teeth of the ecclesiastical world. In all of the mystics we find a superabundant energy that has been schooled and transformed into a single-minded life given over to God.

Poetry often captures something of the mystery that dwells in the heart. Graced day-to-day living almost defies expression and yet the poet often finds words to express the sentiments that rise from the soul. Hopkins gives expression to the miracle of God's presence in daily life when he exclaims: 'The world is charged with the grandeur of God / It will flame out, like shining from shook foil.'[7] Similarly, a God-intoxicated Kavanagh prays for 'faith to be alive / When April's ecstasy / dances in every whitethorn tree'.[8] Both Christian poets sense the compelling energy of God in the universe and bow in reverence towards it. On the other hand, a deformative dynamic in self and global structures can hinder the normal evolution of spirituality, to such an extent that the universe becomes a 'Waste Land', drained of spiritual energy and, in T.S. Eliot's words, we become 'hollowed', 'empty' and 'dried' of significance.[9]

Society can Crush or Foster Spiritual Growth

In many situations in contemporary culture the capacity for mystery in a person can be denied, bruised and ignored. In such cases a person may be reduced to an object, a number, a cipher. Yet the soul can never be obliterated, crushed, annihilated. The pressures of economic development, the pursuit of pleasure and greed can cause a society to become depersonalised, hollowed out and bereft of spiritual flourishing. A living spirituality, on the other hand, recognises the sacredness of each human self and strives to facilitate spiritual emergence and graced development of each person. The need for stillness, space, relationality, solidarity: all are prerequisites for spiritual development. Each person needs time to reflect, to study, to pray, to sit in the presence of mystery in order to deal with the fire of desire that burns within. This is spiritual living which allows the self and others unfold in tune with the earth's resources and the aspiration in all to fullness of life.

Conclusion

A healthy Christian spirituality can lend certain wisdom, even radiance, to life, even when the person is a seeker, uncertain of the goal beyond reach. Spirituality helps us live with as much equanimity as we can muster. When a person lives, faithful to the indwelling, overarching mystery, he or she becomes a locus of inner strength, generating life and energy for others. Spiritual energy operates in a wave-like movement, and in the right conditions envelops the whole personality and life itself in a transforming dynamic. Such is the dynamism of a healthy spirituality that it engages with people and creation in a search for healing, truth, justice and love; it engages with an interiority in all things that extends to limitless horizons.

Before the mystery of each person I occasionally stand in awe and wonder at the magnificence of creation and the extraordinary influence one person can exert in a world starved of spiritual significance. The person is at the centre of spirituality since each person can detect within themselves a goal, a project and a capacity to realise the dream of God implanted in their lives. Of course I too can become empty and despondent and lose sight of the 'star' that guides me. But even if I drift temporarily off course, I also have the capacity to be nudged, guided back onto my pathway to God. Gradually, with awareness of spirit, I begin to sense the ultimate meaning of situations, events, phenomena that present themselves. A spiritual person is more likely to detect missing values in a society, in a community and engage wisely and generously in projects that restore human dignity.

The call of spirituality then is one of awareness, of awakening the spiritual depths of the soul. Stillness can make us either anxious or reflective. When I feel uneasy in silence, it often means that I am unable to listen to my spirit's call. I may need the guidance of a mentor – a soul-friend who understands the initial complexities of engaging in spiritual living. Practicing the art of stillness may be the first step in listening to my inner self and my deepest spiritual longings. Listening to my soul brings inner peace. A reflective life is mindful of self, others and society. Spiritual reading, meditation and spiritual conversation lead to a deeper awareness of God at the centre of the soul. Thus awakened, the spirit engages in lifelong practices that deepen awareness of mystery. By living spiritually we live in tune with God's love at the depth of our being and become more sensitive to the sacredness of others and their needs. Living in tune with self and God gradually makes us aspire to the divinisation of our lives in communion with God and others. Such a life is holy.

Notes

1   William Shakespeare, *Hamlet* Act V Scene II.
2   Patrick Kavanagh, *The Complete Poems*, New York and Newbridge, Co Kildare: 1984, p. 291.
3   *Etty: The Letters and Diaries of Etty Hillesum, 1941–1943*, Wm. B. Eerdmans Publishing Co., 2002.
4   W.H. Gardner (ed.) *Gerard Manley Hopkins: Poems and Prose*, Harmondsworth: Penguin Books, 1953, p. 51.
5   R. Rolheiser, *Holy Longing: The Search for a Christian Spirituality*, New York: Doubleday, 1998, pp. 45–70.
6   D. Hammarskjöld, *Markings*, tr. W.H. Auden & Leif Skjöberg, London: Faber and Faber, 1966, p. 31.
7   *Gerard Manley Hopkins: Poems and Prose*, op. cit., p. 27.
8   Kavanagh, *The Complete Poems*, op. cit., p. 8.
9   T.S. Eliot, *The Poems and Plays of T.S. Eliot*, London: Faber and Faber, 1969.

Further Reading

Agnew, Una, *The Mystical Imagination of Patrick Kavanagh: A Buttonhole in Heaven*, Dublin: Columba, 1998.

Downey, Michael, *Understanding Christian Spirituality*, New Jersey: Paulist Press, 1997.

Dreyer, Elizabeth and Burrows, Mark (eds) *Minding the Spirit: The Study of Christian Spirituality*, Baltimore and London: The John Hopkins University Press, 2005.

Flanagan, Bernadette and Kelly, David (eds) *Lamplighters: Exploring Spirituality in New Contexts*, Dublin: Veritas, 2004.

Gardner, W.H. (ed.) *Gerard Manley Hopkins: Poems and Prose*, Harmondsworth: Penguin Books, (1953) 1963.

Rolheiser, Ronald, *The Holy Longing: The Search for a Christian Spirituality*, New York: Random House, 1998.

SECTION V

CONTEMPORARY CATHOLIC IDENTITY

CHAPTER 22

CATHOLIC IDENTITY: 'LOVE THAT POWERFUL LEAVES ITS OWN MARK'

Anne Hession

Introduction

In the first novel in the Harry Potter series, *Harry Potter and the Philosopher's Stone*, the hero gets an unexpected invitation to attend a school of magic for young wizards called Hogwarts School of Witchcraft and Wizardry. This highly prized gift sets Harry off on a journey to discover his true identity. The story of his quest and his endeavour to live out his identity and bring it to completion forms the basis of the Harry Potter novels so beloved all over the world.

'No one has greater love than this' (Jn 15:13)

Harry, according to the first novel, hears the story of his origins from the headmaster's messenger, Hagrid. He discovers that he was born a wizard even though he spent the first ten years of his life with 'muggles' or 'non-magic folk'. Harry's parents, James and Lily, were also wizards who were killed by the evil Lord Voldemort when Harry was one year old. His mother Lily threw herself in front of Harry on that occasion, thus saving his life: Voldemort's power somehow broke, and miraculously he survived. Harry still bears the scar of that event – 'love that powerful leaves its own mark' – and is known thereafter as 'the boy who lived'.[1] When Harry enters the wizarding world, he discovers that he has been loved and respected there from a very young age. From then on Harry discovers that he has an important role to play in the battle between good and evil, and that his approach to people who are troubled or excluded will shape who he ultimately becomes.

Harry's parents chose to live in a way that seeks transformation through self-sacrifice and love rather than the misuse of power. When he joins

Hogwarts he becomes part of a community of people (Gryffindor) who will help him develop virtues and commitments like theirs. The story of his mother's great love shows Harry the way to pursue good and to overcome evil. Furthermore, the virtues learned in Gryffindor (courage, solidarity, perseverance, fortitude, bravery, self-sacrifice, mercy) sustain Harry in his quest for goodness, enabling him to overcome the harms, dangers, temptations and distractions he encounters along the way. Eventually, when Harry has tackled the various challenges, which provide the novels with their episodes and incidents, his true identity will be revealed.

Identity: Personal and Historical

Like Harry, we all have a deep desire to know who we are and to have the freedom to act in a way that expresses that sense of identity. We sense that each of us lives a life that is our own and no one else's, which has its own particular meaning. The question of who we are is answered by each of us when we face our own personal questions of freedom, responsibility, finitude, anxiety, aloneness, tragedy and death. At the same time our personal quest for identity is carried out in a world overshadowed by the frightening poverty, injustice and discrimination endured by millions of people, most of whom do not have the luxury to reflect on their identity as we are doing now. Yet it could be claimed that our awareness of and response to their suffering and to the future of the earth will play a central part in shaping who we eventually become. In short, how we form and express our identity has both personal and historical consequences: our unique identity and the future of the world are inextricably intertwined.

A Vision and a Way

Each of us seeks to develop a notion of personal identity that has some unity, integrity and constancy. It is a natural human drive to want to know if there is an identifiable 'me' who exists through all the chances and changes of life. A unified personal identity of this kind can only be developed through commitment to some *vision of* what is true, good, beautiful and real. This vision inspires passion and desire, providing an ideal standard by which to live. It enables us to understand our own growth (biography) as well as the human story in which we fit (history). Then it is helpful to discover a *way* in which we can remain true to the vision that guides our lives.[2] The 'way' chosen enables us to develop the intellectual, moral and spiritual virtues that make it possible for us to know and love the vision in our lives and to overcome the obstacles we encounter on the journey.

It is helpful to think of the *vision* as a narrative that links your birth to your life to your death and the *way* as a set of practices and commitments that enable you to shape your own unique narrative, through your ethical choices in the world. The narrative is the more or less consistent story told by your life. It traces your unique destiny and responsibility amidst all the experiences you have. It is in the context of this overarching *vision* and *way* that your life is intelligible to yourself and others.

Catholics believe that the question of who we are and the meaning of our lives cannot be separated from the knowledge of who God is and what God means for every individual person and for the world. The particular manner in which we explain this extraordinary story of love constitutes the *vision* and the *way* that shapes a Catholic's life.

The Vision: God in All Things

The Catholic *vision* begins with the belief that all of reality, human and non-human, is possessed by and rooted in the mystery of God. Furthermore, we believe that God has chosen to reveal Godself to us because God seeks to draw the entire world into God's own life. The best metaphor that describes God is given to us by the writer of the First Letter of John when he says that 'God is love' (1 Jn 4:16). This is because God has revealed Godself as *love* in the incarnation, cross and resurrection of Jesus Christ. To say that God *is* love is to say that God is radically relational and hence person-like. In other words, God freely creates human beings *in order* to enter into a loving relationship with them. This is salvation: God loves us so profoundly that he promises to uphold this relationship of love despite our personal sin and the sin of the world. Catholic identity emerges when we freely respond to a personal invitation to live in communion with God.

Our deepest desire as Catholics is to surrender to God, to glorify God and to carry out God's purposes. This is what it means to say that we are created *in the image of* God. We each have a natural orientation, a force in our nature, leading us to become sharers in the life of God. Eastern orthodox theologians have a nice way of expressing it. Human life, they tell us, is a journey into divine likeness, into *theosis*, which literally means 'becoming

God-like'. Western theologians use the word 'grace' to describe the way God draws us to Godself, calling us to a life of partnership, right relationship and communion. And our final fulfilment, the culmination of who each of us is, is union with God. Catholic identity unfolds when we carry out our vocation (*vocare*, 'to call'): reflecting, worshipping and trusting God.

We can respond to the divine call, by accepting God's presence in faith, by hoping in God's promises and by making love of God and neighbour the touchstone of our lives. This is conversion. We move away from egoism, consciously turn from the self to God, and remain open to hearing a call that comes from beyond ourselves. We no longer search for our identity in terms of fulfilling all our wishes, needs and desires and are willing to relinquish the illusion that we can overcome the brokenness we experience in ourselves and in the world by our own power. Catholic identity is accepting the mandate to participate in a love story: the story of God's salvation of the world.

Love that powerful leaves a mark

Catholics use *the principle of sacramentality* to explain how God draws us into the divine life. This principle states that God's communication with us is not direct but is mediated by the created world. We encounter God as a creative, healing, transforming power in the ordinary experiences and things of life – in our minds and bodies, in our relationships and friendships, in our work and leisure activities, in nature and the whole created order. When we become attuned to the divine presence in the world, we acquire an ability to see that there is a divine dimension to the ordinary experiences of our lives. Such an ability to discern and believe that God is present and active in our lives and in the world is referred to by commentators as a 'sacramental imagination'. It is, as Saint Ignatius of Loyola said, to be able 'to see God in all things'.

To choose to see the world as 'sacramental' is to be able to glimpse God's presence and providence in ordinary moments, places, memories of persons and events. In the depths of every human experience and activity is an opportunity to respond to and attain to God. Whenever we love unconditionally, whenever we are struck by truth, whenever we remain faithful to the claims of our conscience even when it's not popular to do so, whenever we retain our hope when life seems daunting, boring or tiresome, whenever we refuse to act on hateful thoughts – whenever, in a word, we

EXPLORING THEOLOGY

overcome our egoism and despair and acknowledge that God is calling us to Godself in and through our freely chosen responses, *then* we are living out our Catholic identity: our life in God.

Of course we are free to refuse to participate in what God is doing to save the world. This is when we sin. We turn in on ourselves and reject the call to live our lives in right relation to God and neighbour. We deny the power of life and love. But when we accept, we are helped along the way by the law and the grace of God. God opens up our human freedom from the egocentrism of sin to hope, faith and active love. Then, the closer we are to fulfilling our destiny, the more qualities and virtues we display that have their origin in the Spirit of God. We become saints, friends of God and prophets (Wis 7:27), participating in the holiness of God.

The Way: Jesus Christ

If this is the vision of Catholic identity, then what is the *way*? The great orthodox theologian, St Athanasius, writing in the fourth century, answers our question in his famous phrase: 'God became a human being so that human beings might become "like" God.'[3] The *way* to Catholic identity is Jesus Christ. Jesus is the ultimate mark or sacrament in history of the compassionate love of God. Since the beginning of the Church, Jesus' life, death and resurrection have been understood in terms of *God's* very self, reaching out to humankind, fulfilling God's desire to draw all things to Godself. At the same time, Jesus was a fully human person who lived a fully human life. Therefore, in Jesus we see the successful union of the passionate love of God *and* the human quest for identity undertaken by each of us.

Jesus did not make himself the focus of his preaching and mission. The proclamation of the reign of God – God's promise of peace and justice, love and freedom, of fullness of life for all – was at the heart of his work. Anointed and empowered by the Spirit of God, he devoted his ministry to healing and reconciling to building up human persons, especially the poor and downtrodden. When he healed, he expressed his experience that God's desire for human well-being is so strong that God acts against the personal and social evils that prevent people from living full human lives. Today, as then, God's saving, healing presence is encountered by Christians in or through Jesus.

Another key principle of Catholicism is *the principle of mediation*. It affirms that 'created realities not only contain, reflect or embody the presence of God, they make that presence spiritually effective for those who avail themselves of these sacred realities'.[4] In other words, God draws us into the divine life through material realities and objects. The human Jesus forms the central point of mediation for Christian experience of the saving love of God. That is why we worship and pray to God *in and through* Jesus, the Christ. It is through the Spirit of Christ that we experience God's salvation, enabling us to develop the virtues of faith, hope and love. Finally, Jesus reveals and mediates salvation by going ahead of us and showing us the *way* in both personal and social spheres. Catholic identity involves becoming a disciple of Jesus because he is *the way*.

The One who Lived

Jesus is *the way* because he shows us how to live a fully human life. The fact that the absolute Mystery of God became a human person and lived a fully human life is the most extraordinary compliment ever paid to being human. Theologian, Michael Himes, writes that the incarnation points to 'the immense dignity, value and importance of genuine, full and authentic humanity'. It also reveals that 'it is by being fully and authentically human, by being as human as we can possibly be, that you and I become more fully and truly like God, or to put it another way, that we become holy'.[5] Catholic identity is first and foremost about living one's life to the full, developing one's potential and celebrating the gift of life as something essentially good.

Throughout his life, Jesus remained utterly faithful to his relationship with God and to what he understood God to be calling him to. He accepted in faith that God is good to the weak and that this goodness can and will triumph over evil. He *lived* his belief that God would transform the lives of the poor through action against oppression. Most importantly, he freely chose to accept the consequences of this choice – even death on a cross – for the sake of deeper relationships with God and with others. St Paul's letter to the Philippians (Phil 2:5-11) celebrates the fact that Jesus, though equal to God, chose to empty himself (*kenosis*, 'self-emptying') and to share our predicament, our feeling of alienation, our suffering and even our fear of death. In raising him from the dead, God affirmed that the way Jesus lived his life – the way of service and self-transcendence – is the way to full human fulfilment.

The life, death and resurrection of Jesus became known in the liturgical tradition as 'the paschal mystery'. This mystery reveals to us the pattern of living that draws us into the life of God, offering us the possibility of salvation. To experience the paschal mystery is to use our freedom, acquired for us by Christ, to decide to live and die for the sake of others, particularly those in need. Then, in imitation of Christ, we find that our true strength comes from weakness: from letting go of status, strength, power, freedom, possessions and autonomy. Catholic identity is knowing that it is personhood, the ability to transcend ourselves in love, that is determinative of who we are.

Jesus experienced the power of God as Spirit in his life and this empowerment was manifested in his saving actions. With his resurrection, he becomes God's life-giving Spirit for us today. Jesus is who and what we are to become – sharers in the life and existence of God! The Spirit of the risen Christ now brings about the true communion of God and us. The Spirit of God, the Spirit of Christ, the Holy Spirit, incorporates us into the very life of God, leading us to God through Christ. Empowered by the self-gift of God, the Spirit of Jesus Christ, to our human freedom, we can choose to shape our lives on the pattern of Jesus and participate in what God is doing to save the world.

Remaining faithful to Jesus' *way* may lead us where we did not expect to be led. Frequently those who seek to live by love must give up part of their own life. However, because we share in Jesus' crucifixion by surrendering our lives for others, we share also in the hope of resurrection. Just as Jesus' resurrection ensured that all of his actions live on in God, every act of inclusion, every act of hope and love in history, every act of healing and reconciliation carried out by our human freedom will be transformed into the permanent, definitive and ultimate reality of the reign of God. As we dedicate our lives to discipleship of Jesus, in the power of the Holy Spirit, we believe that the responsible character of our identity will be fulfilled in heaven when we will be gathered into a new life of communion with the Triune God.

A Communal Vision and Way

Catholic identity is never achieved alone. Someone must tell us the good news; others have tried the way and found it to be trustworthy. But most important of all, faith in the God of Jesus Christ is impossible without love for one another. God comes to us and we go to God in community. This is a third key principle of Catholicism: *the principle of communion*. We are Catholics because *through the Christian community* we have met Jesus Christ, responded to him in faith and learned the virtues and commitments of his particular 'way'. We come to understand, experience and embody the love of God in and through our love of neighbour and the created world. When we love one another, the presence of the Church in human history is a mark (sacrament) that manifests God's desire to draw *all* people into the divine life. Catholic identity is realising that through our lives, our confessing, our membership of Church, we make salvation manifest sacramentally to the whole human race which has been redeemed by Christ.[6]

Already we noted that our way to God and God's way to us depends on our access to the person of Jesus Christ, his saving words and actions. Some two thousand years after the life of Jesus, we can only achieve this access through the mediation of the community of faith. All the saving acts and words of Jesus are mediated in the church. Words, stories, signs, symbols, music and gestures make present, in a uniquely powerful way, the mysteries of faith. Catholicism's commitment to the mediated nature of God's encounter with us explains our community's historic emphasis on the special mediating functions of Mary (the mother of Jesus), the priesthood, the seven sacraments, the magisterium and the Papacy. Each of these plays a particular role in helping us to relate the *vision* and the *way*, at this time in history, thus enabling us to be formed in the distinctive rhythms of paschal living.

The seven sacraments are specific signs of the irreversible love of God which is effective in forgiving us and drawing us into God's life. At Mass we remember and celebrate what God has achieved in Jesus: the wonderful joining of God and humanity in the mystery of the incarnation, which makes it possible for our awesome sharing in the very life of God. Similarly, our participation in Christian disciplines such as prayer, fasting, pilgrimage and meditation helps us to submit to the paschal pattern of living in imitation of Christ. Having fallen in love with God, the church community enables us to stay in love, mediating our encounter with Christ and of Christ with us.

Conclusion

Harry Potter is marked by goodness from the beginning and his mother's actions display a powerful self-emptying love of her son. It is in the context of a particular community (Hogwarts) and house (Gryffindor) that Harry's capacities to know, love and do are honoured, expressed and tested. He chooses to embody the Gryffindor vision in his own unique way, imitating the model of personhood exemplified by his mother's actions and developing new embodiments of the virtues that unify a Gryffindor life. Paradoxically, as he seeks his own identity through his choices Harry finds that he 'lives into' an identity that was given to him as a gift.

The *vision* of Catholic identity is also a story of the power, promise and possibility of love. It's a story of being called to live our lives in communion with God through the risen Lord Jesus Christ in the power of the Holy Spirit. For each of us personally, the story begins with our origin in God and ends with our meeting with God by the light of glory in eternity. The *way* is a lifelong process of conforming our lives to the history that Christ lived and continues to live among us: a process of transcendence and radical self-giving for the sake of others and for the world. When we abandon ourselves to God and neighbour, we receive the graced gift of a new identity as children of God and brothers and sisters of Jesus Christ. We become more and more capable of knowing and loving the living God who gifts us with identity. Now our identities, because of their openness to God and God's saving activity in the world, will always be more than we can grasp. It is only at the end of the world that we will fully understand its history and it is only when we are indissolubly one with God that we will fully understand our lives.[7]

Notes

1   J. K. Rowling, *Harry Potter and the Philosopher's Stone*, London: Bloomsbury, 1997, p. 216.

2   I am indebted to the brilliant theologian David Tracy for my understanding of vision and way.

3   St Athanasius, *De Incarnatione Verbi Dei*, 54, 3: PG, 192B.

4   Richard P. McBrien, 'Catholic Identity in a Time of Change', *The Furrow*, Vol. 55, No. 9, September 2004, p. 458.

5   Michael J. Himes, The *Mystery of Faith: An Introduction to Catholicism*, Cincinnati, Ohio: St. Anthony Messenger Press, 2004, pp. 23–24.

6   Karl Rahner, 'The Person in the Sacramental Event', *Theological Investigations* XIV, New York: The Seabury Press, 1976, p. 180.

7   Thomas F. O' Meara, 'A History of Grace' in Leo J. O'Donovan (ed.) A *World of Grace*, Washington, DC: Georgetown University Press, 1995, p. 87.

Further Reading

Dulles, Avery, *The Catholicity of the Church*, Oxford: Clarendon Press, 1985.

Cooke, Bernard, *Sacraments and Sacramentality*, Mystic, Conn.: 23rd Publications, 1994.

Hession, Anne, 'Educating for Catholic Identity: Contemporary Challenges' in Hession and Kieran, *Children, Catholicism and Religious Education*, Dublin: Veritas, 2005.

Radcliffe, Timothy, *What is the Point of Being a Christian?* London; New York: Burns & Oates, 2005.

CHAPTER 23

CATHOLIC FEMINIST THEOLOGY

Mary Grey

Introduction: The Maps are out of Date

Feminist theology has permanently changed the face of theology by introducing gendered thinking into the study of religion. This chapter explores the meaning of this specifically for Catholic theology, in its implications for the understanding of the human person, community, relationships and God. First, the origins and reasons for the rise of feminism in theology and society are examined. Second, its main emphases are highlighted and third, some of the key questions it poses for Catholicism are briefly discussed, with a case study, re-examining one foundational doctrine.

The Origins and Rise of Feminism in Theology and Society

For centuries there was an assumption that the human person was a generic male and the word 'mankind' was supposed to subsume both male and female. However, a closer look at the definitions of the human subject reveals that in fact these referred to men. As Simone de Beauvoir put it: 'He is the subject, she is the other.'[1] This is seen in the way that women used to be defined as 'daughter of', 'wife of' or 'mother of', without the right to vote and denied access to education and the professions. It was assumed that women would 'naturally' take a caring or service role in society. In psychology the male psyche was offered as a model for all. Again, Freudian sexuality followed the masculine model, wherein women were defined by a lack and by penis envy. No wonder Freud – who self-confessedly did not understand women – cried, 'What do women want?'

Feminism arose as a secular moment for the liberation of women and only gradually became a movement within theology. It can be defined as the struggle for the rights of women against oppression, the striving for justice

CATHOLIC FEMINIST THEOLOGY   273 and for a different society based on equal rights and full personhood for women. Feminism contributes to transformed patterns of relations in society as a whole. This has developed into not one feminist theology but a global family of theologies whose focus is not exclusively on women. Gradually the understanding has grown that when the aim of feminist theology is to change a social order from one of violence and domination to one promoting justice, peace and transformed patterns of relating, this affects all categories of society, women, men and children, and especially the most vulnerable. The inspiration of the American poet Adrienne Rich has been a vital part:

> My heart is touched by all I cannot save
> So much has been destroyed
> I want to cast my lot in
> With those who
> With no extraordinary power
> Re-constitute the world.[2]

Although there were deeper historical roots to the rise of feminism, for example, the publication of Mary Wollstonecraft's *On the Vindication of the Rights of Women* (1792) in Britain and the Women's Rights Movement and the Movement for the abolition of slavery in the nineteenth century in the US, the more immediate awakening came in the 1960s with the translation into English of Simone de Beauvoir's *The Second Sex,* and the publication of the works of Germaine Greer, Kate Millett, Betty Friedan and Dale Spender, to name but a few.[3]

From the start a key principle evolved: as the Catholic religious sister Maria Riley wrote: 'The symbiosis between personal and political transformation is the basis of feminist praxis.'[4] However, the kinds of feminism that developed manifested different emphases – all of which would come to be reflected in Catholic feminism. For example, liberal feminism (the earliest form, with roots in Enlightenment thinking) stresses equal rights and the achieving of equal access to all strata of society. Cultural or romantic feminism stresses the natural moral superiority of women and the need for that superiority to take shape in public life. It identifies male culture as 'aggressive, competitive, rationalistic, despotic', whereas women, alternatively, are pictured as more caring, patient and reconciling. This is sometimes caricatured as the image of the 'Angel in the House'.⁵ Whereas romantic feminism is usually considered essentialist and idealist, we need to be aware of its ideological appearance in Catholic theology, for example, in John Paul II's Letter, *Mulieris dignitatem*, where the document describes the nature of woman as ordered towards self-giving.⁶ Radical/separatist feminism condemns patriarchy's logic of domination/subordination and develops an alternative female culture. On the one hand this challenges the family as an institution as well as the 'myth' of romantic love, exposing the violent means used to control women such as rape, domestic violence and pornography. On the other hand it celebrates women's culture and women's space with the goal of being liberated from male space. This type does not find favour with most Catholic feminists, who choose to work from within the institutions and communities in which they find themselves, but also because radical feminism tends to ignore other oppressions like racism. The final type, socialist feminism, tends to be the preferred basis for Catholic feminists. Insisting on class analysis, it critiques radical feminism for ignoring analyses of class, race and historical circumstances. Socialist feminism seeks to change the structural relations between men and women within a comprehensive theory of women's oppression. Its central lens is the sexual division of labour, so a structural analysis of work conditions is undertaken, including the invisible work of women in the home and the way that the economic base of women's reproductive work in child rearing, as well as care for the elderly, is rendered invisible.

The Rise of Feminist Theologies

Feminist theologies reflect all strands of secular feminism: we could speak here of the dawn of a new consciousness and the sense that the theological maps they gave us were out of date.⁷ The concept of the human subject, language and the foundations of post-enlightenment thinking had all been gender and context blind. A new cartography was called for, not only in Europe and North America but globally. For Roman Catholic feminists – such as Rosemary Radford Ruether, Elisabeth Schüssler Fiorenza, Mary Daly and Catherine Halkes – the catalyst for the new consciousness was the Second Vatican Council (1962–65). Mary Daly described how the wind of change, which the Council documents caused, created enormous hope that the injustices inflicted on women through the centuries would be replaced by just structures between women and men in the Church.[8]

In the two-thirds world the women's movements were also impacting on theology. Virginia Fabella, a religious sister from the Philippines, refers to the breakthrough of women's voices at the Ecumenical Institute of Third World Theologians' Conference (EATWOT) in Delhi in 1981, now called the 'eruption within the eruption'.[9] As a consequence of this conference the EATWOT Women's Commission was founded. The final statement of the conference included the commitment to take seriously 'the common experience of women in their liberational struggle'.[10] Each region developed features of this new cartography drawn from the specificity of context and history. Latina theologians characterised liberation theology from women's perspective as unifying, relational, free, and identified it as being marked by humour, joy and celebration, and above all, by hope.[11] Asian women theologians denounce the oppression of women as systemic sin, which in their context means, for example, child marriage, dowry deaths, female infanticide, domestic violence and trafficking.[12] For Asian, Latina and African women, their roots in colonialism means that developing a post-colonial theology is of crucial importance. For African-American women theologians, known as womanist theologians, their history of suffering in slavery is crucial and slave narratives are considered as sacred texts.[13] However, at the same time their roots in the bible and church community are equally important. This rootedness in community is shared also by mujerista theologians – the theology of Hispanic American women.[14]

What is Feminist Theology?

Feminist theology is actually a growing family of theologies and is characterised by tremendous diversity. Nonetheless, there are common features, including the ongoing process of awakening to new consciousness, developments in the academy, in culture and society as well as in spirituality. As an academic discipline feminist theology has had a difficult struggle being accepted, sometimes considered as a *changeling* in the academy, of being lightweight, or of substituting political activism for 'solid theology.'[15] Yet when feminist theology manages to keep in creative tension with developments in feminist theory as well as with the concrete struggles of women against oppression, including injustice within the Church herself, then it is at its best.

As an academic discipline feminist theology spans all disciplines, biblical, doctrinal, ethical, as well as pastoral and liturgical areas.[16] Many would identify two movements within feminist theology: (i) a deconstructive or critical analysis of traditional theology as detrimental to the humanity and full becoming of women, and by extension, the whole of humanity, and (ii) a reconstructive moment, when, for example, key doctrines are re-envisioned, factoring in the life experience, dreams and critical reflection of women from diverse contexts. Rosemary Ruether's 'canon' has been very influential:

> The critical principle of feminist theology is the promotion of the full humanity of women. Whatever denies, diminishes or distorts the full humanity of women is therefore appraised as not redemptive.[17]

Methodologically, feminist theology initially placed enormous emphasis on women's experience as theological source and showed awareness of the diversity of contexts and the danger of white, western women speaking as if their experience was normative. Now 'experience' seems a poisoned chalice unless it is qualified by critical, contextual analysis, in a postmodern climate. Yet a very important characteristic of feminist theology is the attempt to 'hear into speech' unheard and silenced voices of women, be they caused by poverty, violence, racism or heterosexism – or a mixture of oppressions. Thus, story-telling, consensus in decision making and a redefinition of power, from that of control and dominance to power as empowerment or as 'mutuality-in-relation' (my own definition) are all prominent features.[18]

Catholic Feminism

How has feminism changed the way Catholic women work as theologians?[19] Many of the names already cited in this chapter are Catholic feminist theologians, although Mary Daly now defines herself as post-Christian. Here I select four dimensions which are important to Catholic theology, and then I give one example as to what the revisioning of a key doctrine might mean.

First, Catholic women theologians – along with others – engage in a 'hermeneutics of retrieval,' engaging with the past, with the Bible, tradition and Church history, to discover and retrieve for today's Church life and spiritual quest 'a usable past' or positive strands for women's authority and leadership.[20] As regards the Bible, this includes both a 'lost coin' approach where stories of the leadership of women, from Miriam to Mary of Magdala are retold, to the ground breaking work of Elisabeth Schüssler Fiorenza who traces the participation of women in the Jesus movement and the early Church.[21] However, it is also an ongoing process of uncovering the contribution of women's leadership and spirituality, for example in the lives of medieval abbesses, the authority of visionaries like Hildegarde of Bingen (1098–1179) and Mechtilde of Magdeburg (c.1240–1298) and the honouring of St Teresa of Avila (1515–1582) and Catherine of Siena (1347–1380) as Doctors of the Church.[22]

The second area where Catholic women theologians are very active is in mining the Church's prophetic traditions – particularly as expressed in encyclicals of Justice and Peace – for transforming the lives of women in Church and society. The Benedictine Abbess Joan Chittister is today active in reclaiming the charisms of Benedictine life as prophetic inspiration not only for women's role but as a challenge to the whole of society. Maria Riley, in *Transforming Feminism*, interprets the encyclical (*Pacem in terris*) and the Puebla documents from Latin America that summon us to read 'the signs of the times' and to include women's rising consciousness of the injustice that the patriarchal mindset continues to impose.[23] In many documents, much emphasis is placed on the dignity of the human person, yet nowhere is gender analysis factored in:

> By including gender analysis in the principle themes of the dignity of the human person, economic and political rights, economic justice, option for the poor, the common good and subsidiarity, women can find in Catholic social ethics a powerful ally in their struggle for liberation.[24]

The strong Church tradition in justice and peace not only inspires women theologians, but also numerous women working in Catholic nongovernmental organisations (NGOs) like CAFOD (in England and Wales), Trócaire (Ireland) and SCIAF (Scotland). The critical analysis of the structural causes of poverty has inspired a prophetic spirituality, sensitive to the female face of poverty, and creatively producing prayers, reflections and liturgies where this is an inspirational source.

If these first two themes sound positive, the next two bring more difficulties. The Catholic sacramental tradition offers a framework for the sacralising of significant moments of human life within the Christian mystery of redemption. Birth, healing, forgiving and being forgiven, the sharing of the sacred meal, giving and receiving in relationship and dying, are all taken up into God's self-giving in Christ. It is the question of the underlying theological anthropology that is the problem. Sacraments are meant to be about valuing bodily life: the Body of Christ is the key metaphor for Church. But, as Susan Ross writes, 'When it comes to embodiment, nearly all of the discussion of body and gender has focused on the appropriateness of male-only ordination.'[25]

One of the problems with the way feminism arose is that its roots lie in the secular search for equality. However, the work of Susan Ross, and more recently, Tina Beattie, show that if sacraments express the embodied nature of Christ's incarnation, then not only does the reality of women's bodily experience and sexuality deserve positive expression, (rather than the damaging way it has been referred to and controlled by centuries of patriarchal theology), but such a positive development would restore theological roots to Catholic feminism.[26] However, this issue leads to the final, troubled issue, of the refusal of the Church to ordain women and allow them to participate in the decision making structures of the Church, despite Pope Benedict's acknowledgment that a greater role for women must be found. Since the theological arguments against this are extremely weak, there is an unmissable groundswell of support for this, provided it is part of a renewal movement for the Church as a whole.[27]

Reimaging the Trinity from a Catholic Feminist Perspective: A Case Study

Nowhere does the maleness of God appear more dominant than in Trinitarian imagery – two men and a bird, as it is sometime facetiously described. An impressive art tradition and symbolism backs this up and there are a host of related problems. The obvious one from a feminist perspective is the exclusively inescapable male imagery. 'If God is male, the male is God,' said Mary Daly, linking male imagery with dominant male authority and violence in society:[28]

> The circle of destruction generated by the Most Unholy Trinity and reflected in the Unwhole Trinitarian symbol of Christianity will be broken when women, who are by patriarchal definition objects of rape, externalise and internalise a new self-definition whose compelling power is rooted in the power of being. The casting out of the demonic Trinity *is* female becoming.[29]

Daly's Most Unholy Trinity – Rape, Genocide and War – details the terrible things done to women by patriarchal society. She calls for the creation of the Most Holy and whole Trinity of Power, Justice and Love to be achieved by a transvaluation of values, almost impossible within patriarchy. In addition to the links between images of God and the kind of world they produce, is the question of language and how it shapes identity and world. John Donne in Sonnet number XIV, on the Trinity, wrote:

> Batter my heart, three-personed God, for you
> As yet but knock, breathe, shine and seek to mend;
> That I may rise and stand, o'erthrow me and bend
> Your force to break, blow, burn and make me new …
> divorce me, untie, or break that knot again,
> Take me to you, imprison me, for I,
> except you enthrall me, never shall be free,
> Nor ever chaste except you ravish me.[30]

Here is a transcendent God battering from the outside, using the language of rape and seduction to take possession of the poet's soul. It was also cited by Robert Oppenheimer's tests with the first atomic bomb in the Nevada desert, code-named 'Trinity'. The question of language legitimising seduction, as well as the nature of religious language as it attempts to explore the relationship between transcendence and immanence is raised here.

Another issue is the comparatively lowly place given to the Holy Spirit by tradition. In the tradition the Holy Spirit is almost an afterthought, appendage or poor relation like 'The Guest who came to dinner and stayed on to be a member of the family' as one writer put it.[31] Elizabeth Johnson points out that a twist to this was that in reformation theology and piety the Spirit became privatised to the individual's experience.[32] Karl Barth would follow this and see the Spirit as the subjective aspect of revelation, the reception of the Word in the heart.

The subordinating of the Spirit has meant a stress on the male bonding between father and son, and the creative power of begetting or generating has been accentuated to the point that female birth-giving has been obliterated from the tradition's imagery. One serious reason for tackling these issues is not simply the discovery of female imagery for the Godhead, but to develop another understanding of Incarnation. Jesus became human as male and man, but in such a way that his humanity is emphasised, so as to encourage and enable the full personhood of both women and men. If women are not able to find an echo, a home for their bodiliness in any of the divine imaging, how can the Incarnation be good news for them and how are women included in the redemptive process? This point is made by Luce Irigaray, who makes a psycho-linguistic critique of western culture, based, she says, on the murder of the mother. She suggests that recovery of Marian symbolism in Catholic theology might be a way to inaugurate a new culture of sexual difference.[33]

One response has been to try to establish the Holy Spirit as female. For example, the late Dominican Yves Congar uses early imagery from Ephrem the Syrian (306–373), imagery that declined by the fifth century.[34] Leonardo Boff, in *The Maternal Face of God*, in an essentialist version of romantic feminism, constructs a link between the being and nature of Mary, women and the Holy Spirit, while he links the being and nature of men with Christ. This is sharply critiqued by Sarah Coakley as re-inscribing biological essentialism and effectively removing women from the Incarnation![35]

Feminist theological attempts have several elements in common, including the re-imaging of transcendence and immanence, and envisioning the Trinity in a functional way, for example, as Creator, Redeemer, Sustainer. There is a new focus on the Trinity as God in movement, as God in relation, whose internal relationships inspire a new form of relating in humanity. Feminist process thought stresses the mutual interaction of God-world:

> When we loose the trinity from its sexist moorings, Trinitarian thought should force us beyond our usual human categories, asking us to intuit a manyness in unity far beyond our experience, yet communicated to us in the deepest reality of communal justice.[36]

But 'loosing the Trinity from its sexist moorings' is not that simple, as I failed to recognise, writing earlier:

> The God we meet in the process toward wholeness, is the God who energises our whole being, in our moments of clearest self-knowledge. The God met in the depths is relationality's deepest core. This is the God who urges us to deepen our connectedness, weave new connections, unravel and re-weave our patterns of relating. The mystery of God's own becoming enfolds and unfolds as we move to new levels of relating and interdependencies.[37]

Of course there is a level on which this is true. Yet it has a tendency to assume that we can reach this depth of relating within the present system. Hence the importance of Irigaray's challenge to recover and create a new genealogy or symbolic matrix for the experience of women. Another dimension developed by many women theologians is a richer theology of the Spirit. Korean theologian Chung Hyun Kyung has been inspirational here:

> Dear sisters and brothers, with the energy of the Spirit let us tear apart all walls of division and the culture of death which separates us. And let us participate in the Holy Spirit's economy of life, fighting for our life on this earth, in solidarity with all living beings …With wild wind of the Holy Spirit blow to us. Let us welcome her, letting ourselves go in her wild rhythm of life. Come Holy Spirit, renew the whole of creation. Amen.[38]

Conclusion

Yet one cannot re-vision the Spirit apart from the entire Trinity. Elizabeth Johnson imaged the suffering of God as belonging to the whole Trinity and as linked with the female figure of Sophia, Holy Wisdom.[39] Sophia is a powerful image for many Catholic feminist theologians, myself included. Sophia's sphere of activity extends to the whole of creation, recalling us to the words of Thomas Berry that in the very structure of the cosmos, there is differentiation, unity and relationality. This suggests that there are dimensions of Trinity yet to be discovered, as there are dimensions of Catholic feminist theology yet to be explored in our shared search for the truth and justice of the kingdom.

Notes

1   Simone de Beauvoir, *The Second Sex*, London: Penguin, 1972, p. 16.
2   Adrienne Rich, 'Natural Resources' in *The Dream of a Common Language: Poems*, New York: W&W Norton, 1978, p. 67.
3   Key figures in the Women's Rights Movement in the nineteenth century were the Grimke sisters, Susan B. Anthony, Matilda Jocelyn Gage and Elizabeth Cady Stanton – the latter responsible for the Bible Project in 1895. In the twentieth century there are many key thinkers, for example, de Beauvoir (1943) 1972 op. cit., Germain Greer, *The Female Eunuch* (London: McGibbon and Kee, 1970), Kate Millett, *Sexual Politics* (London: Jonathan Cape, 1970), Betty Friedan, *The Feminine Mystique* (New York: Norton, 1963), Dale Spender, *Feminist Theorists* (London: The Women's Press, 1983).
4   Maria Riley, *Transforming Feminism*, Kansas: Sheed and Ward, 1989, p. 45.
5   See Tillie Olsen, *Silences*, London: Virago, 1980, pp. 34–37, 213–217.
6   John Paul II, *Mulieris dignitatem*, London: Catholic Truth Society, 1988.
7   The phrase is Adrienne Rich's 'Twenty-One Love Poems' in *The Dream of a Common Language*, New York: W&W Norton, 1978, p. 31; Sara Maitland, *Map of a New Country: Women and Christianity*, London: SPCK, 1980 was also influential in the UK.
8   Mary Daly, *The Church and the Second Sex*, Boston: Beacon, 1968. Later, Daly would come to satirise her own early idealism.
9   Virginia Fabella, *Beyond Bonding – A Third World Women's Theological Journey*, The Philippines: Manila, EATWOT and the Institute of Women's Studies, 1993.
10 Ibid., p. 30.
11 Some of these points are further developed in Mary Grey, 'Feminist Theology: A Critical Theology of Liberation' in *The Cambridge Companion to Liberation Theology*, Christopher Rowland (ed.) Cambridge: CUP, 1999, pp. 89–106.
12 See the journal *In God's Image: Journal of Asian Women's Resource Centre for Culture and Theology*, published by Asian Women's Resource Centre, Kuala Lumpur, Malaysia.

13   The phrase is Alice Walker's in *In Search of our Mothers' Gardens*, New York: Harcourt Brace Jovanovich, 1983.

14   See, for example, Ada Maria Isasi-Diaz, *En La Lucha: Elaborating a Mujerista Theology*, Minneapolis: Fortress, 1993.

15   I invented this word in my inaugural lecture, 'From Cultures of Silence to Feminist Theology', University of Southampton, 1993.

16   As it is impossible here to discuss all these areas, I have had to make difficult choices and restrict the discussion severely.

17   Rosemary Radford Ruether, *Sexism and Godtalk*, London: SCM, 1983, pp. 18–19.

18   Mary Grey, *Redeeming the Dream: Feminism, Redemption and Christian Tradition*, London: SPCK, 1989; Gujurat: Sahitya Prakash, 2000, pp. 103–108.

19   Though my focus here is on women, there are many men – including priests – who, influenced by feminist theology, work in an explicitly feminist-identified way.

20   The phrase is Letty Russell's.

21   Elisabeth Schüssler Fiorenza, *In Memory of Her*, London: SCM, 1980.

22   For Hildegarde, see Barbara Newman, *Sister of Wisdom*, Aldershot: Scolar Press, 1987; for the significance of medieval women, see Caroline Walker Bynum, *Holy Feast, Holy Fast: The Significance of Food to Mediaeval Women*, Berkeley: University of California Press, 1987.

23   Maria Riley, *Transforming Feminism*, op. cit., pp. 87–98.

24   Ibid., p. 97.

25   Susan A. Ross, 'Church and Sacrament – Community and Worship' in Susan Frank Parsons (ed.) *The Cambridge Companion to Feminist Theology*, Cambridge: Cambridge University Press, 2002, pp. 224–242.

26   See Tina Beattie, *New Catholic Feminism: Theology and Theory*, London and New York: Routledge, 2006.

27   For texts and argument for and against the ordination of women, see www.womenpriests.org; for education for the ministry of women, see www.catherineofsiena.net. For the movement for the Ordination of Catholic Women, see CWO, Catholic Women for Ordination, WOW, Women's Ordination Worldwide, and BASIC, Brothers and Sisters in the Church.

28   Mary Daly, *Beyond God the Father*, Boston: Beacon, 1973.

29   Daly, ibid., p. 122.

30   John Donne, Holy Sonnet no. 14, *To the Trinity*, from E.K. Chambers (ed.) *Poems of John Donne*, Vol. 1, London: Lawrence & Bullen, 1896, p. 165.

31   Gerald Priestland, *Priestland's Journey*, Miami: Parkwest Publications, 1983.

32   Elizabeth Johnson, *She Who Is: The Mystery of God in Feminist Theological Discourse*, New York: Crossroad, 1992, p. 128.

33   Luce Irigaray, as cited in Tina Beattie, *New Catholic Feminism*, op. cit.; *God's Mother, Eve's Advocate: A Gynocentric Refiguration of Marian Symbolism in Engagement with Luce Irigaray*, CCRSG Monograph Series 3, Bristol: Dept of Theology and Religious Studies, 1999.

34   See Sebastian Brock, 'The Holy Spirit as Feminine in Early Syriac Literature' in Soskice (ed.) *After Eve*, Marshal Pickering, 1990, pp. 73–88. Critiqued by Coakley in Monica Furlong (ed.) *Mirror to the Church* SPCK, 1988.

35   See Sarah Coakley, 'Mariology and Romantic Feminism' in Teresa Elwes (ed.) *Women's Voices*, London: Marshall Pickering, 1992, pp. 97–110.

36   Marjorie Suchocki, 'The Unmale God: Reconsidering the Trinity' in *Quarterly Review*, Spring 1983, pp. 34–49.

37   Mary Grey, 'The Core of our Desire' in *Theology*, September, 1990, p. 371.

38   Chung Hyun Kyung, 'Welcome the Spirit: Hear her Cries: The Holy Spirit, Creation and the Culture of Life' in *Christianity and Crisis*, 51, July 15, pp. 220–223.

39   Johnson, *She Who Is*, op. cit.

Further Reading

Beattie, Tina, *New Catholic Feminism: Theology and Theory*, London and New York: Routledge, 2006.

Grey, Mary, *Redeeming the Dream: Feminism, Redemption and Christian Tradition*, London: SPCK, 1989; Gujurat: Sahitya Prakash, 2000.

John Paul II, *Mulieris dignitatem*, London: Catholic Truth Society, 1988.

Ross, Susan A., 'Church and Sacrament – Community and Worship' in Susan Frank Parsons (ed.) *The Cambridge Companion to Feminist Theology*, Cambridge: Cambridge University Press, 2002.

CHAPTER 24

FAITH, DIALOGUE AND THE 'CATHOLIC INSTINCT': DISCERNING THE SIGNIFICANCE OF OTHER FAITHS

Michael Barnes

Introduction

What is Catholic about inter-religious dialogue? In mid-September 2006, in the safe recesses of a German university, Pope Benedict quoted an obscure medieval text which criticised the prophet Muhammad. Some commentators called him naïve for straying into an area he did not understand. Others felt that he was too intelligent a man not to know what he was doing. Certainly it is difficult to miss his implied rebuke of Islam for being less rigorous in its account of the relationship between faith and reason than the classical tradition of Catholic Christianity. However, whether or not a robust critique of Islam was intended, the result was an angry response from Muslims across the world. How dare the leader of the Catholic Church, with the blood of crusades on his hands, criticise Islam for nurturing violence? If he wanted to talk about religiously inspired violence, why not choose something closer to home? Surely the point of inter-faith dialogue is to promote peace and reconciliation, not stir up criticism and argument?

These were just some of the responses which were voiced on the BBC's World Service two days after the lecture. I was taking part in a phone-in and it seemed as if half the world of Islam was on the end of the line. To be fair, many comments were carefully thought through and very articulate. Yet not even the mildest comment could disguise the naked reality of our media-saturated, multi-faith, globalised world. When the Pope speaks in Regensburg, his words are picked up in Ankara, Khartoum and Karachi. And flung back. Where inter-religious relations are touched upon, there is no such thing as a 'private' audience. The problem, of course, is that such public prominence comes at a price. It is impossible to control the impact of even the most well chosen words. Gone are the days (if they ever really existed) when 'dialogue' was understood as a reasoned negotiation about common concerns. In the fraught world of the twenty-first century the word has acquired much more diffuse and ill-defined inter-personal connotations. Reason is still there but has to be set in the broader context of history and politics which has formed communities of faith in particular ways. To stray across religious boundaries into the world of the other – whether the movement is deliberate, as in a visit to a place of worship, or more oblique, as in an academic lecture – is to touch upon neuralgic points and to risk misunderstanding. But this is what a properly Catholic commitment to interreligious relations entails. If dialogue is to engage with the 'hard questions' about God and truth and the meaning of human existence and not descend into a fringe activity for a few privileged initiates, then the risk has to be taken.

Whatever else Catholic Christianity is about, it depends ultimately on what I shall call, for the sake of brevity, the 'Catholic instinct'. By this I do not refer to anything definitive of Roman Catholic identity as distinct from the various forms of Orthodox or Protestant Christianity – though there are, of course, areas of overlap. To be Catholic is to bring the virtues learned from a particular pattern of holy living to bear upon the wider world of which Catholic Christians are part. Catholic Christianity, broadly considered, can be understood as a response to God which always seeks out and acknowledges the broadest scope of God's gracious action in the world. In terms specifically of inter-faith relations, this means preferring points of continuity over discontinuity, emphasising convergence rather than difference, looking for what the early Fathers of the Church called 'Seeds of the Word'. It is, in short, a Catholic virtue to want to include rather than exclude, to act with generosity towards 'the other'. Not everything, however, can be included. A sub-text of the Pope's lecture – what caused so much upset – was the implication that unexamined faith may cause violence. There is, to put it bluntly, such a thing as 'bad religion'. The world we experience is shot through with the effects of human sinfulness. In other words, Catholic Christianity will always reflect an instinctive desire to build good relations with others. Nevertheless, the process of discernment, learning to see that which is genuinely of God, is rarely straightforward.

If the naming of 'bad religion' risks misunderstanding, that may be preferable to another danger, that of patronising other faith traditions by reducing them to lesser versions of what is already known within the Catholic tradition. People from the great religious traditions of the world were once unceremoniously lumped together as 'non-Christians', defined by what they were not, rather than as Buddhists and Hindus and Muslims – followers of particular traditions of ancient and life-giving faith and wisdom. Now a growing familiarity and respect accords them the dignity of their own self-designation. The result is that a rather more subtle and elusive question emerges: how can we accept these traditions as genuinely different and 'other', forms of holy living in their own right, something more than immature or incomplete versions of Christianity? And how can we do so without sliding into a vapid relativism?

That question requires that we stand back for a moment and take stock. The days when Catholics could hide behind the old adage that 'outside the Church there is no salvation' are long gone. It does not follow, however, that the alternative is an expanded universalism, a genial assembly of the like-minded – which looks suspiciously like an idealised version of the Catholic Church. This is how Karl Rahner's famous thesis of the Anonymous Christian is sometimes interpreted: Hindus and Buddhists turned into closet Christians – Christians in all but name. It is important to remember that, even when addressing questions which originate within the context of *dogmatic* theology, Rahner writes primarily as a *pastoral* theologian, responding to particular problems which everyday life presents to faith. He is not, in other words, concerned in the first place with the status of other faiths but with the *credibility of Christian faith* in an apparently unbelieving world.[1] It is important for him to show that, despite the reality of human sinfulness, there can be no absolute divide between the particular 'moments' of God's self-revelation in the Incarnation of Christ and the giving of the Spirit and what can be known of God through the mystery of creation *as such*. Thus, Rahner's basic presupposition, spelled out in his theological anthropology is that the relationship between God and humanity contains an immanent dimension; that is to say that within human experience are contained the seeds of our understanding of God. To invoke another important patristic theme, a universal *preparatio evangelica*, a tacit expectation of hearing God's Word in the radical openness of the human spirit's love and searching, forms a sort of 'natural template' within which the self-revelation of Godself in the Paschal Mystery of Jesus Christ can become a reality for human beings. Such a realisation depends, of course, upon God's initiative, but it originates nevertheless as God's answer to the quest for human fulfilment implied *a priori* in the structures of the human spirit and the concrete circumstances of human living in the world. To put it another way, if it is true that only God can make God known, then it must be in and through the actual conditions of existence which people experience. In these terms Rahner would argue that, *potentially*, all of history becomes salvation history and all religious traditions become possible vehicles of revelation, possible articulations of the underlying universal offer of the divine self-communication. What Rahner calls 'categorial' and 'transcendental' revelation have the same purpose and the same content, namely God's communication of himself to human beings.

Rahner's thesis is often referred to as typically Catholic 'inclusivism'. This term has been popularised by John Hick who compares it positively with the hard-edged 'exclusivist' strategy of 'outside the Church no salvation' but negatively with his own more open 'pluralism', religions as equally valid ways to the truth. Hick regards Rahner's inclusivism as a worthy but inadequate step forward. He thus proposes a theological 'crossing of the Rubicon', an irrevocable movement towards exposing the 'myth of Christian uniqueness'.[2] As a short-hand for the 'Catholic instinct' the term is misleading – as is Hick's account of 'theological development'. The crucial question is not how to include all people in some peculiarly Catholic scheme of things but, more precisely, how to acknowledge a continuity between the different patterns of holy living which we call 'the religions' while still allowing for that specificity of Christian faith which recognises that something new or discontinuous has been revealed in Christ. Much of the sometimes ponderous complexity of Rahner's writing arises from the balance he has to maintain between his two principles. Just how Rahner grants the specificity of other traditions of faith while maintaining the integrity of Christian confession cannot be our concern here.[3] Sufficient to note, perhaps, that what Hick's pluralism misses is the *theological* meaning of the inter-religious encounter itself. Rahner's achievement is to shift attention away from the 'problem of the salvation of the non-Christian' to the terms of the Christian life of faithful discipleship, opening up in the process a different but related issue – the *significance* of the other for the Christian.

Since the Vatican Council the official teaching magisterium of the Catholic Church has reflected at some depth on the lived experience of a Church which recognises – to use a term from the Council's Constitution on the Church – that people of other faiths are 'related to' the people of God (LG 16). The word expresses something of the practical, as much as theological, tension which the Council bequeathed to the Church – a tension manifested in the debate about the status of the term with which we began – dialogue. Introduced into Catholic parlance in *Ecclesiam Suam*, the first encyclical of Paul VI, in 1964, dialogue is very often taken along with proclamation as representing two complementary demands which the commitment to mission always makes on the Church. This is what we find in two major Vatican documents on the subject – *Dialogue and Mission* of 1984 and *Dialogue and Proclamation* of 1991. For the most part, they see dialogue as one missionary practice among many (DM 13). Yet there is also something else. At least implicitly, these documents raise the question as to whether the inter-personal 'dialogue' should not be understood as mirroring the *prior* 'dialogue of salvation' which God opens up with human beings through the Word spoken in Christ (DM 22–4; DP 38–41). In other words they shift attention from a purely *instrumental* understanding of dialogue to something more exactly *theological*. To that extent they recognise the force in Rahner's central thesis – what one of the most prominent theologians of religion, Jacques Dupuis, calls the 'operative presence of the mystery of Jesus Christ in other religious traditions'.[4] How is the Word to be discerned in 'the words' spoken by the other and in the dialogue which brings persons of faith into direct contact with each other? Dialogue expresses that engagement with others which leads to a mutual learning, deeper understanding and a conversion to God. This, as DP points out, is the work of the Spirit who brings people to Christ (DP 64–5). The Church needs to note that, before any words are spoken in dialogue, others may already have been touched by God's Spirit – indeed it is that Spirit alone which makes the hearing of the Word possible by human beings. So much of mission, certainly in a pluralist and secular context, is concerned not with direct evangelisation, in the traditional sense of proclaiming the Gospel, but with pre-evangelisation, with a more remote preparation for people to receive the Good News. The

Spirit works *in God's time*. The Church is called first and foremost to be faithful to the God who reveals himself in Christ. Christians speak, therefore, of what they know of this God – yet they will also be open to what the Spirit of Christ may be saying elsewhere, beyond the visible bounds of the Church. Summing up very roughly: the crucial question is not how 'they' fit into 'our' view of the world, but how we are both united *in God's view*.

The practice of dialogue in all its forms – whether this involves theological exchange, the sharing of religious experience or the more mundane practices of common life and common action (DM 29–35; DP 42–3) – brings persons into face-to-face encounters with each other. This is the biggest shift in Catholic thinking about religious pluralism in the decades since the Council: the other is no longer a problem but a partner. This is not to underestimate the very real problems of discerning where the 'seeds of the Word' really lie, or the direction the Spirit is leading in. However, it is to recognise where that discernment must focus – on the relationship itself. In the Spirit human beings not only 'live and move and have our being', but build up a sensitivity towards the other which seeks to be true to God's continuing work of self-revelation. To speak, then of discerning 'seeds of the Word' is not a matter of recognising signs of the Spirit's presence somehow 'out there' (though it may well include this); it is, rather, a matter of an interior growth in the Spirit, becoming a people genuinely fired by the theological virtues of faith, hope and love.[5] Put like this, engagement with the other – however fraught and risky – may well lead to a deepening of faith. Christians are called to speak *in* the Spirit, yet to listen *to* the Spirit: to be faithful to what they know of the God revealed in Christ, yet attentive to the 'seeds of the Word' wherever they may be spoken. But such an engagement, at once nourishing of faith yet profoundly challenging to faith, cannot afford to be unprincipled. It must at some stage lead back into serious theological reflection – in the first place, on the nature of the Church as properly Catholic.

Here two principles commend themselves. On the one hand, the Church is Catholic because it represents, or in some sense mediates, the truth already noted above: the whole of humankind is gathered together and redeemed in Christ. On the other, the Church exists not as some distant ideal, but as *this* community of faith, what Vatican II called a 'pilgrim church' looking forward like all peoples to the time of its fulfilment.[6] Reflecting on the contemporary experience of inter-faith relations, the Church speaks and listens. This community of faith exists 'in the middle', in the world shared with others, a community committed to teaching what it knows of God's self-revelation *and* to learning more of God's continuing purposes for the whole of humankind. The Church speaks of what it knows through the practice of faith in the God who has transformed the world irrevocably by raising Jesus from the dead. Now such a vision of God's purposes has to be tempered by the obvious fact that the Church does not yet know the total reality of what must always remain other and utterly mysterious. Together, these two points, two sides of the mystery of God's self-revelation which characterise an existence which is both 'above' the world yet deeply rooted in the world, give rise to the 'Catholic instinct'. Putting this in terms which speak to the contemporary experience of a pluralist, multi-faith society, Catholic Christianity must at the very least manifest a willingness to allow that God may act in the world in ways of which the Church does not know. Indeed anything less would be to risk putting an arbitrary limit on the action of God.

That may be considered the *sine qua non* of any theological reflection on inter-religious dialogue – the humility which is born of wonder at God's providential purposes for humankind and acknowledges that particular judgements can only be made with care and discernment. Nevertheless, judgements do have to be made; there is, to repeat, such a thing as 'bad religion' and theology has a role to play in making sure that our thinking about the other is robustly critical when necessary. Are we doomed to keep total silence, to speak only of the Christian mystery, to make no comment on how Christian faith may or may not intersect with the beliefs of Muslims and Jews and Buddhists? Clearly not. The 'Catholic instinct' forms a Church sensitive to the continuities between faiths. But it also develops its own specificity and the sense that Christian faith may not lightly be correlated with what is manifestly different. An immediate acquaintance with another tradition often leads to the identification of similarities, which then turn out, on closer inspection, to be problematic. For example, Muslim devotion to Mariam, the mother of Isa, has much in common with Catholic devotion to Mary, the mother of Jesus. For the Muslim, however, the Christian theology of Mary, Mother of God, is impossible to accept while for the Christian the Muslim objection that Christians have deified God's prophet show the limited nature of some Muslim accounts of revelation. Asian mystical traditions such as Buddhism and Vedantic Hinduism are enormously popular antidotes to the materialism of western culture. However, neither is easily reconciled with a theistic account of creation. Facing up to such incompatibilities does not spell the end of the story – or the end of dialogue. More often than not dialogue does not supply 'answers', or even enable conclusions to be reached, but questions the ease with which assumptions about the other – and more particularly about *the* Other, about God – are made. On closer inspection it becomes clear that the disagreement about the identity of Jesus has more to do with certain presuppositions about the nature of God than with different interpretations of the same scriptural material. Similarly in the dialogue with Buddhism, what is at stake is not the status of theism as such but the nature of religious language and the human capacity to say anything meaningful about what is, strictly speaking, beyond words. Islam or Buddhism or Hinduism are not inadequate answers to questions which Christianity addresses with perfect clarity. Muslims and Buddhists and Hindus ask their *own questions* – and very often begin from very different perspectives. In these circumstances, the achievement of dialogue – if one may speak in such terms – is not the negotiation of some elusive 'common ground' but the maintenance of trust and respect even in the midst of sometimes profound misunderstanding and disagreement.

What to do, then, when dialogue comes up against the disarming strangeness of the other? To encounter the very open-endedness of dialogue is to be taken back into the formative experiences of Christian faith and, therefore, to the Paschal Mystery of Death and Resurrection. By living from the story of Christ who himself faced the 'otherness' of the Father in Gethsemane, Christians are motivated to develop not an alternative theory of religious meaning but a contemplative sensitivity to the Word of God wherever and whenever it is spoken – even in the pain of incomprehension. Here, perhaps, in the experience of a Christ-like passivity before the other, is the beginning of a theology of religions.

My argument is that the 'Catholic instinct' grows out of a deep trust in God's own act of generous self-giving manifested in Christ which sustains the virtues necessary for a life which is lived, in a very real sense, on those uncomfortable edges between what is known and what is unknown. Such trust is not to be confused with a stoic obduracy or a romantic optimism which fails to take account of the effects of human sinfulness. Rather, understood in terms of the life-giving action of God's Spirit, which forms Christians after the manner of Christ, engagement with the other always brings about a deeper *self*-conversion. The challenge, of course, remains. How to discern the Word in the midst of the 'seeds of the Word'? There is no easy answer. This chapter has argued that 'answers' begin to arise only in and through the actual practice of faith.

I finish with a thought from my own Ignatian tradition. In his Spiritual Exercises, Ignatius of Loyola (1491–1556) wrote various rules for the discernment of spirits. The aim was to become sensitised to the guiding presence of God's Spirit, and therefore to God's will. Ignatius was concerned to show how God worked through people's feelings and desires. If we would know the will of God then we must trust interior movements, such as strong attractions and aversions to this or that object or way of action. Such a claim caused a great deal of suspicion in its time. But Ignatius was careful to show that no one could claim to discern the signs of God – the 'seeds of the Word' – if they were not making honest efforts to lead the Christian life with complete integrity. So he proposes a principle at the beginning of the Exercises. This states that, since all things are given to human beings so that they may realise the end which God wishes for them, then ultimately there can be no difference between great gifts and few, riches and poverty, a long life or a short one. The key question is how human beings *use* things for the purpose for which they are created – in Christian terms, to love and praise God. So the most important quality of Christian living – and the key to correct discernment – is what Ignatius calls indifference or detachment. It may sound negative, but it is the very opposite of an uncaring dismissal. Rather he is speaking of a balanced openness to whatever is *given* in experience. Without this quality of peaceful equanimity it is impossible to enter into the immediate experience and to recognise there something of God.

Conclusion

Listening to angry Muslims does not naturally lead to peaceful equanimity. More likely, it will provoke what Ignatius called desolation – a decrease in faith, hope and love, not its growth. However, that in itself is not a reason to avoid interreligious dialogue and the conflict which it may bring. For even, and perhaps especially, those most desolating of human experiences – loss, isolation, diminishment, opposition, misunderstanding – do in God's good time lead back to an awareness that all is grace. Such is the promise of Christian faith. In the end nothing counts against that deeply Catholic vision in which all human activity, all human experience, all people of faith, are gathered to God. Yet the only way it is possible to translate that vision into something which is learned and known in the heart is through a persevering trust which is prepared to wait and see, to test the fruits, to refuse to jump to conclusions. That does not give a neat answer to 'hard questions', but it does propose a way of living with what is always, in the best sense, other – beyond our power to control. And maybe that is enough.

Notes

1   Karl Rahner, *Theological Investigations*, Volume 5, London: Darton, Longman and Todd, 1966, pp. 3–22.

2   John Hick and Paul Knitter (eds) *The Myth of Christian Uniqueness*, London: SCM, 1988, pp. 16–36.

3   Rahner, ibid., pp. 311–321.

4   Jacques Dupuis, *Toward a Christian Theology of Religious Pluralism*, Maryknoll: Orbis Books, 1997, p. 123.

5   Michael Barnes, *Theology and the Dialogue of Religions*, Cambridge: Cambridge University Press, 2002, pp. 3–28.

6   Michael Barnes, *Walking the City*, Delhi: ISPCK, 1998, pp. 20–37.

Further Reading

Barnes, Michael, *Walking the City*, Delhi: ISPCK; 1998.

_____ *Theology and the Dialogue of Religions*, Cambridge: Cambridge University Press, 2002.

Dupuis, Jacques, *Toward a Christian Theology of Religious Pluralism*, Maryknoll: Orbis Books, 1997.

'The Attitude of the Church towards the Followers of other Religions' ['Dialogue and Mission'], *Bulletin* (of the Secretariat for Non-Christians) Vol. 19, No. 2; 1984, pp. 126–141.

'Dialogue and Proclamation: Reflections and Orientations on Inter-Religious Dialogue and the Proclamation of the Gospel of Jesus

Christ', *Bulletin* (of the Pontifical Council for Interreligious Dialogue) Vol. 26, No. 2; 1991, pp. 210–250.

Tanner, Norman P. (ed.) *Decrees of the Ecumenical Councils*, London: Sheed and Ward, 1990.

CHAPTER 25

CATHOLICISM AND ECUMENISM
Paul D. Murray

Introduction

In exploring the relationship between 'Catholicism and Ecumenism' we engage with issues touching on the very character and self-understanding not just of Roman Catholicism but of the Christian churches and vocation more generally. Here we deal with matters relating to the calling and mission of the Church of Christ, the quality and manner of the Church's witness and its tragic disfigurement through sin. We also explore the need for continual conversion within the Church itself and the key role this should play in the Church's proclamation of the Gospel of reconciliation in a world of violent difference.

A straightforward look at the respective linguistic roots of 'Catholicism' and 'Ecumenism' suggests there is a certain overlap, even necessary interrelationship, between these concepts. On the one hand, 'catholic' derives from the Greek adverbial phrase *kath'holou*, literally meaning 'according to the whole', and with connotations of universality and completeness. On the other hand, 'ecumenical' derives from the Greek word *oikoumene* (past participle of *oike*, to dwell/to inhabit) which was variously used to refer to the extent of the Greco-Roman empire, the entire inhabited world and – subsequent to the establishment of Christianity as the religion of the empire – the whole Christian Church.

So, when applied to the Church, or to any particular aspect of Christian practice and belief, 'catholic' and 'ecumenical' are each concerned with expressing the deep-rooted Christian claim for the universal significance and relevance of Jesus Christ as the deepest story of all things. With this, the labels 'catholic' and 'ecumenical' also express the claim that the Church's practices and beliefs are themselves situated within, orientated towards and expressive of, something of this fullness of truth in Christ. As example of this, in the *Niceno-Constantinopolitan Creed*, the great common creed of the Christian Churches, catholicity is confessed, along with unity, holiness and apostolicity, as an identifying mark of the entire Church of Christ. Similarly, the 'Ecumenical Councils' (e.g. Nicaea in 325 and Constantinople in 381) are those which are generally regarded as giving definitive articulation to core, identifying beliefs of the entire Church.

On this basis it might be assumed that the story of 'Catholicism and Ecumenism' necessarily unfolds as one of unremarkable harmony, even simple identity: the catholic Church of Christ simply is the *oikoumene* without distinction.

In contrast, the significant tensions that arose even within New Testament communities (cf. Gal 2:11-21), combined with the long-standing rejection by some professing Christian communities of the teaching of the Ecumenical Council of Chalcedon in 451, should remind us that claims to identity and totality are inherently unstable, requiring to be pressed with subtlety and allowing for due differentiation. Indeed, following the emergence of the modern ecumenical movement in the late nineteenth and early twentieth centuries under largely Protestant inspiration – with ecumenism now understood in the more specific sense of seeking to find ways for the divided Christian Churches to think and act together as the one Church of Christ – far from the story of 'Catholicism and Ecumenism' unfolding as one of harmonious identity, it seemed rather, to a significant stretch of Roman Catholic perception at least, to be a story of competing claims to totality.

Even during the period following the Second Vatican Council (1962–1965), when official Roman Catholic thinking eventually took a decisive turn away from its previous stance of isolationist self-sufficiency and towards far greater ecumenical engagement, significant elements still proceeded with formal caution; excessively so in the disappointed judgement of many. Others, however, including Pope Benedict XIV, when he was Cardinal Prefect of the Congregation for the Doctrine of the Faith, viewed such caution as a necessary prudence that has been subsequently vindicated by various developments – most notably in relation to women's ordination and homosexuality – which collectively serve to push any hopes for the re-establishment of structural and sacramental unity between Rome and the Protestant churches way beyond the foreseeable future.

This poses a dilemma for Roman Catholicism. On the one hand, as Benedict XVI himself powerfully expressed in his first statement as pontiff on 20 April 2005 and many times since,[1] Roman Catholicism is irrevocably committed, precisely on account of its sense of catholicity, to the strong ecumenical aspiration for a structurally and sacramentally united Church. On the other hand, and again precisely on account of its understanding of the demands of Catholic integrity, it is now extremely difficult for the Roman Catholic Church to envisage any realistic way forward towards this non-negotiable goal. Read with the eyes of faith, the challenge here is to find in this problem fresh possibility, fresh opportunity for growth into a deepened, expanded and enriched – not diminished or compromised – Catholic identity.

With such concerns in view, this essay proceeds in five stages. Attention first focuses on the emergence of the modern ecumenical movement, and official Roman Catholic resistance, through to the surprise calling by Pope John XXIII (1958–1963) of the Second Vatican Council. Attention then turns to elucidating the key shifts in understanding enshrined in the Vatican II documents. Following this is a sketch of some of the most significant developments that have followed in the wake of Vatican II. This, in turn, leads into a discussion of various factors contributing to a more recent disappointing of earlier ecumenical hopes. Finally, the question will be aired as to the appropriate strategy for the churches now to adopt. With reference to the recently introduced notion of 'Receptive Ecumenism',[2] the essay concludes by suggesting that the growing into and showing forth of genuine catholicity is the greatest contribution Roman Catholicism can make to the ecumenical endeavour and, with this, that receptive ecumenical learning represents an essential resource for Roman Catholicism's own destined growth into the fullness of the catholicity of the Church of Christ.

Emergence, Resistance and Openings

The modern ecumenical movement has its origins in the nineteenth-century missionary activities of many of the Protestant churches which served to draw them out of the regionally/nationally demarcated existence that had, for the greater part, become their norm and into a common but separately pursued task of evangelisation. Here, the stark contrast between the Gospel being proclaimed and the multiple divisions actually marking

Christianity came to be felt as a contradiction that diminished the churches' witness. These concerns came to formal expression in the landmark 1910 Edinburgh world missionary conference, with calls also being made that year for a world conference on faith and order focused on the differences in doctrine and Church order between the churches. This call was, in turn, given renewed impetus in 1919, after the First World War, when the Ecumenical Patriarch expressed his commitment to formal meetings taking place between the Protestant and Orthodox churches. The respective first meetings of the Life and Work movement and the Faith and Order movement subsequently took place in Stockholm in 1925 and Lausanne in 1927, between them constituting the two main streams that would flow into the first assembly of the World Council of Churches (WCC) in 1948.

Throughout this period, the highest levels of Roman Catholic officialdom consistently declined to participate in ecumenical conversations. Indeed, the peace-loving Pope Benedict XV (1914–1922), generally noted for his commitment to reconciliation, had it enshrined in the 1917 Code of Canon Law that Catholics were forbidden, in lieu of formal permission, from participating in meetings with other Christians (Canon 1325). The mindset here was that the one true Church of Christ is to be straightforwardly and exclusively identified with the Roman Catholic Church and association with other Christians is to be consequently rejected as appearing to suggest a false equivalence. The only genuine way forward, it was believed, was that of unidirectional return to Rome. This deeply-held conviction came to clearest expression in Pope Pius XI's 1928 encyclical *Mortalium Animos*, 'On Fostering Religious Union', where we find:

> There is only one way in which the unity of Christians may be fostered, and that is by promoting the return to the one true Church of Christ of those who are separated from it; for from that one true Church they have in the past unhappily fallen away.

But such was not the only story. Notable Catholic contributions of a more creative sort include the proposal in 1908 by Paul Wattson, convert founder of the Franciscan Friars of the Atonement, to establish an octave of prayer for Christian unity between the feasts of the Confession of St Peter (18 January) and the Conversion of St Paul (25 January). Whilst originally imbued with the then standard theology of return, this Catholic initiative was subsequently broadened by Abbé Paul Couturier of Lyons in 1935 into a more nuanced Universal Week of Prayer for Christian Unity 'as Christ wishes and by the means which he desires'. Between these points, the early 1920s witnessed a remarkable series of conversations between Anglican and Roman Catholic theologians in Malines under the presidency of Cardinal Mercier of Belgium. First articulated there was the imaginative idea of 'united but not absorbed' to speak, in a manner prescient of related thinking at Vatican II, of a model of reconciled unity in diversity that would preserve the valid distinctive gifts of each tradition. Similarly, despite official strictures, many Roman Catholic scholars engaged with energy and imagination, and typically at considerable cost to themselves, in close dialogue with Protestant theology and practice during this period, concerned as much for the renewal of Catholicism as for the enrichment of Protestantism. Pre-eminent amongst such figures was the French Dominican, Yves Congar (1904–1995) who, although later one of the major influences on Vatican II, had to endure a prolonged period of official silencing during the mid 1950s.

Whilst a period marked, in the light of Pope Pius XII's 1950 encyclical *Humane generis*, by the repression of theologians variously seeking to overcome the limitations of neo-scholastic theology, the late 1940s and early 1950s also witnessed a number of tentative ecumenical openings on Catholicism's behalf. In the wake of the first assembly of the WCC in 1948, the Holy Office (later renamed the Congregation for the Doctrine of the Faith) issued a letter, *Ecclesia Sancta*, in 1949 acknowledging the ecumenical movement as deriving 'from the inspiration of the Holy Spirit' and opening the way for Catholic theologians to join in ecumenical conversations. Although such openings still stopped short of supporting Roman Catholic participation in the second assembly of the WCC in 1954, they did lead to the formation of the Catholic Conference for Ecumenical Relations in 1952, itself a forerunner of the Secretariat for Promoting Christian Unity (SPCU) which Pope John XXIII established in 1960 as a preparatory organ for Vatican II. By the time of the third assembly of the WCC in New Delhi in 1961, it was deemed possible for an official delegation of observers from the SPCU to participate. But this is to run ahead in our narrative.

On 25 January 1959, just three months into his papacy, whilst visiting the Basilica of Saint Paul Outside the Walls, to close the Week of Prayer for Christian Unity, Pope John XXIII made the surprise announcement of his intention to call a Second Vatican Council. When he subsequently clarified his aims in so doing, he identified within one breath the need for renewal within the Catholic Church and the need to serve the goal of Christian unity. The appropriate reception of Vatican II is still, perhaps unsurprisingly, a matter of disputed interpretation within contemporary Roman Catholicism. What cannot, however, be denied with credibility is that Vatican II was, indeed, an occasion of unparalleled significance within modern Catholicism. Nowhere is this clearer than in relation to the shift in ecumenical perspective that Vatican II embraced and promoted.

Catholicity and Ecumenicity in Vatican II Perspective

An exploration of the relationship between 'Catholicism and Ecumenism' must focus on two key documents from Vatican II. *Lumen gentium*, 'The Dogmatic Constitution on the Church', was promulgated on the 21 November 1964 as one of the four central documents of the Council, and *Unitatis redintegratio*, 'The Decree on Ecumenism', also promulgated on 21 November 1964 and representing the most authoritative charter to date of the participation of the Roman Catholic Church in the ecumenical movement.[3]

Within these documents, the central principle lending shape to everything else in Vatican II teaching on ecumenism is to be found in LG §8. Prior to this point in *Lumen gentium* it is the Church of Christ that is in focus, situated within the perspective of salvation history, with its origin in and orientation towards the Trinitarian communion of God, and without any specific mention being made of the Roman Catholic Church. When the document does turn in 8 to discuss the relationship between the one Church of Christ and the Roman Catholic Church we find a subtle but highly significant distinction being drawn relative to the standard pre-Vatican II claims for a strict and exclusive identity in this regard. What we find is not the straightforward claim that the Church of Christ simply *is* (L. *est*) the Catholic Church but the deliberately more nuanced claim that: 'The Church, constituted and organised as a society in the present world, subsists in the Catholic Church ...'

The specific context of usage, combined with the historical records of the conciliar debates and the broader background of association in Trinitarian theology all strongly indicate that 'subsists in' (L. *subsistit in*) here was intended to maintain that all that is essential to the Church of Christ can be found in the Catholic Church – indeed, found, in key respects, most adequately there – but not exclusively so. As we find in the very next sentence: 'Nevertheless, many elements of sanctification and of truth are found outside its [the Roman Catholic Church's] visible confines' (cf. UR 3 for a similar statement). Equally significant is the recognition that whilst the Roman Catholic Church might not lack any of the essential marks of the Church of Christ, they cannot be thought of as being present there in perfect form. With definite overtones of the Protestant Reformers, the Roman Catholic Church is described as being 'at once holy and always in need of purification' and as following 'constantly the path of penance and renewal' (LG 8, compare UR 6). Again, relinquishing the previous attitude of one-sided fault, the Catholic Church's own complicity in the historic breaks of the sixteenth century is acknowledged (UR 3), as is the need for conversion on all sides (UR 6-7), and the consequent possibility of the catholicity of the Church itself being enriched (UR 4).

In the latter regard and resonating with the earlier Malines' idea of 'unity without absorption', *Lumen gentium* explores the unity and catholicity of the Church not as a strict uniformity but as a differentiated communion of local churches around the world, with differing cultures, customs and practices, in structural and sacramental communion with the Bishop of Rome (see LG 13). As regards the ecumenical implications of this, Avery Dulles finds explicitly advocated in UR 14-18 a view of the redeemed unity of the Church as one of 'reconciled diversity'.[4] In short, this is a principle with significant implications both for the future of ecumenical relations and for the internal health of Catholicism itself, relating closely to disputed issues such as collegiality, consultation, subsidiarity and inculturation.

Significant Initiatives, Documents and Developments

Given the relative tardiness of Catholicism's entrance upon the ecumenical stage, the level of activity in the years following the Council was quite staggering, prompting in some high hopes for realisable Christian unity in the foreseeable future. In 1966 the SPCU was made a permanent office of the Roman curia, subsequently renamed the Pontifical Council for Promoting Christian Unity (PCPCU) by Pope John Paul II in 1989, and widely regarded as one of the best functioning curial departments.[5] The year 1966 also witnessed the inaugural annual meeting of a Joint Working Group between the Roman Catholic Church and the WCC, followed, two years later, by full membership of the Faith and Order Commission. With this, the SPCU (and later the PCPCU) engaged upon a wide-range of formal bilateral dialogues with other Christian traditions, aimed at promoting increased mutual understanding and seeking ways to overcome historic areas of disagreement. The first of these, and in some respects the most successful to date, was initiated with the Lutheran World Federation in 1965, eventually leading in 1999 to the historic *Joint Declaration on the Doctrine of Justification* declaring that clarification and understanding had developed to such a point that the doctrine of justification need no longer be regarded as a cause of division. Similar bilateral dialogue processes began in 1966 with the Anglican Communion (following a visit of Archbishop Michael Ramsey to Rome, during which Pope Paul VI famously placed his own ring on the Archbishop of Canterbury's finger), the World Methodist Council and the Old Catholic Churches, and, in 1968, with the World Alliance of Reformed Churches. Subsequent dialogues were also instituted with the Pentecostals in 1972, the Orthodox in 1979, the Baptist World Alliance in 1984 and the World Evangelical Fellowship in 1993.

These dialogue processes have resulted in an impressive body of documents dealing with the entire range of Christian practice and belief and representing some of the best constructive Christian theology in recent years. Perhaps most significant for the Irish context is the body of jointly agreed reports that have been produced by the Anglican-Roman Catholic International Commission (ARCIC).[6] Here, the concern has not been simply to find ways of holding together differing emphases traditionally regarded as incompatible, but to ask how each challenges the other to fresh learning. Also reflecting this concern, the most recent document of the Joint International Commission for Dialogue Between the World Methodist Council and the Roman Catholic Church, entitled *The Grace Given You in Christ: Catholics and Methodists Reflect Further on the Church*, focuses less on seeking to articulate a resolved agreed theology of the Church and more on seeking to identify the particular gifts that each could fruitfully receive from the other.

Similarly, the SPCU/PCPCU has, over the years, produced a considerable number of other documents providing general norms to guide local ecumenical initiatives and pastoral practice, e.g. the 1993 revised *Directory for the Application of Principles and Norms of Ecumenism.*[7]

Without question, however, the single most important Roman Catholic document since the promulgation of *Unitatis redintegratio* is Pope John Paul II's 1995 encyclical *Ut unum sint*, 'On Commitment to Ecumenism'. In this encyclical he famously extended a remarkable invitation to theologians and leaders of other Christian traditions to help re-imagine the papacy so that it might once again become the focus for Christian unity rather than the continuing cause of division it currently is (95-6).

Difficulties and Disappointments

Despite, however, the very real progress since Vatican II, the widespread – perhaps over-optimistic – hopes and enthusiasm of an earlier generation have now given way in many circles to a sense of tiredness, disappointment, even disinterestedness. Many, for example, felt disappointment at the tardy and largely negative judgement of the Congregation for the Doctrine of Faith on the first phase of ARCIC's work, which contrasted starkly with the very public way in which the relevant texts had already been discussed, and largely enthusiastically welcomed, by mixed groups of Anglicans and Roman Catholics in parishes throughout the UK and far more widely. For the detractors, the Congregation's criticisms betrayed a misplaced concern simply to bring all to the point of understanding and agreeing with traditional Roman Catholic formula rather than seeking together to find appropriate ways of giving fresh, joint expression to a faith essentially held in common. Equally, read charitably, the concern of the Congregation was to avoid any ambiguity that simply served to cover-over continuing substantial differences. Allied with this has been a concern also for consistency across the various bilateral agreements a given tradition might enter into, and – more recently at least – a concern also that dialogue partners should not take unilateral action in relation to significant fresh developments (e.g. women's ordination) that cannot be approved by all.

More generally, the relative waning of the strong ecumenical concern to work for full structural and sacramental communion reflects, in part, a sense of frustration with the slow pace of official processes compared to the urgent need for shared witness on the ground. Such an attitude found formal expression in a shift within the WCC under the leadership of Konrad Raiser from a model prioritising issues of doctrine and Church order to one prioritising matters of mission and evangelisation and offering the structurally distinct yet fraternally associational character of the WCC as an adequate representation of the unity in diversity and universal catholicity of the Church of Christ.

Within the Catholic instinct, however, 'reconciled diversity without structural unity' can simply never be a sufficient equivalent to the intended unity and catholicity of the Church. Whilst the ecumenical aspiration for forms of unity that appropriately reflect this calling will necessarily be a long haul, to give up on it for that reason would be like giving up on the aspiration for economic justice which will likewise always be elusive in this order. The point is to ask what it means to live orientated upon such goals. It is to this question that the recently proposed strategy of *Receptive Ecumenism* seeks to respond.

Conclusion: Receptive Ecumenism and the Call to Catholic Learning: An Ethic for the Ecumenical Long Haul

Inspired by and seeking to generalise the self-critical openness to receptive learning that features increasingly strongly in the ARCIC documents, the most recent Methodist-Roman Catholic statement and Pope John Paul II's *Ut unum sint*, *Receptive Ecumenism* brings to the very forefront of the Christian ecumenical agenda the self-critical question as to what, in any given situation, one's own tradition can appropriately learn with integrity from the other traditions? Moreover, it does this in the conviction that if all were pursuing this question, then all would be moving, albeit somewhat unpredictably, but moving nevertheless, to places where more may, in turn, become possible than appears to be the case at present. As such, it is a way of long-term, hope-filled conversion rather than immediate convergence.

Viewed in this way, the present, interim situation begins to appear less as a problematic derailment of the ecumenical agenda and more as a long-term learning opportunity in which the churches might progress towards their calling and destiny in the only way possible – by slow and difficult growth in maturity. Again, from the Catholic perspective, this much needed process of ecclesial growth and maturation through receptive ecumenical learning is not a matter of becoming *less* Catholic but of becoming *more* Catholic, precisely by becoming more appropriately Methodist, more appropriately Anglican, more appropriately Orthodox, etc.

Herein lies both the challenge and the promise that ecumenism holds for contemporary Roman Catholicism. On the one hand, Catholicism's greatest gift to the ecumenical movement lies precisely in its potential for holding a rich and full catholic diversity within a unity of communion with the Bishop of Rome. On the other hand, for this catholicity to be released and realised in a manner genuinely appealing to other traditions, Catholicism first needs to receive of the particular gifts of such traditions. Furthermore, lest any are inclined to think that the responsibility for such transformative learning lies simply at the level of Church officialdom, it should be recognised that *Receptive Ecumenism* bespeaks a commitment that is of direct relevance to *all* in the churches, with implications for every possible level of Church life. It is, in short, a total ethic that is as simple yet all-pervasive as the Gospel it represents. Like the Gospel, it holds the promise of life within it and is worth making the greatest of efforts to walk in its way.

Notes

1   Available at: www.vatican.va/holy_father/benedict_xvi/messages/pont-messages/ 2005/documents/hf_ben-xvi_mes_20050420_missa-pro-ecclesia_en.html. See also 'Address of His Holiness Benedict XVI to the Delegates of Other Churches and Ecclesial Communities and of Other Religious Traditions', 25 April 2005, at www.vatican.va/holy_father/benedict_xvi/speeches/2005/april/documents/hf_ben-xvi_spe_20050425_rappresentanti-religiosi_en.html.

2   See Paul D. Murray (ed.) *Receptive Ecumenism and the Call to Catholic Learning: An Ethic for the Ecumenical Long-Haul*, Oxford: Oxford University Press, 2007.

3   See *Vatican Council II: The Conciliar and Post Conciliar Documents*, Austin Flannery, O.P. (ed.) Leominster: Fowler Wright, 1980 (1975), pp. 350–423, 452–70.

4   See Dulles, *The Catholicity of the Church*, Oxford and New York: Oxford University Press, 1985, pp. 21–24.

5   For further on what follows, see Tom Stranksy, 'The Secretariat for Promoting Christian Unity', *Modern Catholicism: Vatican II and After*, Adrian Hastings (ed.) London: SPCK, 1991, pp. 182–184.

6   See www.prounione.urbe.it/dia-int/arcic/e_arcic-info.html.

7   Available at: www.vatican.va/roman_curia/pontifical_councils/chrstuni/general-docs/rc_pc_chrstuni_doc_19930325_directory_en.html.

Further Reading

Gros, Jeffrey, FSC, McManus, Eamon and Riggs, Ann, *Introduction to Ecumenism*, New York/Mahwah, NJ: Paulist Press, 1998.

Kasper, Walter Cardinal, *That They May All be One: The Call to Unity Today*, London: Burns & Oates, 2004.

Murray, Paul D. (ed.) *Receptive Ecumenism and the Call to Catholic Learning: Exploring a Way for Contemporary Ecumenism*, Oxford: Oxford University Press, 2007 (forthcoming).

O'Gara, Margaret, *The Ecumenical Gift Exchange*, Collegeville, Minn.: The Liturgical Press, 1998.

CHAPTER 26

HOW 'CATHOLIC' IS
CATHOLIC THEOLOGY?

Patricia Kieran

Introduction

Who can do Catholic theology and why would anyone do it? These questions are often posed to those engaged in theological studies by people who fail to see the social relevance, intellectual excitement or practical application of studies in theology. However, these simple questions raise a series of further questions about the status, function and legitimacy of Catholic theology as a discipline as well as the motives and purposes of those doing theology. Since these are important questions it is vital for those 'doing' theology in the Catholic context to give them further consideration.

WHO CAN DO CATHOLIC THEOLOGY?

Theology as a Formal, Professional, Academic Activity

Theology reflects upon the nature of God, humans and the world. If we reply to the question 'who can do Catholic theology?' by stating that only a professional theologian with an appropriate qualification can do Catholic theology, then theology is immediately defined as a formal academic activity carried out by a minority group, who think and talk about God. In this model of theology as a formal professional academic activity, the vast majority of people become the subjects of theology (theologians reflect upon them and their faith experience) but are incapable of initiating, engaging or sustaining theological reflection themselves. In one sense it is unsurprising that some people may operate exclusively from this restrictive model. The history of theology can throw some light on this. For centuries the study of theology was part of a vocational preparation for religious or clerical life. The Christian community's need to think theologically and prepare clergy for ministry gave rise to the establishment of formal learning environments with dedicated theologians. In western Europe most universities emerged out of monastic institutions and Church schools. In the twelfth and thirteenth centuries great institutions were dedicated to theological learning. In the high middle-ages theology was the main subject of study (alongside *Trivium* or the three basic subjects of Grammar, Logic and Rhetoric) at universities (called *Studia Generale*) such as Paris, Oxford, Cambridge, Montpellier and Bologna.[1] Other academic subjects (e.g. *Quadrivium* or the four subjects of Arithmetic, Geometry, Music and Astronomy) as well as Philosophy, Medicine and Law were viewed as aides to theology, which was seen as the 'Queen of the Sciences'.[2] With the rise of modernity, theology's status in the university underwent considerable change, and increasing secularisation meant that it no longer towered above all other subject areas. After the Enlightenment a broad range of subjects were taught at universities from what could generally be termed a humanistic perspective, that is, without reference to religion or God. In subsequent centuries the legitimacy of theology as an academic discipline in a university context was challenged.[3]

As we will see in this chapter, Catholic theologians argue that theology undoubtedly belongs in a formal academic setting. Aidan Nichols comments that theology, along with all other academic disciplines, requires three things:

> First, it requires the ability to follow an argument; second, it requires the capacity to remember a certain number of facts; third, it requires a basic flair or sense for the subject that enables us to be creative in thinking up hypotheses in its regard.[4]

Not everybody has the opportunity or the inclination to engage in the formal study of theology in an academic context. Ascribing this particular type of scholarship to the word 'theology' inevitably sets limits on who can do theology. Indeed, in its long history the Church has only given the title 'theologian' or 'Doctor' (L. *docere*, 'to teach') to a handful of people 'exceptional for the quality of their personal faith' and their capacity to make sense of that faith.[5] While the use of the word theologian is widespread today, John Macquarrie maintains a qualitative emphasis on theological reflection when he reserves the term 'theology' for 'the most sophisticated and reflective ways of talking about God'.[6] Clearly theology, in this sense, does not refer to all types of reflection about God. There is a huge difference between someone who discusses questions of faith 'over a pint of beer at the local pub … and the person who makes a serious lifelong commitment to struggling with them and turns that commitment into a part of his or her very self-definition'.[7] In this model of theology as a formal professional academic activity the word 'theology' is used specifically to designate a sophisticated and informed, self-critical, intellectually coherent and reasoned discourse on God.

Having a specifically designated, identifiable and dedicated group of 'professional' theologians whose job is to think, talk, teach and write about God and God's relationship to the world ensures that high standards of scholarship prevail, theological specialisation is fostered, interdisciplinary dialogue is nurtured and the Church is served by theologians with widely recognised competency. For the theologian who is intoxicated with questions of faith and knowledge, 'theology is the highest of the habits of mind that a Christian man or woman can acquire'.[8] The work of academic theologians in this formal context has been vitally important in the history of Christianity. As Karl Rahner states 'The Catholic Church cannot and ought not be a "Church of professors", but it cannot be today a Church without professors'.[9] Neither the Catholic Church nor the academic world is served by the marginalisation or dumbing down of theology. Theology has a vital function to play in a formal academic environment. The scholarly study of theology is concerned with questions of meaning and truth and rightfully belongs in the academy. Academic theological reflection emerges from the raw ingredients of the lived experience of faith in all its variety and complexity as it engages in dialogue with the Christian tradition, the disciplines of the academy and contemporary culture. This type of theological reflection is a vital sign of a healthy academy as well as a healthy Christian faith community and it provides a much-needed dialogue with, and a critique of, contemporary life.

However, if we operate exclusively from the model of theology as a formal professional activity, by reducing theology to a component in the preparation for ministerial life or by viewing it as the exclusive preserve of a group of professional theologians, it becomes evident that the professionalisation of theology can have more negative than positive consequences. Academic exclusivity brings with it the danger of theological reclucivity. One of the side effects of ascribing the term 'theologian' to a professional group is that those around them abdicate responsibility for thinking about theological issues. The professionalisation of theology for the minority can unintentionally lead to its irrelevance for the majority. If theology is *only* an activity that is undertaken by a minority of professional academics, with very specific formal academic training, it quickly becomes marginal and meaningless to many. In the Catholic tradition people are sometimes inhibited by the fear that their God-thought and God-talk is rudimentary and uninformed in comparison to the 'expert' theologians. In response to this it is crucial to remember that it is not necessary to engage in a formal study of a discipline in order to know something about it. For example, people can behave in a responsible manner without studying ethics. Likewise it is unnecessary to study sports sciences in order to be physically fit. It goes without saying that people can reflect meaningfully upon their faith in God without ever engaging in formal theological study.

The Inclusive or 'catholic' Model of Theology – Theology as an Essential Activity of the believing Christian

Once we broaden the notion that theology belongs in the academic world but is by no means restricted to it we are at liberty to acknowledge a second model of theology. This more inclusive or 'catholic' (Gk *katholikos*, 'according to the whole' or 'universal') model of theology presents theology as an essential human activity which all people of faith spontaneously engage in. As in the previous model, faith in God is the raw ingredient out of which theology emerges. From the early days of the Church the faith of believers was reflected upon, communicated to others, discussed and written down. Christian theology did not originate in a formal academic environment; it was first articulated in conversations, letters and written testimonies between believers struggling to make sense of the life, death and resurrection of Jesus Christ. The experience of faith is always accompanied by some attempt, no matter how rudimentary, to make sense of that faith. The word theology affirms the link between *logia*, meaning 'words' or 'discourse', and *Theos*, God. Faith (personal knowledge of God) is a primary pre-requisite for the Catholic theologian and theology is always a retrospective response to the lived experience of faith. The experience of faith is so laden with meaning that it invites subsequent reflection. From this perspective theology is done at a variety of levels by a range of people in a multitude of different ways. In some sense every person of faith does theology. Richard P. McBrien comments that faith and theology should not be polarised or separated as faith 'exists always and only in some theological form'.[10] If we accept St Anselm's (1033–1109) notion of theology as 'faith seeking understanding', then the moment a person of faith develops curiosity about faith and begins to self-consciously reflect upon faith they are doing theology.[11]

Why should anyone do Theology?
If reflection on faith is part of being a person of faith then theology is relevant to all believers. Faith needs to be quizzed over, unpacked and teased out as all believers struggle to understand and accept aspects of their faith. Therefore, any attempt to make sense of and understand an experience of faith or an expression of faith is an engagement in theological reflection. In this inclusive 'catholic' model of theology the believer who puzzles over the meaning behind a scriptural passage, who responds in a thoughtful manner to a child's enquiry about a religious topic, who unravels confusing words found in a prayer, or who engages in a discussion about a controversial moral issue, is doing theology. This is qualitatively (different levels of analysis) and contextually (not necessarily in an academic environment) different from the type of theological reflection engaged in our first model of theology.

However, theology is not limited to any one form of theologising or way of doing theology. Just as faith cannot be constrained and relegated to any one aspect of human life neither can reflection upon faith. The person of faith approaches a religious tradition with a history of religious culture, language and belief that they try to make sense of. In the Christian tradition the ways in which people make sense of their faith are pluriform. Theology is not restricted to the written text or the spoken word. In this 'catholic' model, theology involves attempts to make sense of faith including, among other things, a variety of creative and interpretative acts such as the copying and illumination of manuscripts, the composition of poetry, music, dance, literary texts, works of art and architecture. Theology also encompasses the transmission of faith, teaching, engagement in rational discourse, works of devotion, preaching and prayer, in so far as all of these emanate from a desire to make sense of the Christian faith.[12]

People doing Theology: Laity and Clergy working together

For those who erroneously think of Catholic theology as an exclusively or predominantly clerical enterprise, it is useful to look at Vatican II's *Apostolicam actuositatem*, the Decree on the Apostolate of the Laity. Here the Church actively calls its members to become apostles and to spread the kingdom of Christ throughout the earth so that all humans can be saved. The Catholic Church calls lay people to work in tandem with the clergy and it sees lay people's consciousness of their responsibility to serve Christ and the Church in all circumstances as a manifestation of 'the unmistakable work being done today by the Holy Spirit'.[13] Part of the work of the laity and the clergy involves theological reflection and the Church teaches that the laity 'share in the priestly, prophetic and royal office of Christ and therefore have their own share in the mission of the whole people of God in the Church and in the world'.[14] Vatican II issues a universal call to holiness and exhorts the laity to work actively as members of the body of Christ to spread the good news of Jesus Christ. This involves doing theology by way of reflecting upon faith, engaging in conversation about it as well as applying it to the contexts in which people find themselves. The document states:

> this sacred synod earnestly exhorts laymen – each according to his own gifts of intelligence and learning – to be more diligent in doing what they can to explain, defend and properly apply Christian principles to the problems of our era in accordance with the mind of the Church.[15]

The impact of this quotation is not to reinforce division between clergy and laity but to invite those who tend to see theology as a professional and largely clerical activity to recognise their own capacity to engage in theological reflection. Perhaps the time has come for Catholics to take seriously the idea of the democratisation (Gk *demos*, 'the people' and *kratia*, 'power') of theology by recognising the power of ordinary people to think, imagine and do theology, at different levels and in different ways.

Approaches to Catholic Theology

If faith is essential to theological reflection this raises the question of whether it is possible for atheists or non-believers to study, research and explore Catholic theology. As an academic discipline Catholic theology is not restricted to people of faith and often atheists, agnostics and unbelievers engage in fruitful theological research. One can be a film critic without being a film-maker. The non-believer can study Catholic theology from a descriptive, analytical and critical perspective, for example, from what may be termed a Religious Studies or Religious Science perspective. However, phenomenological and social science approaches are distinguished from the approach of a Catholic theologian who operates from within a living faith tradition. Catholic theology does not fracture the relationship between reason and faith, hence the Church teaches that 'reason and faith cannot be separated without diminishing the capacity of men and women to know themselves, the world and God in an appropriate way'.[16] In the Catholic tradition, theology is the study of God's revelation which is grasped in faith. For a Catholic theologian to *generate* Catholic theology it is necessary to have reflected upon a prior personal faith experience. The Catholic theologian engages in dynamic and faith-inspired dialogue with the sources of Catholic theology, that is, the scriptures, tradition and the teaching Magisterium of the Church.

Who does Catholic Theology speak to and why?

Theological reflection should not be privatised and it cannot consist entirely of the personal opinion of the believer. The believer who seeks to understand their faith encounters diverse public theological expressions such as church architecture, religiously inspired music, sacred literature, formal Church teaching and theological scholarship. Interpretation and expression of faith can be shared in a variety of ways. David Tracy argues against a view that theology is a private activity carried on in a marginal realm of human society. He countenances the privatisation of religion with the notion of the public nature of theology. Tracy explores the public nature of authentic theology:

> To speak and mean God-language is to speak publicly and mean
> it. Theologians must speak of many matters. And yet, if they are

not also speaking of God while they address these other issues, they are not doing theology. Theologians can and must speak in many forms and genres. But if they are not articulating a public position, they are not speaking theologically.[17]

When people think and talk about God and human relationship to God they are part of the much greater ancient yet ongoing theological conversation of the Christian tradition. They are also part of a wider contemporary cultural context where their expression of their understanding of God is significant for others who also seek to understand God.[18] Tracy explains that when theologians write or speak they address three distinct and related publics: (i) the wider society, (ii) the academy and (iii) the Church.[19] While individual theologians may primarily address one of these publics, if they are practicing what he calls an 'authentic' theology, they should participate in and address all three publics.

Theologians, along with all other human beings, are social selves and they belong to a particular society. Thus, theology should address the major issues of that society such as social justice, law, technology, citizenship and economics.[20] The Catholic Church must be 'expert in humanity' and 'has a perennial interest in whatever concerns men and women' who live in society.[21] For instance issues of social injustice, global warming, economic policy and war are crucially important in Catholic theology. Society provides the context in which theology teases out the meaning of faith. The second public which theology addresses is the academy (for example, the university) where reasoned debate and interdisciplinary dialogue about meaning and truth are vital. The academy represents the formal context where scholarly study occurs. In Tracy's view theology is legitimately located in an academic context but unlike the first model of theology, which we explored, it is not restricted to it. For Tracy, the final public which theology addresses is the Church. Authentic theology operates from within a particular denomination and it addresses that faith community, thereby strengthening religious commitment and Church participation.

Different ways of doing Catholic theology

Both professional theologians and believers seeking to understand their faith cannot bypass both the positive (falling in love, birth of a baby, personal

EXPLORING THEOLOGY

achievement) and negative (disability, sickness and death) aspects of human experience. Theology involves people telling the story of their experiences of God while simultaneously attempting to interpret them. There is theological meaning latent within and revealed by these ordinary human experiences which theological reflection unpacks. In recent years theologians have spoken of 'theological reflection' as a way of doing theology. Robert L. Kinast sees that lived human experience is crucial to theology as theology always emerges out of a specific context rather than from abstract generic truths:[22]

> It [theological reflection] begins with the lived experience of those doing the reflection; it correlates this experience with the sources of the Christian tradition; and it draws out practical implications for Christian living.[23]

Only when we have explored the nature of human experiences and understood how they connect with the Christian tradition can we understand and practice our faith more effectively. Kinast encourages all those doing theology to take human experience seriously. We must, however, resist the temptation to view theology as a purely subjective or private interpretation of an individual's experience. Theology engages in dialogue with a faith tradition which in turn challenges, critiques and places human experience in a larger context. Finally, theological reflection always emerges from a practical context and should lead to praxis or reflective action. Theology is not a theoretical construction divorced from the world. It should lead us to change our lives and challenge us to live out our faith in a particular historical context.

Reclaiming Theology as a Universal Human Activity arising from Faith

To return to our opening questions, 'who can do Catholic theology and why would anyone do it?', we can respond by saying that Catholic theology is a discipline that is open to investigation and research by everybody (believers and non-believers) but that all Catholic Christians are called to engage in some level of theological reflection on their experience of faith. This book began by stating that theology is not an arid discipline but an interesting, creative field of investigation for anyone who attempts to make sense of their faith. Theology arises from the curious desire to know more about the God who loves us and who calls us to be more fully human. To hold fast to a fully worked-out notion of God, humanity and the world, to have answers to all the fundamental questions of life, is antithetical to the exploratory, critical, theological spirit.

In 399 BCE just before his death Socrates declared to a jury in a court in Athens, 'The unexamined life is not worth living'.[24] These words have particular relevance for all people of faith today. Surely if we profess belief in God and proclaim the good news that Jesus is the Christ, this means that each believer, from childhood to old age, is called to explore, examine and make sense of that faith – or indeed, at times, the lack of it. A mature faith is not one that is grafted onto a passive recipient by some external religious or theological authority. A mature faith struggles with its own religious ideas and questions and expresses them to others in a variety of forms. People of faith should not view theology as an IQ test that calibrates their sophisticated or rudimentary understandings of God. Theology is deeply personal and thoroughly enjoyable if we liberate ourselves to dare to think about, imagine, question and explore our faith in God.

Conclusion

The seeds of faith that are planted in the believer grow in various ways if they are nurtured through prayer, thought and action. Doing theology is not the preserve of an exclusive professional minority. All believers are called to make sense of their faith in ways that emerge from their own context and reflect their own giftedness. One of the internal requirements of faith is that the believer needs to experience, reflect upon, express and share that faith. This can take many forms (e.g. verbal, written, artistic, practical). Faith is not an exclusively private, subjective reality and neither is theology. The classical sources of theology (revelation, scripture, tradition) help the curious believer to understand their own faith experience. Believers need to make sense of their faith and to communicate the nature of their faith in a coherent, intelligent, creative manner to others in society, Church and, in the case of professional theologians, academy. The fact that there is a designated group of professional theologians who engage in highly specialised, systematic and innovative theological reflection should not deter but rather encourage every believer to make more sense of their own faith. Catholics need to take seriously the notion that people of faith are empowered by that very faith to think, imagine and do theology, at different levels and in different ways. Catholic theology should indeed be truly 'catholic' or universal. This whole book has attempted to explore theology in a manner which invites the reader to enter into the theological enterprise with energy, creativity, enthusiasm and confidence.

Notes

1   Medieval universities aided greatly in the task of preserving, translating and interpreting ancient texts, among them the works of Aristotle and other ancient Greek texts. The Vatican bestowed the title *Studium Generale* or 'university' on the most prestigious centres of learning in medieval Europe. In the thirteenth century eight *Studia Generale* received a papal bull formally confirming their university status and these are generally recognised as being the universities of: Paris, Bologna, Oxford, Cambridge, Montpellier, Palencia, Reggio Emilia, Vicenza and Salerno.

2   In the High Middle Ages a good university education, equivalent to a contemporary B.A. and M.A., comprised of seven subjects, combining the *Trivium* (coming from the Latin word for 'three roads') and the *Quadrivium* (L. 'four roads'). Cf. Wolfhart Pannenberg, *Theology and the Philosophy of Science*, Philadelphia, Westminster: John Knox Press, 1976, pp. 228–297 for an account of the emergence of theology as a science in the medieval university.

3   Cf. Claude Geffré and Werner Jeanrond (eds) *Why Theology?* London, SCM, 1994.

4   Aidan Nichols, *The Shape of Catholic Theology*, Edinburgh: T & T Clark, 1991, p. 14.

5   Doctors of the Church must be formally recognised by the Church as exhibiting outstanding learning and holiness – '*eminens doctrina, insignis vitae sanctitas, Ecclesiae declaratio.*' Among those thirty-three listed as Doctors of the Church (L. *Doctores Ecclesiae*) we find St Gregory the Great, Saint Ambrose, Saint Augustine, Saint Jerome and Saint Thomas Aquinas. In 1970 St Teresa of Ávila and St Catherine of Siena became the first female Doctors of the Church and in 1997 St Thérèse of Lisieux was given the title. Cf. Nichols, p. 17.

6   John Macquarrie, *God-Talk*, London: SCM, 1973, p. 11.

7   Nichols, p. 18.

8   Y.M. Congar, *La foi et la théologie*, Desclée & Co., 1962, p. 192.

9   Karl Rahner (ed.) *Encyclopedia of Theology*, London: Burns & Oates, 1981, p. 1694.

10   Richard P. McBrien *Catholicism*, London: Geoffrey Chapman, 1980, Vol. 1, p. 26.

11   The original title of Anselm's work *Proslogion* (meaning 'to speak to' or 'address') was *Proslogion fides quarens intellectum*, translating as 'to speak to God, faith seeking understanding'.

12   'Theology, in the broad sense of the word, may emerge in many forms: a painting, a

piece of music, a dance, a cathedral, a bodily posture, or, in its more recognisable form, in spoken or written words.' McBrien, p. 26.

13   *Apostolicam actuositatem*, Decree on the Apostolate of the Laity, 1.

14   Ibid., 2.

15   Ibid., Chapter 11, 6.

16   John Paul II, *Fides et ratio* (Faith and Reason) (1998) 16.

17   David Tracy, 'Defending the Public Character of Theology' in *The Christian Century*, 1981, pp. 350–356.

18   David Tracy, *The Analogical Imagination: Christian Theology and the Culture of Pluralism*, London: SCM, 1981, p. 104.

19   Ibid., p. 5.

20   By society Tracy means technoeconomic structure (organisation and allocation of goods and services), polity (social justice and the use of power) and culture (art and religion among others), ibid., p. 7.

21   *Letter to the Bishops of the Catholic Church on the collaboration of men and women in the Church and the world*, Congregation for the Doctrine of the Faith, 2004, Par. 1.

22   There are many different ways of doing theology and Kinast outlines five distinct types of theological reflection. These include: Ministerial, Spiritual, Feminist, Inculturation and Practical Theology, cf. Robert Kinast, *What are they Saying About Theological Reflection?* New York: Paulist Press, 2000.

23   Ibid., p. 1.

24   *Apology* by Plato, 38a.